Pilot Studies
for a **New Penang**

Socio-economic and Environmental Research Institute
Pulau Pinang, Malaysia

The Socio-economic and Environmental Research Institute (SERI) was established by the Penang State Government to supply it with solid policy recommendations and to aid its strategic planning. The think tank seeks to contribute to the building of a caring and sharing society through research approaches that are comprehensive and challenging, and conducts research into social, economic, and environmental issues. Its other core activities include the preparation and dissemination of information, and the facilitating of various programmes specially structured to help it achieve its goals.

Institute of Southeast Asian Studies
Singapore

The Institute of Southeast Asian Studies (ISEAS) was established as an autonomous organization in 1968. It is a regional centre dedicated to the study of socio-political, security and economic trends and developments in Southeast Asia and its wider geostrategic and economic environment. The Institute's research programmes are the Regional Economic Studies (RES, including ASEAN and APEC), Regional Strategic and Political Studies (RSPS), and Regional Social and Cultural Studies (RSCS).

ISEAS Publishing, an established academic press, has issued more than 2,000 books and journals. It is the largest scholarly publisher of research about Southeast Asia from within the region. ISEAS Publishing works with many other academic and trade publishers and distributors to disseminate important research and analyses from and about Southeast Asia to the rest of the world.

Penang Studies Series

Pilot Studies
for a New Penang

Edited by Ooi Kee Beng & Goh Ban Lee

Socio-economic and Environmental Research Institute
Pulau Pinang, Malaysia

Institute of Southeast Asian Studies
Singapore

First published in Singapore in 2010 by ISEAS Publishing
Institute of Southeast Asian Studies
30 Heng Mui Keng Terrace
Pasir Panjang
Singapore 119614
E-mail: publish@iseas.edu.sg
Website: http://bookshop.iseas.edu.sg

for distribution as an e-book and print in all countries except Malaysia.

ISEAS Library Cataloguing-in-Publication Data

Pilot studies for a new Penang / edited by Ooi Kee Beng and Goh Ban Lee.

    Papers presented at the Penang Outlook Forum 2009 on "Restructuring and Reshaping Penang" held on 1-2 June 2009 in Penang, jointly organized by the Socio-economic and Environmental Research Institute (SERI) and Institute of Southeast Asian Studies (ISEAS).

    1. Pulau Pinang—Economic conditions—Congresses.

    2. Pulau Pinang—Economic policy—Congresses.

    I. Ooi, Kee Beng.

    II. Goh, Ban Lee.

    III. Socio-economic & Environmental Research Institute (Pulau Pinang)

    IV. Institute of Southeast Asian Studies.

    V. Penang Outlook Forum (2009 : Penang, Malaysia)

HC445.5 Z7P4P64   2010

ISBN 978-981-4279-69-7 (soft cover)

ISBN 978-981-4279-70-3 (E-Book PDF)

Cover Design, Content Format and Typeset by PM Wang

Printed by Vinlin Press Sdn Bhd (25680-X)

No.2, Jalan Meranti Permai 1,Meranti Permai Industrial Park, Batu 15,

Jalan Puchong,47100 Puchong, Selangor Darul Ehsan.

[CONTENTS]

[ACKNOWLEDGEMENT]

The papers presented in this volume were first discussed at the Penang Outlook Forum 2009, titled "Restructuring and Reshaping Penang", held on 1-2 June 2009 at the E &O Hotel in Penang.

We wish therefore to thank everyone involved in making that conference a success, especially the directors and the able staff of the Socio-economic and Environmental Research Institute (SERI) of Penang and the Malaysia Study Programme at the Institute of Southeast Asian Studies (ISEAS), Singapore.

Thanks also to all the contributors, chairpersons and discussants for their inspiring participation in the debate to improve the standard of living in Penang, and in Malaysia.

Heartfelt gratitude goes to the main sponsor, BSG Property, and to Khazanah Nasional, the Penang Development Corporation, InvestPenang, SERI and ISEAS for their support.

Last and certainly not least, a special hurrah must be shouted for Liew Chin Tong, MP for Bukit Bendera, for conceptualizing the project and for being the key person in its realization.

The Editors

[CONTRIBUTORS]

Dr Chan Chee Khoon is professor of health and social policy at Universiti Sains Malaysia. He graduated from the Massachusetts Institute of Technology with degrees in life sciences, and has a Doctor of Science degree in Epidemiology from Harvard University. Among his awards is an Institut Pasteur fellowship which supported his doctoral research on the epidemiology of nasopharyngeal carcinoma, teaching and research fellowships at MIT and Harvard, as well as a Nippon Foundation API senior fellowship in 2004-2005. Dr Chan has served as consultant and technical adviser to the World Bank, European Commission, World Health Organization, UNESCAP, UNESCO, Japan International Cooperation Agency, and the Ministry of Health, SERI, Malaysian Medical Association, Federation of Malaysian Consumer Associations (health policy adviser), and the Department of Environment in Malaysia. His current research interests include emerging and re-emerging infectious diseases, ethical and policy issues in science and technology, environment and development, and health systems in transition.

Dr Chan Huan Chiang received his Ph.D. in regional science from the University of Pennsylvania. He is a SERI Fellow and was an associate professor at the Centre for Policy Research, Universiti Sains Malaysia. He taught finance, econometrics and public sector economics in USM's School of Social Sciences. He is an associate research fellow with the Malaysian Institute of Economic Research (MIER) and also a member of the economic policies committee of the Federation of Malaysian Manufacturers (FMM) Northern Branch. He is a member of the editorial boards of Kajian Malaysia and the International Journal of Asia and Pacific Studies. At the international level, Dr. Chan has also served as a member of the combined methods task team as well as the economic policies task team of Global International Waters Assessment (GIWA) a GEF/UNEP funded project based at the University of

Kalmar in Sweden, and has acted as economic consultant in missions involving the development of export processing zones in Kenya and Sri Lanka on behalf of the World Bank and the Asian Development Bank respectively.

Dr Goh Ban Lee is a SERI Fellow. He is also a columnist for the-Sun newspaper in Malaysia, focusing on issues related to urban governance, housing and urban planning. He has a Bachelor of Social Sciences and Master of Social Sciences from Universiti Sains Malaysia and a Ph. D. in Urban Planning from the University of California, Los Angeles. He was an associate professor in Universiti Sains Malaysia and vice principal of Tunku Abdul Rahman College. He also served on the first National Economic Consultative Council (1989-1991) and was a councillor in the Penang Island Municipal Council (1989-1995). He was involved in projects conducted by United Nations Centre for Regional Development (UNCRD), Urban Management Program of the United Nations – Asia Pacific Region, and Asian Productivity Organization (APO). Among his publications are *Urban Planning in Malaysia* (1991), *Non-compliance – A Neglected Agenda in Urban Governance* (2002) and *Counselling Local Councils* (2007).

Encik Hamdan Abdul Majeed currently heads the department overseeing Khazanah investment activities in the Northern Corridor. Prior to that, he was actively involved in developing new investment initiatives for Khazanah both in Malaysia and abroad. Before joining Khazanah, he was the founding director of a corporate advisory group, where he was involved extensively in debt capital markets advisory specializing in structured finance and project finance. Prior to that, he was attached to HSBC Investment Banking as a specialist in equity capital markets, covering the Malaysian equity market. He has an interest in the development of civil society in Malaysia, the political economy of Third World nations and Islam. He holds a degree in Economics and Management from the University of London.

Dr Francis Hutchinson is a consultant specializing in governance, public sector management, and decentralization. He holds a Ph.D. in Public Policy and Administration from the Crawford School of Economics and Government of the Australian National University. His dissertation entitled 'Can Sub-national States be Developmental?' looks at industrial policy at the sub-national level in Malaysia and In-

Contributors

dia, taking the states of Penang and Karnataka as case studies. He has carried out applied research on state capacity, decentralization, state-level industrial policy, anti-corruption, and social policy for the World Bank, UNDP, UNICEF, UNESCO, the Australian International Aid Agency as well as political risk consultancy firms such as Oxford Analytica and Control Risks. A political scientist by training, he also holds degrees in Social & Political Sciences and Development Studies from the Universities of Cambridge and Sussex, respectively.

Ms Hwa Yue-Yi is studying for a B.A. in political economy and a certificate in Arabic at Williams College in Massachusetts. Her research interests include education policy and inter-ethnic relations. As part of her B.A. programme, she spent a semester on exchange at the School of Oriental and African Studies (SOAS) in London. She has also completed internships at SERI and theSun.

Ambassador K Kesavapany is the Director of Singapore's Institute of Southeast Asian Studies. He was Singapore's High Commissioner to Malaysia from 1997 to 2002. In his 30-year career in the Foreign Service, he served as Permanent Representative to the United Nations in Geneva (December 1991 - March 1997) and held key staff appointments in Singapore's Ministry of Foreign Affairs.

Dato' Lee Kah Choon is the Director of investPenang and of the Penang Development Corporation. Dato' Lee served as Parliamentary Secretary of the Ministry of Health from 2004 to 2008, and as Member of Parliament for the Jelutong Constituency from 1999 to 2008. Prior to his political career, Dato' Lee was Seberang Perai Municipal Councillor 1997-1999. He was a practicing lawyer with his own private legal practice from 1987 to 2004, after being called to the Bar of Malaysia in 1987 and Bar of England & Wales in 1986. He holds an LLB from Southampton University, and an MA from City University London. He is a alumnus of the Royal Military College Kuala Lumpur and Chung Ling High School, Penang.

Mr Liew Chin Tong is the Member of Parliament (DAP) for Bukit Bendera, Penang, and also policy advisor to Penang's Chief Minister, Mr Lim Guan Eng. He is Executive Director of the Socio-economic and Environmental Research Institute, and also heads Research for Social Advancement (REFSA). He was formerly a Visiting Research Fellow at ISEAS, Singapore. He graduated with a degree in Political Science and an Honours degree in Asian Studies from the Australian National University and holds an International Masters in Regional Integration from the Asia-Europe Institute, University of Malaya.

Mr Lim Guan Eng is Chief Minister of Penang. He has a degree in economics from Monash University, Australia, and is a qualified professional accountant. He is the Member of Parliament (DAP) for Bagan, Penang, and state assemblyman for Air Putih. He is the secretary-general of the Democratic Action Party (DAP).

Dr Lim Mah Hui is a SERI Fellow and Visiting Senior Fellow at ISEAS. Prior to that, he served as Senior Specialist at the Asian Development Bank in the field of private sector debt and equity recovery. Dr Lim also has extensive banking experience in the area of investments and corporate loans, having held various portfolios in prominent financial institutions within the Asia Pacific region. His distinguished contributions in academia cover research and lecturing positions at Universiti Malaya, Temple University and Duke University in the United States. His recent publications have focused on the US subprime mortgage crisis as well as labour concerns in developing economies.

Prof Suresh Narayanan holds bachelor and master degrees in economics from Universiti Malaya, and received his Ph.D. in economics from Boston University. He is currently Professor of Economics at USM's School of Social Sciences. His fields of research include indirect taxation, labour migration, foreign labour issues and technology transfer. He was a Visiting Professor at El Colegio de Mexico, and Aalborg University in Denmark. He was also a Visiting Scholar at Harvard University, Uppsala University (Sweden) and the Technical University of Denmark. He has served as a consultant to several local agencies such as the National Economic Action Council (NEAC), the Ministry of Finance, the Economic Planning Unit of the Prime Minister's Department, the Penang Development Corporation (PDC), the Institute of Strategic and Social Studies (ISIS) and the Malaysian Institute of Economic Research (MIER). He was a consultant to UNDP and ILO and has just completed a study for the NEAC on reducing the Malaysian dependence on foreign labour.

Dr Nungsari Ahmad Radhi joined Khazanah as Executive Director, Research and Investment Strategy, in 2007. After ten years in academia, he resigned as Dean of the School of Economics at Uni-

versiti Utara Malaysia before winning a Parliamentary Seat in 1995. Besides representing the Malaysian Parliament in a number of international organizations, he was also a Board member of Bank Pertanian Malaysia, Yayasan Pelajaran MARA and the National Library. Prior to joining Khazanah, he had a brief stint at Sime Darby Berhad and was an Associate Director of Innovation Associates. His areas of interest have been in industrial organization, applied game theory and public economics. He also writes regularly for The Edge and the most recent book he edited was *New Challenges Facing Poverty Eradication and Rural Development* (2005). He holds a PhD from the Krannert School of Management, Purdue University.

Dr Ooi Kee Beng's entire tertiary education was done at Stockholm University, with Public Administration being his first degree. After several years studying Practical Philosophy, he concluded his studies with a doctorate in Sinology. He is a Fellow at ISEAS, and is adjunct associate professor at the Southeast Asian Studies Programme at the National University of Singapore and also visiting associate professor at the Department of Public and Social Administration at Hong Kong's City University. His books include *Arrested Reform: The Undoing of Abdullah Badawi*; *March 8: Eclipsing May 13*, *Malaya's First Year at the United Nations*, *Lost in Transition: Malaysia under Abdullah; The Era of Transition: Malaysia after Mahathir*, *Chinese Strategists: Beyond Sun Zi's Art of War*, *The Reluctant Politician: Tun Dr Ismail and His Time*, and *Continent and Coast and Ocean: Dynamics of Regionalism in Eastern Asia*. He is a columnist for Today Newspaper, Singapore, and editor for the Penang Economic Monthly.

Prof. P. Ramasamy is currently Second Deputy Chief Minister of Penang. Before entering politics, he was professor of political science at Universiti Kebangsaan Malaysia until his retirement in August 2005. He was subsequently visiting professor at Kassel University, Germany, and a senior visiting research fellow at ISEAS.

Ms Sin I Lin is a PhD student in Sociology at the University of Edinburgh whose key research interests are social mobility aspirations, higher education, study-work transitions and international migration. She is presently studying Malaysian middle-class practices of social distinction in the education and labour market. Working on related themes in her Masters and Honours years, she published in *Studies in*

Higher Education and *the Asian and Pacific Migration Journal*. She studied for an MSc in Sociological Research at the University of Manchester (2007) and a BA (Hons) in Sociology at the Australian National University (2005). She previously worked at the Department of Sociology in the National University of Singapore, assisting in research on migrant integration and social indicators in Singapore.

Mr Ajit Singh Jessy, Advocate and Solicitor, has over 30 years of Personnel-Industrial Relations experience. Prior to going into legal practice, he was Group Human Resources Manager and Legal Advisor of Palmco Holdings. He is ranked among the Top Industrial Relations Lawyers in Malaysia, advising both leading corporate and multinational companies and representing senior litigant clients. He is Chairman of the Penang State Human Resources Liaison Committee, which advises the State Government on labour and industrial relations issues and is also a member of the Bar Councils Industrial Court Practice Committee. He is a past Chairman of Malaysia Employers Federation (Northern Region), Malaysian Institute of Personnel Management (Northern Branch) and Electrical Industry Employers Association.

Dr Wong Poh Kam is Professor at National University of Singapore (NUS)'s Business School and concurrently serves as Director of the NUS Entrepreneurship Centre. He also holds joint professorship appointment at the LKY School of Public Policy and the Engineering School's Division of Engineering & Technology Management (DETM). He obtained two BSc.s., an MSc. and a Ph.D. from MIT. Prior to joining NUS in 1988, he co-founded two IT companies and a consulting firm in Malaysia. As director of the NUS Entrepreneurship Centre, he spearheads the university's entrepreneurship education and outreach programs and various university technology spin-off support programs including incubator facilities, seed funding and mentoring. He also directs the centre's research program on technology entrepreneurship and innovation strategy. He has published in numerous international journals on high tech industries, innovation strategy/policy and technology entrepreneurship, including, among others, the Journal of Business Venturing, Entrepreneurship Theory & Practice and Journal of Management.

Contributors

[FOREWORD]

A Blueprint for
Sustainable Development

Speech by Lim Guan Eng
Penang Chief Minister
(Penang Outlook Forum 2009)

Progress! That's what most people wish for. But real progress, progress that sees impressive improvements in the quality of life for everyone, cannot take place only at the personal level. It has to happen at the social level as well.

That's why you need politicians! And you need the civil service, you need the businessmen, you need the thinkers, you need the NGOs, and you need the people.

Progress is a collective undertaking.

Now, no other state in Malaysia has done more than Penang in pushing itself forward. Penangites have worked hard for two centuries, and they have survived. But surviving is not enough. Surviving is not the goal. What we need to do today is to put brains and muscles together to achieve a prosperity that transforms Penang from a sweat shop into a smart shop.

Once upon a time, not long ago, Penang was already a Brand Name that was instantly recognizable abroad. Penang's progress signaled the coming progress of Malaysia. Penang was ahead of other states. It was the state that defined Malaysia's future.

But I am sad to say this so openly to a room full of proud Penangites: All that was a long time ago. We have gone backwards since then. Do you know that Penang family incomes increased the least among all the states over the last ten years? I repeat, all the states, including Sabah and Sarawak!

Between 1999 and 2004, Penang family incomes grew by 2.5% annually, while the average for the whole country was 6.6%! In 1999, our income was 85% of what people in Selangor were making. Only five years after that, in 2004, we are only 68% as rich as those same people in the Klang Valley.

Penangites have not only been losing in relative income; we have also been losing our relatives. Now, even if you do not trust statistics, you have to agree that Penang families have been sending their sons and daughters abroad, down to the Klang Valley, down to Singapore, and out into the great wide world. These young people had to leave because there was a sorry lack of opportunities for them here at home. Our talents leaked away, and one can imagine the family heartache behind every such leakage. It is because of the failures of the past that I was elected as the surprise choice for Penang Chief Minister.

Looking ahead, it is critical to reverse the trend. That is the point of this conference, and of many others like it that we are planning for the near future. Before we act, we have to discuss things. We have to plan, and we have to visualize what the future is to be; and we have to visualize the path we have to take to get there.

And that is why we are gathered here today. The Penang Outlook Forum represents one further step towards creating a blueprint for the reshaping of Penang, a process already begun in many ways. We will use the ideas aired over the next two days to decide the next steps to take to bring change to Penang. These are the first steps towards a Penang Blueprint, towards turning Penang into an International City and State.

We have been there before. We have had experiences with globalization for over 200 years! Penang has the resources it needs to transform itself. I am sure you agree with me on that point. But there is one thing I must stress this morning: we are not transforming Penang simply for Penang's sake. Transforming Penang into an International City and State is simply the first step in our long-term strategy to transform Malaysia as a whole.

That is our vision – making Penang a model for others to follow. We need intelligent and experienced people to realize this blueprint. This is why this Forum has brought together some of Penang's smartest people, sons and daughters of Penang who are based either locally

or overseas, who can help us define what this new blueprint should be. Most importantly, this blueprint must rest solidly on a local system that is properly regulated and monitored, one that is transparent so that neglect and incompetence cannot hide within it. Such a structure depends on certain cornerstones being properly laid.

The first cornerstone is the quality and integrity of the political leadership. Clean, efficient and effective governance must always remain our practice and our goal. This must be a distinguishing factor of Penang as an International City and State. Hence, change starts with a change in the substance of the political leadership and the state institutions.

The second cornerstone for our transformation is the economy. The economy of an International City and State will simultaneously be competing in and complementing the global economy. Penang's economy must be ready to rise to the challenge. Cities and entire regions are locked in stiff competition with one another today, creating a multi-layered playing field. If Penang wants a leading role in this new economy, it must restructure its economy accordingly.

The present crisis is affecting all nations big and small, developed and developing. But the dark cloud has a silver lining. It is during moments like this that we can seriously rethink old economic models and reassess our own capabilities. An economic restructuring could endeavor to free us from our exports-dependent role, and bring a healthy diversification to our economy.

A restructuring must boost local employment opportunities, raise the median income level and disposable income, and lead to greater purchasing power for the people of Penang. Penang has been in the so-called middle-income trap, bordered on one side by low-cost competitors in poor countries who are competitive in mature or sunset industries and on the other by high-wage innovators in rich countries who are competitive in new or sunrise industries. To get out of this trap, we need a new holistic approach that links Penang's unique logistic position, its scenic beauty, rich and cultural heritage, social harmony, even good food with our talented human resources and strong work ethic.

The third cornerstone is definitely the most important one in the long run – the development of Penang's human capital. International Cities may boast high-tech and Space Age infrastructure, or obscene material wealth, but to be truly successful they must have one important resource: a dynamic and happy people. To attract talent, Penang must be seen to be an attractive enough place to call home. It must be a great place to work, and a great place to live. Now, cities like New York and Tokyo may be expensive places to live in, but it is in those cities that human talents are allowed to thrive. That is why they continue to be talent magnets. If we want to attract new blood to Penang, the environment here has to change as well. There must be a good environment where people feel comfortable expressing themselves, artistically or otherwise.

We must have healthy income levels in order to make their relocation here worthwhile. There must be affordable housing, good infrastructure, efficient public transportation, and good public services in general. Only then can we consistently revitalize our human and other precious resources. And not only shall we strive to train and retain local talent, we also want to bring in NEW talents to Penang. Penang needs to change for that purpose, too. Nothing kick-starts change faster than bringing in fresh new blood with new ideas and energy, and adding them to a growing talent pool.

To recap, there are eight key measures that we need to look into:

1.   Institution building as a source of growth; there is a need to respect rule of law and good governance based on CAT (competency, accountability and transparency);

2.   A sound education system that promotes a culture of excellence that is relevant to the demands of industry and economy. Emphasis naturally centers on ICT and computer knowledge. To facilitate the creation of more computer literate knowledge workers, Penang has launched a new initiative to be the first wifi state in Malaysia where wireless services will be provided free and wimax at affordable rates in 2 years time;

3.   A civil society encompassing the triple transformation of political transformation to achieve political equality, respect for human rights, supremacy of people's power and democracy; economic transformation that provides equal opportunities and relies on the energy, expertise and enterprise of our human resources; ethical transformation that establishes

integrity in public life, checks corruption and pursues socio-economic justice.

4. Encouraging creativity, innovation, research and development with new ways of thinking and new ways of doing things;

5. Establishing international benchmarks that make development sustainable – where resources that are used today in a manner that will allow them to be still available for our future generations. Penang was voted as the 10th most livable city in Asia amongst 254 cities throughout Asia;

6. Trusting in the ability of any state's greatest resource – our human resources by investing in retraining and human development;

7. Moving towards a government that works better, but that costs less. The explosion in the number of civil servants and public spending on the civil service without a corresponding rise in quality of services requires the adoption of best business practices. Such spending must be curbed not only to increase savings but ensure a value for money approach where as long as the civil service approaches international benchmarks they shall be provided with international rated pay scales.

8. Adopting a public-private partnership model of a win-win formula where public interest is upheld without sacrificing the private sector's necessity for profits. Open tenders and capping the private sector profits at a reasonable rate of return will ensure the protection of public interest without sacrificing efficiency and productivity.

A Penang Blueprint for sustainable development based on eight key measures on government, economy, society and environment to transform Penang into an international city. A blueprint only describes to us what can be a workable system. No matter how well crafted it is, it is only as good as the results it actually produces. This is the litmus test the Penang Blueprint must pass.

We must be innovative in all four areas simultaneously if we are to succeed. And the only way to do that is for us – all of us – to be stakeholders. We need smart and willing partnerships across the board. Let us begin this labour of love for Penang as equal partners where we learn together, grow together and enjoy the fruits of our labour together.

With that, I declare the Penang Outlook Forum 2009 open. Let us now air our views.

[FOREWORD]

Two Islands with Similar Experiences

Speech by Ambassador K. Kesavapany

Director of ISEAS

(Penang Outlook Forum)

ISEAS has been happy indeed in working with the Socio-economic and Environmental Research Institute (SERI) of Penang to organize this pioneer event that we are all participating in today.

I have many fond memories of my time as a young teacher here in the 1960s at the Westlands Secondary School. As a historian, I am naturally cognizant of the intimate ties that have existed between Penang and Singapore. Besides such personal ties, let us not forget that Singapore and Penang are close in many more general ways, starting with the Straits Settlements.

The people-to-people relations have always been intimate. A number of Penangites worked in Singapore and contributed greatly to Singapore's early development, such as the late Minister of Finance, Mr Hon Sui Sen from Balik Pulau.

Cultural, historical and geographical ties continue to the present day with Penang-born Singaporeans figuring prominently in Singapore's parliament. Two such individuals are Mr Khaw Boon Wan, our Minister of Health, and Ms Irene Ng, a Member of Parliament who is just finishing a book on S. Rajaratnam, one of modern Singapore's founding fathers. Indeed, you also find many old schoolboys' associations in Singapore, such as Old Frees, Old Xaverians and Chung Ling Old Boys.

Notwithstanding the old ties, both Singapore and Penang are working on new approaches to strengthen the relationship. The dynamics following the March 2008 general elections in Malaysia have made this possible. Singapore had the pleasure of receiving a visit by YB Lim Guan Eng recently. Hopefully, this will soon lead to an increase in such visits from both sides.

In the economic sector, I believe that Singaporean companies – such as the township-building company, Surbana – are involved more intensively in Penang's economy than is normally assumed. That involvement is bound to increase further in these changing times.

Culturally as well, our ties go deep. And I do not mean just the Peranakan culture that defines so much of both Penang and Singapore. Our role in the pre-war economy was similar, and our historical position as favoured ports-of-call for traders, missionaries, adventurers, and political exiles such as Sun Yat-sen and many others were also similar. Indeed, many of our experiences are similar.

Ladies and gentlemen;

There is much that we can learn from each other, and in many ways, we do act as mirrors for each other, reminding each other about values that we share and that we may be in danger of losing, caught up as we are in the political economy of the global age.

For this particular forum, we are pleased to collaborate with SERI in the formulation of new strategies to cope with the challenging times ahead,

Thank you.

Foreword

[INTRODUCTION]

Political Masters and Master Plans

Goh Ban Lee & Ooi Kee Beng

Most of the chapters in this volume are first presented at the Penang Outlook Forum 2009, held on 1-2 June 2009 at the E &O Hotel in Penang. A few others have been added because of the salience of the topics discussed, to complement those debated at the conference. Tellingly, that convention was entitled "Restructuring and Reshaping Penang".[1]

Indeed, the change of government following the General Elections of March 8, 2008, provides good reasons for a review of Penang's development, despite the fact that the existing plan, namely the Second Penang Strategic Development Plan (PSDP2), ends only in 2010.

As any student of planning learns in Planning 101, the first step in the preparation of a development plan is to understand its context. So let us briefly revisit the history of development planning of Penang and the major plans that helped to shape its economy.

As a settlement of the British East India Company and later a British colony until 1957, Penang's economy was strongly linked to regional and international trading activities. Furthermore, as a free port until the early 1970s, it was also the international link between the Malay Peninsula and resource-rich countries like Burma, Thailand and Indonesia on the one hand, with European markets on the other. While it lost its pioneer status after the founding of Singapore in 1819, for

---

1   *This was organized by the Socio-economic and Environmental Research Institute of Penang and the Institute of Southeast Asian Studies of Singapore, and was sponsored by BSG Property, with support from Khazanah Nasional, the Penang Development Corporation and InvestPenang.*

almost 170 years, it was generally economically healthier than other states on the peninsula, not to mention Sabah and Sarawak.

When Malaya achieved independence in 1957, the focus of attention was the new national capital, Kuala Lumpur. It was only natural that Port Swettenham, since renamed Port Klang, would become the main port of the country and receive all the attention and all the financial support from the federal government. Penang could not continue to depend on its free port status for its growth.

Penang Master Plans

By the early 1960s, it was abundantly clear that Penang's economic health was in a bad way. A Colombo Plan advisor, A.M. Munro, was engaged to prepare a master plan. The Penang Master Plan (commonly referred to as the Munro Report) was completed in 1964. In it, the state's poor economic conditions were made very clear:

> From being the major port and trading centre on the China run, Penang – having ousted Malacca – has itself yielded pride of place, successively, to Singapore and Hong Kong and, in recent years, has been bypassed through centralisation of development and capital investment in Port Swettenham and the Klang Valley. Port development, industrialization and vital communications have all been delayed, and have been granted little priority within the National sphere. Finally, the Island's Free Port status is now threatened with extinction. The inevitable end products of such a train of circumstances are: depression, spiralling unemployment, labour unrest and political instability (p. 132

The Munro Report called for a structural shift in the economy of Penang. More specifically, it called for an intensive programme of industrialization, focusing on the mainland portion of the state. This recommendation to locate factories on the mainland was a first as Seberang Perai, formerly known as Province Wellesley, used to be the back-water of the state, despite being the food basket for the islanders.

The Munro Report is not widely acknowledged although it did lead to the development of the Mak Mandin Industrial Estate in Butterworth and the setting of import substitution industries, such as textile, cables and wires, flour, mattresses and laminates. Furthermore, a sugar factory

and a steel mill were also built in Perai. There were also the Deep Water Wharves in Butterworth.

Despite serious efforts by the Alliance state government led by Tan Sri Wong Pow Nee, the economic situation of Penang remained bad. According to a Memorandum prepared by the Chairman of the Penang Branch of the State of Malaya Chamber of Commerce, it was actually dismal (Engel, 1968).

The Alliance lost Penang in the May 1969 general elections to the newly formed Gerakan Rakyat Malaysia (Gerakan), led by Tun Dr Lim Chong Eu, who thus became the Chief Minister of the state.

In 1970, a new master plan was prepared. It is not clear whether this was done at the request of the new state government or whether it was initiated by the earlier administration. Popularly known as the Robert Nathan Report (1970), this plan also called for a basic shift in the economic structure of the state. More specifically, it recommended the promotion of manufacturing industries, tourism, fisheries and educational, health, and research facilities was needed to pull Penang out of its economic doldrums. Most importantly, it argued that Penang would not be able to break the "poverty trap" of low productivity coupled to high unemployment. This meant that Penang would not be able achieve economic development if it merely concentrated on the import-substituting manufacturing industry as had been recommended by the Munro Report. The Robert Nathan Report suggested that Penang linked its economic activities with robust economies outside the country.

Here, it is useful to quote substantially the insightful observations made in the Robert Nathan Report. It suggested the following:

1. The redirection of Penang's economy to establish market linkages with broader, more rapidly expanding demands than those afforded by local, national and regional markets. Development in Penang is considered to have been limited by the deficiency of demand for traditional goods and services in the production of which its resources have been employed. Therefore, the Plan calls for Penang's very considerable potential for growth to be realized by "plugging in" its resources to growth industries with rapidly expanding world markets. In effect, the strategy is designed to break the self-perpetuating circle of low income, deficient

demand, stagnant production, unemployment, low incomes, etc., by introducing elements of demand that are not a function of incomes in Penang.

This is by no means a novel approach to accelerated economic growth; it is precisely the approach that has been successfully applied in other Asian Countries beset by labour redundancy and limited natural resources, such as Japan, Taiwan, Hong Kong, South Korea and, more recently, Singapore.

2. The mitigation, or removal, of constraining influences which inhibit the development of a more dynamic economy. These include some physical elements of the resource base, but perhaps more significantly, economic policies, administration and attitudes that have evolved in response to circumstances that no longer exist (1970: 37).

The significance of both the Munro Report and the Robert Nathan Report was not only in development strategies and policies, but also in infrastructure in development planning. For instance, according to the Munro Report, "One of the greatest dangers to the successful implementation of any such policy lies in the current lack of planning control within the boundaries of the State and the consequent, widespread speculation in land " (1964: 133).

Both plans stressed that in order to ensure the successful implementation of policies, there was a serious need to have a good land use plan and development control procedures. Among other things, the Robert Nathan Report recommended that a State Development and Planning Council be established to act as a "plan-formulating and policy-making body of representatives from State, Local and Quasi-Government bodies" (1970, Vol. 111:233). The State Government did actually set up a State Planning and Development Planning Committee (SPDC). It is interesting to note that in making the recommendation for a state-wide planning committee, the master plan was ahead of its time. The present powers and functions of the State Planning Committee which are provided for in the Town and Country Planning Act of 1976 are similar to those of the SPDC.

The Gerakan state government also set up a vehicle to spearhead stae development. The Penang Development Corporation (PDC) was

established in 1972 under the leadership of Datuk Chet Singh, who was then the State Financial Officer. It is also important to note that in 1972, Gerakan also became a component of the Barisan Nasional, a coalition of the Alliance, made up of Umno, MCA, MIC, PPP, PMIP and several parties from Sabah and Sarawak.

In 1974, the two local authorities in Penang Island were abolished and the island was placed under a single municipal administration, which was called the Board of Management of Penang Island. Thus, after a lapse of 86 years, the whole island was once again brought under a single municipal administration.

On the mainland, the three district councils were merged to form a single local authority. In 1976, the nomenclature of the two local authorities were changed to Penang Island Municipal Council and Seberang Perai Municipal Council.

Penang underwent rapid development in the 70's. Real GDP grew annually by 8.3 percent in 1970 to 1975, led by the manufacturing sector which grew by an average of 18 percent. The utilities and transport, storage and communication sectors also grew by 14.9 percent and 13.2 percent respectively (PSDP: 1-2). For the period 1976-1980, the growth was also equally remarkable. The GDP grew by an annual average of 11.2 percent, again led by the manufacturing sector which recorded a growth of 29.2 percent (PSDP: 1-2).

It was not always smooth sailing. In tandem with a worldwide economic slow down, the manufacturing sector registered only a two percent growth in the first half of the 1980s. However, it rebounded impressively to "almost 12 percent" after the 1985-1986 recession (PSDP: 1-2).

As a result of the robust growth of the manufacturing industries, the economic structure of Penang changed dramatically within a span of 20 years. In 1970, manufacturing accounted for only 12.7 percent of the GDP while by 1990, it was estimated that the figure had increased to 46.0 percent (PSDP: 1-9) (This figure was subsequently corrected to be 43.0 percent).

Physically, the development was largely confined to the Bayan Lepan Free Trade Zone. In other words, in less than 10 years, Penang Island was transformed from a sluggish commercial and primary product area into a vibrant industrial centre with electronic factories taking the lead. More specifically, the South-eastern part of the Island changed from a paddy and coconut area into an industrial estate producing goods used all over the world. In the northern coast of the island, small fishing villages were replaced by facilities catering to local and international tourists. In other parts of the island, particularly on the outskirts of the city, housing estates were replacing agricultural areas with indigenous attap/zinc-wooden houses.

But there were other problems facing the island. Despite the generally high per capita income, it was found that about 30 per cent of households had less than $500 household income per month. Housing for the poor was still in short supply. The physically handicapped and the aged were often ignored in planning strategies and building design. Transportation was still a problem and so was the occurrence of flash floods in the city. Environmental destruction and pollution were becoming very visible and were being painfully felt.

Despite the economic success, the Barisan Nasional component parties did not do well in the 1990 General Elections. The DAP won 14 out of the total 33 state constituencies. More importantly, Chief Minister Tun Dr. Lim Chong Eu, the man generally credited for the rapid growth of the state into Silicon Island, lost his seat. However, despite the total loss of all the MCA candidates, the Barisan Nasional still had the majority and Tan Sri Dr Koh Tsu Koon of Parti Gerakan Rakyat became the chief minister.

Penang Strategic Development Plan

The installing of the new state government coincided with the preparation of a new development plan, the Penang Strategic Development Plan (PSDP), to chart Penang's development efforts for 1991-2000. It was jointly prepared by the Institute of Strategic and International Studies (ISIS) and the Penang Development Corporation (PDC).

Although the plan maintained that manufacturing should continue leading the development of Penang, it also proposed that the state broadened its economic base. More specifically, it recommended that the state placed emphasis on the service sector through promoting higher order services such as finance, education, information technology and medical services. It also called for deepening the industrial base through the promotion of skill intensive, technology intensive and

high-value added industries. Towards this end, the plan also called for upgrading the training skills of the workforce and promoting local entrepreneurship and the growth of small and medium scale industries.

On the whole, Penang's economic performance from 1991 to 2000 was impressive, despite the 1998 Asian financial crisis that hit the state, the country and indeed many countries in East and Southeast Asia. On the whole, it registered an average growth rate of 8.2 percent per annum which was higher than the 7.3 percent growth rate provided for in PSDP (PSDP2: 2-1).

During the last decade of the 20th century, the leading sector was still manufacturing. In fact, this sector even registered a growth from 43.0 per cent to 45.7 percent in the GDP (PSDP2: 2-2). The contribution of employment by the manufacturing sector was 39.4 percent in 1999, an increase of nearly two percent from the 1990 figure. The bulk of the employment was in the electrical and electronics and textiles and garment industries.

Although Penang could boast of its robust manufacturing sector, it is important to note that the single biggest sector in terms of contribution to the overall GDP in 2000 was the service sector. It accounted for 49.5 percent in 2000, down one percent from that of 1990 (PSDP2: 2-2).

Second Penang Strategic Development Plan (PSDP2)

The Second Penang Strategic Development Plan (PSDP2) is for charting development strategies from 2001 to 2010. As stated in the first paragraph of the plan, the emphasis of development for the state is on "economic competitiveness, ecological balance, caring and sharing, cultural vibrancy and good governance" (PSDP2: 1-1). Among its ambitious targets is achieving a per capita GDP of RM25,631 by 2010 (in 1990 prices) (PSDP2: 1-4). According to the plan, this means that Penang would have achieved a "developed status" ten years earlier than stated in Vision 2020 (a target set in 1990 for the whole country by former prime minister Tun Mahathir Mohamad). As noted in the plan, "Penang can be confident of reaching the Vision 2020 target ten years earlier" (PSDP2: 1-4).

In order to achieve "developed status" with an ecological twist, the plan calls for the following "development trusts":

- Enhancing economic competitiveness;
- Improving productivity growth;
- Developing a Knowledge-based economy;
- Consolidating and e-enabling the manufacturing sector;
- Enhancing the quality of the service sector;
- Strengthening the tourism cluster;
- Revitalizing the agricultural sector;
- Providing an enabling environment for development;
- Expanding the usage of information and communication technology;
- Enhancing human resource development;
- Ensuring a sustainable transport system;
- Providing quality infrastructure;
- Sustaining ecological balance;
- Building a caring and sharing society;
- Encouraging the participation of Bumiputras and other disadvantaged groups in the economy;
- Enhancing the quality of life;
- Promoting cultural vibrancy;
- Practising good governance.

A detailed analysis of the PSDP2 will have to wait for some postgraduate student eager to do a thesis of the subject. Here it is useful to point out that the plan tries to touch all bases and thus does not provide a focus on certain areas that the state should concentrate on.

In the March 8, 2008 General Elections, for the second time in the history of Penang, Penangites voted for a change of state government. As a result, the Pakatan Rakyat, under the Chief Minister Lim Guan Eng, replaced the Barisan Nasional as the government of Penang.

Nevertheless, it would be a mistake to conclude that it was the mismanagement of the economy of Penang that caused the people to reject the Barisan Nasional at the polls. While there may be some truth that the Penang state government was wobbling in the pursuit of development and a better quality of life for the people, it is more correct to say that the voting pattern of Penangites was more strongly influenced

by what was taking place in Kuala Lumpur and Putrajaya than by Penang's economy.

At present, there is no authoritative study on Penang's current economic conditions. There is some evidence showing that Penang was not doing well in the first half of the first decade of the new millennium, compared to the past or to the rest of the country. For example, according to the Ninth Malaysia Plan (2006-2010), the rate of growth of the monthly household income of Penang from 1999 and 2004 was only 2.5 percent, the lowest among the states in the country (9MP: 378). The average for the country was 5.6 percent while the next lowest was Johore which registered a growth of 3.1 percent. The highest was Pahang with 10.2 percent.

However, it would be negligence on our part not to question the robustness of the figure of 2.5 per cent monthly household income for Penang. It is important to note that the state recorded a 5.0 per cent average growth rate for the same period when the national figure was 4.5 per cent. Those involved in producing the data should provide some explanation for this incongruence. Was there a sudden population increase? Furthermore, it should also be noted that the potential employment for Penang from 2001-2005 for Penang was 69,146, a number that was lower only to those of Selangor and Johore (p. 359).

It should be noted that Penang was still one of the richer states in 2004, with an average household income of RM3,531, up from RM3,128 in 1999. It would be expecting too much to anticipate the average household income in Penang to continue to grow at a rate of five to seven percent per annum, especially with a base figure as high as that for 1999.

It is also useful to note that Penang did relatively well in the eradication of hard-core poverty. In 2004, it registered a rate of only 0.3 percent, down from 0.7 percent in 1999 (9MP: 378). The 0.3 percent was the lowest in the country, compared to 1.5 percent for Kuala Lumpur and 23.0 percent for Sabah and 15.4 percent for Trengganu. Having said the above, the low growth rate should be a matter of concern. After all, both Kuala Lumpur and Selangor did register a growth rate of 4.1 percent and 6.9 percent from 1999 to 2004.

There is cause for worry about Penang. Being a small state and relatively far away from Putrajaya, it has to be at the forefront of innovation to keep its development momentum going. The fact that it is ruled by a coalition that is in the opposition to the national government only adds to that burden.

Conclusion

Success in development efforts depends on having a good plan and having effective leadership. Other factors such as availability of funds, efficient civil servants, availability of land and productive workers, are also important, but these are mitigated next to the first two factors.

So far, there has been no study on why Penang did so well not only in achieving very respectable growth rates in 1970 to 1990 but also in transforming the economy from a basically business and agricultural one into a manufacturing giant. Was this thanks to good planning, especially the Robert Nathan Report or a very effective leadership in the person of Tun Dr Lim Chong Eu, or both? Indeed, could a very effective leadership succeed even if the plan is of mediocre quality?

References

Engel, B. "Notes on the Economic Situation in the State of Penang", Memorandum to the State Government by the Chairman of the Penang Branch of the States of Malaya Chamber of Commerce, 1968.

Goh Ban Lee. *Urban Planning in Malaysia*. Petaling Jaya: Tempo Publishing, 1991.

Jabatan Perancangan Bandar dan Desa. *Rancangan Struktur Negeri Pulau Pinang 2020*. Pulau Pinang, 2007.

Kerajaan Negeri Pulau Pinang. *Rancangan Negeri Pulau Pinang Pertama (2001-2005)*. Unit Perancang Ekonomi Negeri Pulau Pinang, 2001.

Ninth Malaysia Plan 2006-2010. Unit Perancang Ekonomi, Jabatan Perdana Menteri, 2006

Munro. *The Penang Master Plan*, 1964.

Penang Strategic Development Plan 1991-2000. Institute of Strategic and International Studies (ISIS) and Penang Development Corporation (PDC), 1991.

Penang Development Corporation (undated) Penang – *Looking Back, Looking Ahead Years of Progress*. Georgetown Printers.

Robert Nathan. *The Penang Master Plan*, 1970.

State Government of Penang (undated) *The Second Penang Strategic Development Plan 2001-2010*.

[1]

Moving Penang from Past to Present

Lee Kah Choon & Chan Huan Chiang

Introduction: Economic Transformation in Malaysia

In 1994, a group of scholars at the Research School of Pacific Studies, Australian National University (ANU), published the findings on Malaysia from their study on industrial transformation in South-East Asia.[1] Their scholarly interest was in the scale and speed of the transformation of Malaysia's economy – exceeded in the region only by Singapore – from the 1950s through to the end of the 1970s, largely driven by the export production of commodities: originally tin and rubber, and later palm oil, timber and petroleum. By the 1980s, the export of manufactured goods had taken over as the leading sector, turning Malaysia into a high-growth economic performer. The transformation was not only economic, but had been accompanied by both social impacts as well as physical changes to the urban and rural landscape. In some ways, the publication was a revisit of the study by Silcock and Fisk,[2] thirty years before. Back then it was the familiar transition from primary production into low-level manufacturing aimed at reducing income leakages due to imports and to diversify the employment base. In the decades that followed, the process of transformation had become much more complex and called for the need for a more comprehen-

---

1   Harold Brookfield, ed., *Transformation with Industrialization in Peninsular Malaysia* (*Kuala Lumpur: Oxford University Press, 1994*).

2   *T H Silcock and E K Fisk, The Political Economy of Independent Malaya: A Case Study in Development (Canberra: Australian National University, 1963).*

sive view of the process of transformation from different perspectives, something the scholars undertook in 1994.

One view was to look at the transformation not as an economy going from one stage of production to the next in response to economic growth, but to trace the transformation back further by arguing that in fact an industrial structure organized with the export trade in mind had been developed as early as during colonial times. There had already existed such things as backward and forward linkages, say from agriculture to production and commerce, as well as an understanding of economic impacts such as labour pricing and the urban-rural dichotomy. Another view was that different insights are revealed when we try to understand transformation from a macro perspective as opposed to a micro one. Broad indicators about the macro economy sensitize us to structural changes on an aggregate basis: the urban-rural divide, the agricultural sector versus the manufacturing one, low, middle, and high income earners and so on. But also within these categories were the man-on-the-street stories, learned from case-studies, about individuals whose livelihoods have been altered by larger structural changes to the economy. A third angle on the transformation took into consideration the alteration of geographical space that economic analysis usually fails to take account of. Our understanding often stops at what and how much has changed and neglects the fact that sometimes it is where changes took place that the most profound impacts requiring intervention and policy prescriptions can be found. Finally, there was also the political account of the economic transformation – initially this was an economy under colonial rule and then, during the post-independence years, Malaysia became an uniquely multi-racial as well as multi-cultural economy, quite unlike its Asian and Southeast Asian neighbours.

There might not have been much more to learn about the Malaysian economic transformation story had it not been for international events that impacted on Malaysia's economy in the nineties. One might agree that globalization is synonymous with the concept of the international division of labour that occurs as a result of multinational companies locating offshore by way of foreign direct investments or FDI. Centres of production are traditionally located either at the site of raw materials or at the market place, depending on which is cheaper to transport, raw materials or finished goods.[3] With globalization, labour costs became a key factor, and with the development of the jumbo jet, economical and time-saving transport allowed raw material inputs to be flown into new production sites around the globe; from where the round trip back would be made, bringing finished products into the markets of the North and the West. Because of globalization, Penang could, as far back as thirty years ago, be proud of the words Made in Malaysia stamped on computer chips used all over the world, for Penang soon became one of the biggest suppliers in the world.

The nineties, however, saw a series of events that altered the process of globalization in ways that may not have been imagined by researchers who had been trying to understand and explain the phenomenon up to this point. Many of these events were technological such as the Internet. Computer networks, file sharing and emails had already been in existence for many years even then, but the take up and penetration rates brought by very efficient internet protocols to link remote computers together, higher data transfer rates, as well as a very much lower cost of equipment has taken global communication to a degree quite unimaginable then. To multinational companies, FDI was no longer simply production in some strange new land that might be hard to coordinate and control. Instead, global communication meant instantaneous inventory control, making purchasing orders and production planning infinitely quicker. Other events, however, are developmental, such as that of China joining the World Trade Organization to become the formidable presence it now is, a country with such enormous capacities and low wage rates that more and more foreign direct investment funds are diverted there. Global country to country competition had taken on a new dimension; it is no longer just a matter of making oneself an attractive investment location through tax incentives, because exports now play a more dominant role in a country's economy and growth. Losing one's competitiveness can spell recession and job losses. Policy making and strategizing to ensure an efficient and effective export production base have become critical success factors.

Then in the middle of 1997, somehow what was seen as the Asian miracle played by Asian tigers and mini-tigers was thought to have

---

3   See William Alonso, "Location Theory", in Regional Policy: Readings in Theory and Applications, edited by John Friedman and William Alonso (Cambridge: MIT Press, 1975).

come to a quick and merciless end with the Asian financial crisis. The phenomenal annual economic growth rates experienced in the years before 1997 at near or beyond double digit rates proved too good to be lasting. The International Monetary Fund or IMF was there ready to perform its mandated function, imposing financial disciplining conditions on countries hurt by the crisis as part of its rescue regimen. It had not been many years previous that the IMF had performed similar tasks among the tequila economies that were suffering from the so-called peso-problem involving rising money supply in the face of falling foreign exchange reserves that had created a runaway inflation effect. Following the IMF prescriptions, the tequila economies moved to free-floating exchange rates so that the issue of domestic currency was no-longer dependent on available foreign reserves.[4]

Many people were therefore surprised that the Asian economies recovered quickly, in a matter of a few years. Malaysia's economic recovery plan went smoothly despite having defied the IMF prescription and pegging the ringgit to a fixed exchange rate against the U.S. dollar and imposing capital control from 1998 until 2005. Unfortunately, the recovery in the Asian economies did not last long. When prices shot past USD$100 per barrel early in 2008, there was fear of an even greater oil shock. Oil has become somewhat decoupled from the gross domestic product in today's economies compared to previous oil shocks because energy inputs have fallen for every value-added dollar earned and thus cushioning the fall of the economy due to the high price of oil. Today, oil has fallen to the US$50 range but the global recession (demand levels not keeping up with potential output from the employment of production resource) or deflation (fallen nominal rates of growth that prevent financing and investments) that looms over economies around the world is threatening jobs especially in export oriented economies like Penang, bringing the even more serious threat of depression (fallen asset values that fuel bankruptcies, destroying productive capacities multiplying the depth of the recession and prolonging beyond the period of normal business cycles).

The research question of this paper is how much of our understanding of the past is relevant (or useful) as we prepare for the future? This

4   When the exchange rate is fixed, the value of a currency depends on the size of the country's foreign reserve. But if a free exchange rate is adopted, then value is just a function of supply and demand.

is Penang transiting from the past and into the future. Should we keep reinventing ourselves, rather like how viruses mutate or how species evolve through adaptation to become resilient in the future, or should we keep looking back to our past with the intention of harvesting whatever resources we can find and use these as leverage to propel us forwards? Culture and traditions are intrinsic features of our lives that give us identities we often romanticize about and preserve as heritage. But are there lessons in history that also say progress usually occurs at the price of getting rid of the old and adopting the new? What should we think of tribal societies or conservative societies like the Amish people in Lancaster County in Pennsylvania that ignore changes in the world, preferring instead to keep traditional lifestyles that have gone unchanged for centuries?[5] It would seem that most modern societies have become secularly pragmatic, embracing progress in the form of modern technologies and lifestyles while still holding dear their cultural identities in spirit if not in practice except maybe occasionally during cultural festivities.

Employment of Resources

Traditional growth theories that led to our early understanding of how countries trade, are based on the concept of comparative advantage.[6] Economic production is closely linked to natural resource endowment. In colonial Malaya, rubber and tin formed the original pillars of the economy. The rubber species originated from Brazil but thrived in Malaysia as an economic crop. Penang was not an important producer of these commodities but the industrial-commercial structure that had developed during colonial times gave Penang the role of a shipping port and perhaps it is also for this reason that tin ore from neighbouring Perak was brought by railroad to Penang and there smelted into ingots before export. The industrial organization that developed during colonial times had a spatial dimension patterned out of regional specialization. Comparing employment in Penang with Perak (see Table 1), the difference in specialization of labour in the primary, secondary and tertiary sectors can be clearly observed between the two

5   See "The Amish and the Plain People" <http://www.800padutch.com/amish.shtml>

6   Philippe Aghion and Peter Howitt, Endogenous Growth Theory (Cambridge: MIT Press, 1998).

states, revealing the backwards-forwards industrial linkage as well as a geography that has not changed very much with time.

Table 1: Employment in Penang and Perak (1921-1980) ;
Percentage by Sectors

PENANG	primary	secondary	other
1921	46	11	42
1931	38	11	52
1947	35	14	51
1980	14	34	53

PERAK	primary	secondary	other
1921	71	5	24
1931	68	5	27
1947	78	8	24
1980	43	17	40

Source: based on numbers found on Table 1.3 of Brookfield (1994)7

It must not be forgotten that the abovementioned linkages and geography were based on production for export, while the success of the pattern over time would suggest that as long as industrialization and exports go hand in hand, such a pattern will likely continue. As Table 2 shows, the distribution of Penang's employment in percentage across the different sectors in 2008 had not deviated much from the 1980 pattern found on Table 1.

Table 2: Employment in Penang (1990-2008) ;
Percentage by Sectors

	1990	2000	2004	2008
agric	8	2	2	2
mining	0	0	0	0
manuf	34	41	37	33
construction	7	6	7	7
services	52	51	54	57

Source: Penang Statistics SERI Penang, various issues
http://www2.seri.com.my/Penang%20Statistics/2008/Q4%20Oct-Dec%202008%20II.pdf

---

7   Harold Brookfield, *"Transformation Before the Late 1960s"*, Transformation with Industrialization in Peninsular Malaysia, edited by Harold Brookfield (Kuala Lumpur: Oxford University Press, 1994).

This thrust to industrialize Penang's export sector may be seen as a centre-periphery model[8] where production "sweatshops" in Asia are dependent on America as the chief export market. The sustainability of such a model for trade is highly questionable given the chronic twin (budget and current account) deficits that the U.S. has been suffering and which has caused advocates to ask for a policy and strategic shift away from export dependence.

However, MIER[9] executive director, Mohamed Ariff, has argued that the present "export-led growth strategy is not an option, but a must for the country" and "domestic demand is no substitute for external demand".[10] Not only is Malaysia's population small compared to Indonesia, India and China, but given that foreign economic interest in Malaysia is due to the country's vast trade linkages, should trade be de-emphasized, foreign economic interest will falter. The position of Quah Boon Huat, also from MIER, is that if deindustrialization were to occur in Malaysia, it would be for the wrong reasons.[11] The country's economic development continues to be driven by investments and imported technology and designs, with the nation's competitive advantage lying in efficiency and manufacturing.

Manufacturing in Malaysia is at a crossroads. The manufacturing share of the gross domestic product or GDP was 27 percent in 1990, climbing to 32 percent in 2000, and then falling to 30 per cent in 2007. Even though the manufacturing share of total employment has risen (20% in 1990 and 28% in 2000), the rate of increase has fallen by such a degree that in the new millennium, the manufacturing share of employment had only risen to 29% by 2007. While the waning of manufacturing is suggestive of Malaysia evolving into a tertiary stage economy, the real indication of this evolution does not lie in contributions by these sectors to the GDP alone. The falling share of employ-

8   Michael Dooley, David Folkerts-Landau and Peter Garber, "An Essay on the Revised Bretton Woods System", NBER working paper no.9971 (Cambridge Mass. 2003).

9   Malaysian Institute of Economic Research.

10   Quoting Mohamed Ariff in Cecilia Kok, "Search for a new growth model", in biz. thestar.com.my, April 2009 <http://www.halalfocus.com/artman2/publish/asia/Search_ for_a_new_growth_model.shtml> (accessed 26 April 2009).

11   Quah Boon Huat, "Deindustrializing for the Wrong Reason" <http://www.mier.org. my/newsarticles/archives/pdf/quah20_4_2009.pdf> (accessed 20 April 2009)

ment in the overall economy by the manufacturing sector has been the result of higher productivity levels, leading to a need for fewer workers in manufacturing. This has been coupled with a reduced demand for exports from abroad. Falling demand results in a slow-down in manufacturing output and productivity, preventing full employment and in turn leading to inefficiency in resource utilization. The term being used is negative deindustrialization associated with stagnating real incomes and rising unemployment.

The labour productivity numbers for Malaysia from Public Bank given on Table 3 are indicative of negative deindustrialization as suggested by MIER analysts.[12] At growth rates of between two and three percent a year, labour productivity is only moving in tandem with population growth rates, implying that if we were to ignore other sources of economic growth, labour input alone is merely offsetting inflation rates, keeping welfare levels at 1980 levels.

Table 3: Labour Productivity And Productivity Growth Rates, Malaysia, 1980-2005

RM million	1980	1990	2000	2005	
Manufacturing	13.5	19.5	26.3	26.7	
Pvt. services	17.6	17.5	28.1	30.2	
Other sectors	9.9	13.2	18.6	20.8	
% growth p.a.	1980-1989	1990-1999	2000-2005	1980-2005
Manufacturing		3.9	2.4	2.8	2.8
Pvt. services		0.3	5.2	2.5	2.5
Other sectors		3.7	2.9	3.2	3.2

Source: Based on numbers found in Public Bank Economic Review August 2005

If, as Professor Mohamed Ariff states, labour inputs have not led to welfare gains in Malaysia, then real per capita income gains must have largely come from capital investments. Capital led growth is quite unlike growth obtained from labour inputs. In the case of labour, the amount available can only come from population increase and labour

---

12 Quah Booh Huat, "Services sector in Malaysia: Part 1", in Public Bank Economic Review, August 2005 <http://ww2.publicbank.com.my/cnt_review77.html>

participation rates (unless labour is imported) and therefore welfare gains are very much dependent on increased labour productivity that must surpass growth in the population. Capital inputs, on the other hand, can be increased through financing systems such as capital markets development, but, unfortunately, as technology levels increase, capital efficiency (the capital to output ratio) tends to fall, requiring more and more capital for each unit of output.

Analysis conducted by the Public Bank that attempted to link the nominal growth of Malaysia's gross domestic product or GDP to manufacturing investment figures found the correlation coefficient between these variables to be 0.729 (a value of 1 shows perfect link and 0 shows absolutely no link).[13] Fitting a regression line using GDP as the dependent variable and total investments as the independent variable for data between 1980 and 1999, resulted in parameters estimates .= 55,771 and .5.624 (t statistics 4.523 and therefore significant). The regression line assumes a fixed relationship between GDP and capital investments throughout the period covered by the data set and says nothing relevant about how this relationship is changing over time. The Public Bank report, however, did say that "in the 1980s, total approved manufacturing investment was increasing at a compounding rate of 28.5 per cent per year, before it stabilized at a relatively high level in the 1990s". This means that if economic growth or, more specifically, manufacturing sector growth occurs below 28% annually, then the need for capital has been rising disproportionately to growth. Our own rough calculations using the same data show that in the period 1980 to 1999, investments rose at 12% annually, whereas nominal GDP growth rose by only 8% a year, lending, therefore, further evidence that capital inputs do become less efficient over time.

Primary to Secondary to Tertiary Transitions

As mentioned, Penang has had a much smaller primary production sector compared with the rest of the country. Still, there are some insights to be gained by looking more carefully at the primary to secondary to tertiary transitions undergone. The stereotyped account is the enclave (territory under foreign dominion) in which production

---

13 *"Manufacturing investments in Malaysia", Public Bank Economic Review <http://ww2.publicbank.com.my/cnt_review17.html> (December 2000).*

amounted only to resource exploitation to satisfy foreign rather than domestic demand with little indigenous potential for either human resource development or capital formation. Consequently, the gaining of independence in 1957 provided the needed freedom from colonial exploitation for local potential to be developed. An alternative thesis has been argued by Overton and by Abdul Samad (1994).[14] Rather than seeing independence as a watershed event that enabled the transition away from rural peasantry and urban working class to the social vibrancy and economic growth we are familiar with in Malaysia today, the alternative is to view post-independent development of the agriculture industry and of the service sector as merely a continuing and gradual extension from the past into the present. It has been argued that such inter-sector linkages were already present throughout much of colonial times and that post-colonial development merely built on the existing structures. In other words, independent Malaya, and later Malaysia, did not start at point zero but merely continued down an existent path.

Seen in the light of such an alternative thesis, Penang's industrialization had not been a post-independent creation but can instead be explained as being the result of the agriculture to industry to commerce inter-sector linkage. It may be true that the passing of the Free Trade Zone Act in 1971 acted as an incentive to attract foreign direct investments by multinational companies to places such as Bayan Lepas, Penang, to produce computer chips, rather than build on existing agricultural and manufacturing practices. Yet, the industrial base that eventually emerged in Penang did not begin in 1970, but was perhaps an adaptive evolution of the existing industrial organization at the time. The foreign technology, capital and modern management that came with FDI provided the means for such an adaptation to occur.

Land Use and Regional Development

Inter sector linkage forwards and backwards has a geography and as such, industrial organization will also imply a spatial organization. In this linkage, Penang has not been a primary commodities producer in

---

14 John Overton, "Agriculture and Industry in Colonial Malaya" and Abdul Samad Hadi, "Agriculture and Industry: Towards Vertical Integration", in Transformation with Industrialization in Peninsular Malaysia, edited by Harold Brookfield (Kuala Lumpur: Oxford University Press, 1994).

comparison to other states. Despite this, even at a time in the country's history when commodities formed the pillars of the country's economy, Penang was a key element within this industrial organization. Produce came by train and was semi-manufactured in Penang and then serviced by local commerce (banking, insurance, legal services, freight forwarding). The country had long been involved in international trade using Penang as one of the region's major shipping ports.

The geography of industrialization along the lines of a centre (production and service focus) and a hinterland (natural resource focus) gives rise to the concept of growth-triangles involving different production locations synergizing together and creating multiplier effects due to inter-sector and hence inter-location linkages. Since rubber and tin are no longer the main commodity exports from the country but palm oil, petroleum and timber are, the traditional geographical pattern of Penang's inter-sector linkages with Perak and the other states are no longer observable. Instead, new variants of the concept of spatial linkages are being developed as part of an industrial and developmental strategy. A large scale version is the ASEAN Free Trade Agreement (AFTA) which is actually more relevant to Malaysia than Penang since much of Penang's trade is outside of the ASEAN[15] region. On a smaller scale is the Indonesia-Malaysia-Thailand Growth Triangle or IMT-GT launched in 1993 with the aim of liberalizing and integrating the combined market of a population of nearly 70 million to complement economic activities across the region, hopefully thereby making efficient use of the region's vast resources, lowering logistics costs and improving small scale economies.[16]

On a much smaller scale is the development of the Northern Corridor Economic Region or NCER development programme, covering the four northern west-coast states: Perlis, Kedah, Penang and Perak. This

15 The Association of South East Asian Nations is made up of ten nations in Southeast Asia. AFTA is the phased reduction of intraregional trade tariffs being implemented. Its scope has been extended to explore issues such as customs standards harmonization and financial swap mechanisms.

16 See the IMT-GT homepage for additional information <http://www.imtgt.org/About.htm> The Asian Development Bank undertook a detailed feasibility study and formulated a framework for cooperation across the three nations in six priority areas: Infrastructure development; agriculture and fisheries; trade; tourism; human resource development, and professional services. See <http://www.adb.org/IMT-GT/about.asp> and in <http://www.adb.org/IMT-GT/partnership.asp> .

programme is aimed at the transformation and expansion of industries to accelerate economic growth and elevate income levels. Modernizing agriculture is one of the focal development priorities. As of March 2009, 17 projects of the 40 programmes had taken off under the supervision of the Northern Corridor Implementation Authority (NCIA).[17]

A Note about State Economies: Production Output versus Income[18]

Because Malaysia is a federation, it is often looked at as being comprised of many independent state economies that unite to form an overall national economy. The European Union is a huge counterpart example where many individual economies of independent nations unionized themselves to form a larger bloc. In doing so, a degree of economic management has to be surrendered by the different sovereignties and transferred to a central body like the European Central Bank located in Brussels where monetary policies are conducted. In Malaysia, it is Bank Negara that undertakes economic management centrally on behalf of all the different states.

But Malaysia's states are not complete economies (except for Sabah and Sarawak) when it comes to the demand side. The relevant demand components: consumption, government spending, investments and exports-imports are not individually tracked. Tracking the performance of these demand components allows for economic policy (fiscal, monetary and trade) prescriptions to address their twin goals: economic growth and economic stability. Although individual states have their state economy planning units (unit perancang ekonomi negeri or UPEN) their role is more narrowly focused on overseeing development investment proposals by the private sector and on coordinating public (fiscal) investment projects in their respective states.

Beyond the role of the UPENs, much of Malaysia's economy is centrally managed with a single set of policies that do not give special considerations to individual states. For this reason, the national accounts are also centrally assembled, and it is thereby that the gross

---

17 See the NCER homepage for more information <http://www.ncer.com.my>.

18 See Chan Huan Chiang, "Population Growth and Distribution: Impact on Regional Development", MIER National Outlook Conference, Kuala Lumpur, 27-28 November 2007.

domestic product (GDP) numbers are calculated. From the Third through to the Fifth Malaysia Plan, covering the period from 1976 to 1990, there were dedicated chapters on regional development within which the state equivalent of the national GDP numbers (the correct term is gross regional product or GRP) were officially reported according to broad sectors of the economy: agriculture, mining, manufacturing, construction, utilities, and services. The technique that was used to obtain GRP numbers was devised by a consultant engaged by the Economic Planning Unit (EPU) that used a disbursement formula that apportioned national GDP numbers for each sector into their individual state contributions.[19] A wide range of information was used to determine the apportioning formula: population, employment, productivity, land area, survey statistics of manufacturing industries, etc. From these data items, one immediately sees that state GRP estimates are supply side (potential GRP) numbers.

The Sixth Malaysia Plan 1991-1995, however, did not have a chapter on regional development. All that was mentioned was a one and a half page, five paragraph section entitled "regional development strategies" without reports of any numbers on the state economies. When the regional development chapters were resumed in the Seventh and Eighth Malaysia Plans, covering the period 1996 through to 2005, official GRP figures for the different states, by sectors, were no longer made available. In these plans, only the overall state GRP numbers, without sectors, were reported. In the Ninth Malaysia Plan, 2006-2010, official state GRP numbers were not made available, with only overall state GRP growth rate numbers being given.

Many reasons may be offered for this policy by the government not to make more detailed state GRP numbers available to the public as of the Ninth Plan. Lack of know-how, or statistics, as to how to estimate these numbers cannot be the reason, since the government has made these numbers available before. The more plausible explanation is that without looking at components on the demand side, and the ability to mitigate them through policy prescriptions, state GRP numbers are less relevant. The issue of disaggregating the national economy to the different states is more meaningful if we refer to states as people

19   See Robert Turgoose, "Gross Regional Product: A Review", mimeographed (Kuala Lumpur, Economic Consultant Ltd., 1980).

rather than places. Thus the concern should be on income levels of people from different states rather than where production was carried out.

In this regard then, the attention should be on the state equivalent of the gross national product GNP and not the GDP. The GNP is the measure of national income and therefore the concern should be on how we are to measure state incomes. Economically speaking, incomes are factor payments: profits, wages, interest and rent. The GNP is GDP net of factor payments abroad, i.e., subtracting profits, wages, interest and rent to non-nationals participating in Malaysia's economy and adding similar payments to Malaysian nationals earning these from economies all over the world. GNP numbers are important because per-capita income, which is a measure of economic welfare and its change over time, is GNP divided by population and not GDP divided by population as it is commonly mistaken.

When we consider state incomes, therefore, in the GNP sense, our concern is not whether there is more production output located, say, in Kelantan than Terengganu but whether Kelantanese are earning more factor payments than Terengganuites regardless of where such income is earned. There is little impediment for Malaysians to make their homes anywhere in the country and population gets redistributed as a result of economic opportunities. In many cases, the people who populated the various states in 1957, when the federal constitution was framed, and the people who now live there, fifty years later, are no longer the same in terms of their origins. Is development of regions across the country delivering the constitutional promise of more equitable growth in the different states, or is it for all Malaysians, leaving sentiments of statehood aside, to instead embrace the sentiment of nationhood? In other words, is Malaysia a federation only in name but operationally a single nation?

Fiscal Federalism

Fiscal federalism in Malaysia is described in eight chapters found in Part VI of the Federal Constitution that covers articles 73 through to 91.[20] These delineate relations between the federal and state gov-

---

20 *Legal Research Board, Laws of Malaysia: Federal Constitution, International Law Book Series. (Petaling Jaya, Selangor: Legal Research Board, 2007).*

ernments, within which Article 74 pertains to the subject of federal and state laws. Here, the constitution divides the making of laws into the First (federal), Second (state) and Third (concurrent) Lists, and declares that the federal government has jurisdiction over the first and third lists while the states are only given authority over the second list (such lists can be found in the Ninth Schedule).

Access by states to public monies held by the federal government has undergone a long debate in Malaysia and elsewhere.[21] Shankaran Nambiar[22] observed that because of the limited scope of the second (state) list, states could do little to direct the nature or course of their own development, citing examples such as communication, transport, education and health that are federal concerns outside the control of states, resulting in a situation where development becomes very much at the discretion of the federal government. He said that Penang, for instance, has long complained about worsening traffic congestion and a need for a second bridge link to the mainland. A second bridge would fall under the jurisdiction of federal allocations for improvement in transportation, which falls in its turn under the country's five year development plan. Federal allocations to the states follow various formulae under various grants: the launching grant which is based on population and land area, the annual equalization grant which is to bridge the gap between fiscal capacity and fiscal need in terms of performing obligatory duties of service extension and small infrastructure development and the balancing grant which mainly concerns deficits from civil servant salaries and other administrative costs.

However, the ongoing debate appears to overlook the fact that even though there is a method (formula) for making allocations to the states, the federal government can go further to "subvert" this by spending money disproportionately through its many ministries (all of

21 Paul Hobson, "Federal-State Fiscal Relations in the Malaysian Federation: An Evaluation of the Existing Arrangements and Some Proposals for Reform," commissioned work for the Malaysian Institute for Economic Research (MIER), funded by the Canadian International Development Agency as part of an Institutional Co-operation Program between MIER and Queen's University (1989). See also John Kincaid and Anwar Shah,eds. The Practice of Fiscal Federalism: Comparative Perspectives. McGill-Queen's Press (2007), and Jonathan Rodden, "Reviving Leviathan: Fiscal Federalism and the Growth of Government", International Organization 57 (2003), pp.695-729.

22 Shankaran Nambiar, "Malaysia", in John Kincaid and Anwar Shah (eds.) Ibid. (2007).

which have "presence" at the state level). One example put forward is the locating of University Sains Malaysia's medical hospital in Kelantan in 1983, apparently as a "reward" to Kelantanese for electing the same party coalition that formed the federal government to form the Kelantan state government during the 1978, 1982 and 1986 general elections. Kelantan has since the 1990 elections come under the opposition rule of Parti Islam or PAS. Basically, the federal government can either squeeze or flood Kelantan with money by spending via ministries rather than through the state fiscal allocation mechanism.

The state government which is formed by the same party coalition as the federal government is obviously subservient. The chief minister will likely listen to the prime minister. But if the state government is from the opposition party coalition, as in Penang today, then how can the state sidestep efforts by the federal government to squeeze funding to the state? The Penang bridge issue mentioned by Shankaran and the rapid transit system are cases in point. The state makes a lot of publicity saying that all the analyses show that a second bridge and a transit system are needed, so much so that the federal government cannot refuse to take up the matter, or risk appearing incompetent. The federal government then faces a dilemma. On the one hand, the federal government wants to discredit the state government, formed by the opposition, by making it ineffective through lack of funding so that the party may lose in the next election. But if the federal government oversteps, then the people in the state may become so angry with the federal government because of a lack of government delivery in education, health, safety, etc. (the various ministry functions), that it may be difficult in the future to recapture the state from the opposition party.

Micro Level Impacts

On an aggregate basis, policy advocates talk about prescriptions for structural changes aimed at "tweaking" the economy to bring about increased resiliency and competitiveness in response to external challenges. Change, however, especially those brought by interventions, affects different individuals and households in different ways. For even though those in authority may be sensitive to and sympathize with those who become worse off, there is really little that policy prescriptions can do to ease the sufferings of these individuals or households. The reason is policy analysis can only look at data on a group basis, for which sometimes there are only very few categories. For example, when the government decided to ease the burden of high petrol prices in 2008, it only divided the people groups into two categories: those who own two-litre cars and above and those whose cars have capacities below this cut off. The first group gets a reduction of RM200 in their annual road tax, meaning that if one happens to get caught near the low end of this cut-off, one ends up paying around RM200 instead of the more common rate of about RM400. On the other hand, if one is fortunate enough to fall below the minimum of this two litre cut-off even by a few cubic centimetres, one ends up receiving a cash-back rebate of RM625 after the road tax is paid. This means pocketing more than RM200 after paying the road tax of about RM400. This scheme makes no distinction between whether one is wealthy or poor but merely assumes that the wealthy will tend to own big capacity cars and vice versa. Imagine a wealthy person who owns many cars below two litres driven by different members of the family. This person might possibly receive a couple of thousands worth of government financial assistance when the money might prove more useful to someone else.

Policies and Plans

From the above assessment of Penang's development history and present circumstance, we are now in position to evaluate the kinds of policies and plans that have been announced to address the development of Penang. The policy thrust has long been to attract investments for economic growth and sustenance by leveraging on a list of Penang's essential qualities: a vibrant city on a tranquil island, an appealing lifestyle, reliable infrastructure and logistics, an educated workforce, and cost-wise very competitive. The Penang story is often told as starting in 1786 when it was called Prince of Wales Island by Francis Light. Over the centuries, Penang has evolved to become the multiracial, multilingual and truly Asian island it is today, with diverse cultural events being held throughout the year, events which are promoted eagerly for tourism as part of the year-long Pesta Pulau Pinang (Penang festivities) programmes. These cultural events help celebrate and preserve traditions that link younger Penangites to their forefathers. Despite this, many people today have forgotten that in the nineteen century Penang was a Straits Settlement free port. In fact, so important a port was it

along the international trade route that it came to be referred to as the Pearl of the Orient.

Today Penang is more often called the silicon valley of the East – implying an industrial zone teeming with multinational firms linking backwards to a supply chain of local subcontractors and original equipment manufacturers or OEMs existing alongside the services sector that supports trade and commerce (banking, insurance, legal services) on the one hand, and tourism (hotels, restaurants, retail outlets) on the other. These varied economic activities are leveraged on Penang's heritage of a colonial past that fused Penang's rich and diverse cultures of local folks with foreign presence and, in some ways, domination. They are also leveraged on the island-mainland landscape and natural ecology that offer both seashore beaches as well as hills from which the tourism industry is developed. More recently, the concept of tourism has been reinterpreted to cover foreign visitors who come to Penang for treatment (medical tourism made up two thirds of the nation's total fetching revenues of RM400 million in 2007) or to attend college (education tourism). Regional development thus involves harmonizing the economic role of Penang, as made up of the above industries and services, with the household sector, which is made up of a population of one and a half million people (5.5% of the national population), their housing, their daily commuter movements and their recreational needs, as well as desire to enhance and preserve Penang's beauty and its environment.

Amenities in Penang are modern. There are good health services available and an adequate supply of both public and international schools, as well as recreational and sports facilities. Policy makers like to publicise reports in which, for example, Penang has been voted twenty-second best destination to visit in the New York Times 44 Places to go in 2009 list or Georgetown has been ranked tenth place in the European Expats Top Preferred Asian Locations by ECA International.[23] The idea being to woo foreign participation by saying Penang is a good place to stay if one were to make investments here compared

---

23 Seth Sherwood and Gisela Williams, "The 44 places to go in 2009", The New York Times, January 2009 <http://www.nytimes.com/interactive/2009/01/11/travel/20090111_DESTINATIONS.html>; Administrator II, "European expats' top 10 preferred Asian locations", Visit Penang, 13 March 2009, <http://www.visitpenang.gov.my/portal/latest-news/1-latest-news/550-european-expats-top-10-preferred-asian-locations.html>.

to just another low cost location on the globe. For many years now, the property development sector in Penang has been shifting its market focus to target foreign buyers in response to the Malaysian My Second Home or MM2H programme by building profitable high-end residential properties. The MM2H offers non Malaysians a ten-year renewable visa along with a variety of incentives. Some 12,000 people have been approved, with the majority being those wishing to retire in Malaysia or to spend extended periods in Malaysia.[24]

Given these policy thrusts in Penang's development, its production capacity was examined by looking at available and missing portions of the value chain by Anna Ong (2000).[25] She explained the emergence of industrialization in Penang by noting that the state had no natural resources endowment. When the Investment Incentives Act was passed in 1968 to allow foreign direct investments to enter into the country as part of a strategy for the export orientation of industries, Penang offered cheap and easily trained labour[26]. In one way Penang was selected as a favourable investment location because of the comparative advantage that labour availability offered. But other issues, such as the strategy by multinationals to develop linkages with local industries as outsourcing partners and to undertake vendor development such as technology transfer along the supply chain and the role of government incentives and institutional strengthening, appear to be more important factors underlying the success of Penang as one of the nation's industrial bases. These "partnerships" between multinational and local firms and the "partnerships" between the public and private sectors have been keystones, with the role that the government has played continuing to be undeniable.[27]

---

24   See MM2H homepage, <http://www.mm2h.com>.

25   Anna Ong Cheng Imm, "Building Penang's competitive advantage in sustaining growth and foreign direct investments", unpublished M.A. thesis (Penang: Universiti Sains Malaysia, 2000).

26   Donella Caspersz, "Globalisation and Labour: a Case Study of EPZ Workers in Malaysia", Economic and Industrial Democracy 19 (2) (1998).

27   Jason Brown, "The Role of the State in Economic Development Theory, the East Asia Experience, and the Malaysia Case", Asian Development Bank Staff Paper No. 52 (Manila, 1993).

Increasingly, policy makers are realizing the importance of soft issues such as knowledge, environmental correctness, political transparency and public accountability as well as the need to be socio-culturally robust. The Higher Education Ministry began to implement the teaching of the soft-skills module in 2006 and the race-relations module in 2007 in Malaysian public universities which have specific social objectives as part of their national development priorities.28 In 2008, the entrepreneurship module was also added.29 Apparently, not enough was done as far as voters were concerned. The last general elections on 8 March 2008 saw, for the first time in the nation's history, the loss of the two-thirds parliamentary majority (required for constitutional amendments) by the ruling party coalition as well as the loss of more state legislatures than had been traditionally possible. The electorate's confidence is not merely gained through feeding and clothing the masses and facilitating modernity. After fifty years of independence, developments in education, income levels, information technology and political maturity have raised public expectations significantly.

Conclusions

One may feel disappointed that policies and plans in Penang, as outlined in the previous section, appear incoherent. On the one hand, there is the tendency to make reference to the legacy of past merits and longing for ways in which our heritage can, somehow, form part of the resource upon which Penang's future potential can be built. On the other hand, there is also a tendency to stretch our imagination by venturing out and trying new things. As a result, all sorts of rhetoric and actions in the name of policy making and planning transpire, each framed and set in motion to achieve a certain policy objective with little concern for how one set of actions might either aid or disrupt another.

---

28 Karen Chapman, "Undergrads to learn soft skills from next month", The Star Online, 13 June 2006 <http://thestar.com.my/news/story.asp?file=/2006/6/13/nation/14517221&sec=nation>; Suzieana Uda Nagu, "Ethnic relations module not given due importance", New Straits Times, 12 May 2009, <http://www.nst.com.my/Current_News/NST/Sunday/LearningCurve/20090201135639/1>.

29 Juhaidi Yean Abdullah, "Malaysian public universities and new approaches to meeting global challenges", Islam Hadhari, 5 January 2009 <http://islamhadhari.net/?p=1922>.

What this paper has attempted to do is to suggest a pause in order to take stock not of physical or social factors that we might use to allow Penang to grow and develop further, but rather to suggest that it might also be useful to factor in various persisting issues that we should begin to address so that formal policies can be framed that will allow plans to be implemented to fulfil specific objectives. For instance, can the centre-periphery model continue to operate given the American economy crisis? The alternative domestic-led growth appears infeasible, based on the analysis by MIER, unless positive deindustrialization is achieved. Unless we begin to attempt to answer these questions, our policies amount to a wait-and-see attitude, because there is no clear strategy to either push for more exports (by addressing the American problem) or wean ourselves off them.

The other issue is linkage development. True, Penang is now well beyond rubber processing and tin smelting before shipment in its position both along the industrial chain as well as in spatial organization. Instead, growth triangles have since developed both internationally, as in the case of IMT-GT and AFTA, as well as locally, as in the case of NCER. Such multilateral government-to-government arrangements are only half the story because industrial linkages are firm-to-firm interconnections. So far, growth triangles form the platforms for promoting industrial linkage, but more than that, without careful coordination firms might end up competing against rather than complementing each other.

Then there is the issue of income versus production across the different states in Malaysia. In the development of the NCER, for instance, should the policy be to ensure that all "member" states: Perlis, Kedah, Penang and Perak have a somewhat fair share of the physical development or, alternatively, should investments be concentrated at the most efficient location inside the NCER but ensuring fair access to matters like jobs and business opportunities by "citizens" from all four states? In the case of fiscal federalism, is the NCER the concern of the federal government or should it be under the discretion of the local and state governments? In other words, have economic regions in Malaysia become miniature federal territories that are funded and

controlled directly by Putra Jaya?[30] Finally, there is the issue of specific individuals. When we talk in terms of Penang as opposed to other parts of Malaysia, we have to be mindful that intra-group disparities among Penangites are also important because often these can be more pronounced than inter-group disparities when we compare Penang with other states in the country.

If we begin to factor in these issues when we put strategies and plans together, not only will there be more substance but there will also be more consistency across such strategies and plans. Take tourism as an example. Given that Penang has come under the view of international travellers, with the New York Times, for example, including Penang in their destination listings, the strategizing of tourist sites and products must begin. The first issue is: do we see an increase in foreign visitors to Penang as export-led or domestic growth? Is more spending by tourists a form of deindustrialization? What kinds of inter-industry links can be fostered both within Penang and across a wider region in the tourist trade? Can there be a one-stop tourist package in which, for example, airport transfers are supplied by a Penang operator, accommodation is provided by a hotel in Kedah, a tourist attraction is located in Perlis and tourist paraphernalia (slippers, hats, umbrellas, the proverbial batik shirt, etc.) is made by factories in Perak? Finally, when we think foreign spending in Malaysia, are we limiting ourselves to high-end products, as is the case with the MM2H programme?

Maybe there is also space to encourage foreigners to spend more time in Malaysia by highlighting the cultural exoticism that Penang also offers so that the small man on the street also plays a part. At the top of such a list, we would all agree, is Penang's hawker food – not served in hotel restaurants, but by the road side, local style. How can policy actions ensure that street food is bacteria free and more aesthetically presented so that the street hawker is not associated with urban impoverishment? The Penang street hawker is, undeniably, a sifu – a master-chef who can bless your tongue with history and tradition, transporting you to a time long gone when cultures merged and ingredients were shared. The tourist should taste this culinary experience as well.

---

30 *The seat of the federal government in Malaysia, located just south of Kuala Lumpur.*

[2]

Asia's Shift towards Innovation and Its Implications for Penang

Poh-Kam Wong& Ho Yuen Ping

Introduction

Over the last two decades, a number of Asian economies have made great strides in their economic development, achieved in large part through strong emphasis on developing their technological capabilities. *Technological capability* is the ability to use and innovate technologies to develop, make and deliver cheaper or better products and services. In essence, technological capability comprises 3 key elements: (a) operating capability; (b) process innovation capability; and (c) product innovation capability (Wong, 2003). Technological capability is in turn crucial to a nation's continual development of its *industrial capability*, which is fundamentally about developing and deploying progressively more advanced technological capability to expand/improve existing industries and create/enter new industries. While learning to use existing technologies is important in the early economic development phase, the capacity to innovate becomes more critical in later phases.

The only way for an economy to sustain economic growth in the long-run is to continuously enhance her productivity and competitiveness (Porter, 2000). For late-comer nations, this necessitates catching-up with the more advanced nations in terms of industrial and technological capability. This catch-up process requires sustained investment

in two phases of learning – first, acquiring the ability to do what others have done; and second, innovating new capabilities (technologies, products, services) Furthermore, late comer nations also need to develop specialization in certain economic activities to differentiate from other competing nations/regions. Such specialization typically needs to be at a sufficient scale to achieve critical mass and agglomeration economies through industrial clustering.

This paper examines the shift towards innovation in various Asian economies in the last 2 decades, highlighting the key indicators of achievement made in science, technology and innovation by the three Asian Newly Industrialized Economies (NIEs) of Taiwan, Korea and Singapore and to some extent China and India. The paper will compare and contrast the performance of these economies with those of the ASEAN4 economies (Thailand, Indonesia, Malaysia and Philippines) in general and Malaysia in particular, to show that the latter has fallen significantly behind the three NIEs and in some cases the emerging economies of China and India. Implications of these observations for Penang's economy are discussed.

Moving towards an Innovation-Driven Economy: The R, I and E Framework

All late-industrializing economies need to move beyond catching up on using existing technologies, and shift more towards an innovation-driven economy. The *Research-Innovation-Enterprise (RIE) Framework* (Wong (2009)) is one useful way to highlight the key routes for an NIE to develop competitive industries through its investment in science, technology and innovation capabilities. Figure 1 illustrates the RIE framework, showing how R&D can be translated through various mechanisms into enhanced competitiveness of existing industries and growing new knowledge-based industries.

Figure 1: Research, Innovation & Enterprise (RIE) Framework

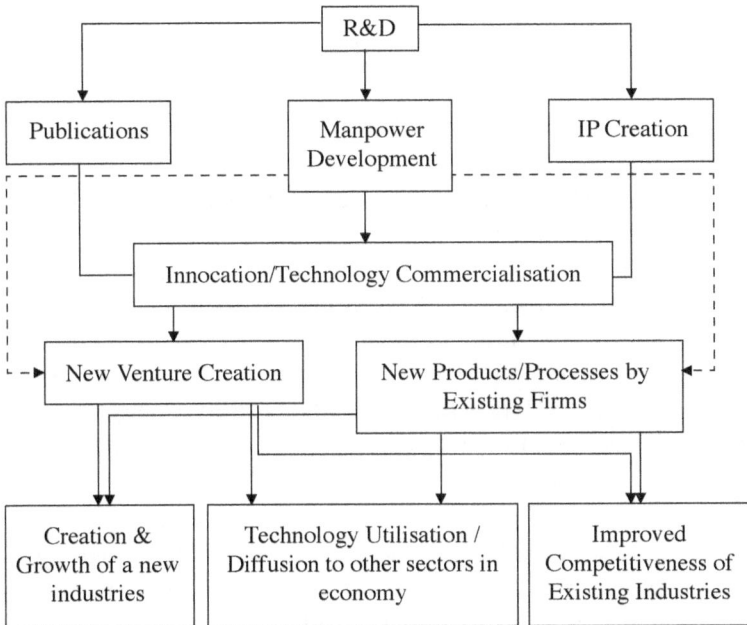

Source: Wong (2009)

The RIE framework emphasizes the link between research, innovation and competitive enterprise development. Particular emphasis is placed on developing the capacity for generating new knowledge through R&D, and strengthening the mechanisms for R&D *Commercialization*, including the focus on converting scientific and technological invention into *intellectual property*, especially patents, and their subsequent commercialization through licensing to existing firms or new spin offs.

From a macroeconomic policy perspective, the RIE framework highlights the significance of innovation to provide economic stimulus and encourage growth. Compared to the prevailing approach in many developing economies, which highlights the role of market liberalization and reducing the involvement of the state, the framework emphasizes an active role for the state in developing the innovative capability of both public research institutions and private enterprises. The rapid

industrial capability development records of the Asian NIEs – Taiwan, Korea and Singapore – show the relevance of the RIE framework, although each has adopted a different mix of policies within the framework (Wong and Ng, 2001, Wong and Ho, 2007b).

Shift towards Innovation among Asian Economies

We will examine in this section the empirical evidence for how Asian economies have progressed in terms of innovation and technological capability development, using a variety of indicators highlighted in the RIE Framework. The key findings presented here draw heavily upon our prior work (Wong 2008, Wong and Ho, 2007a and 2007b). In summary, over the last 2 decades, the three Asian NIEs (Taiwan, Korea and Singapore) and more recently China and India have increasingly invested in developing their innovative capacity. Comparably, the ASEAN-4 economies in general and Malaysia in particular, are lagging significantly behind.

The success stories of the three East Asian NIEs – Korea, Taiwan and Singapore – are particularly compelling based on the available empirical evidence. These were among the poor LDCs at the beginning of the 1960s, with per capita income significantly below the advanced OECD countries. However, over the last 50 years or so, these late-comer economies have achieved not only the highest economic growth rate among LDCs over the last 50 years, but they have also done so through a rapid catching-up of industrial and technological capabilities in specific industrial clusters where they have now become globally competitive. The accomplishments of the three Asian NIEs in technology capability development are reflected in their performance on a number of key innovation indicators, as detailed in the following sub-sections.

Intensity of R&D Investment

Table 1 shows a number of R&D intensity indicators for Asian economies as well as the developed industrialized economies of the OECD. Among the OECD nations, the average ratio of Gross Expenditure on R&D (GERD) to GDP was 2.24% in 2003, with values ranging from 1.2% in the smaller economies of Ireland and New Zealand, up to 4.5% in Israel. An important observation is that the 3 Asian NIEs – Singapore, Korea and Taiwan – have all three recorded GERD/GDP intensity ratios that are on par with the OECD average. The R&D spending intensity levels in the Asian NIEs are in fact higher than a number of large G-5 economies, specifically France and the UK. All three economies have also expressed ambitions to further increase the level of R&D intensity, with Korea setting a target of 5%, while Singapore and Taiwan are aiming for a more modest goal of 3%.

Table 1: Comparative R&D Indicators, Selected OECD/Asian NIEs

Grouping	Country	Year	R&D/GDP (%)	Researchers per 10,000 Labour Force	Target for R&D/GDP (%) Year	Target
OECD	OECD Average	2003	2.24	79		
G-5	Japan	2003	3.2	101		
	Germany	2003	2.5	68	2010	3%
	U.S.A	2003	2.6	91		
	U.K	2003	1.9	55[a]	2015	2.5%
	France	2003	2.2	71	2010	3%
Industrialized Small Countries	Finland	2003	3.5	159	2010	3%
	Switzerland	2001	2.6	63	2010	3%
	Sweden	2004	3.7	106	2010	3%
	Israel	2004	4.5	Na		
	Ireland	2004	1.2	57	2010	3%
	Netherlands	2004	1.8	45	2010	3%
	Denmark	2004	2.6	90	2010	3%
	Norway	2003	1.8	88	2010	3%
	Australia	2002	1.7	74		
	New Zealand	2003	1.2	76		
Asian NIEs	Korea	2004	2.6	66	2007	5%
	Taiwan	2004	2.5	67	2008	3%
	Hong Kong	2002	0.6	na		
	China	2004	1.4	12	2020	2.5%
	India	2001	0.8	4[b]		
	Malaysia	2006	0.6	N.A.		
	Singapore	1990	0.8	28		
	Singapore	2006	2.4	87	2010	3%

a 2001 figure; b figure for 1998; c RSEs per 10,000 labour force
Source : OECD Science, Technology and Industry Scoreboard, OECD Main Science & Technology Indicators 2006

There is also a strong presence of R&D personnel in the labour forces of the Asian NIEs, comparable to levels observed in the OECD economies, as also shown in **Table 1**. In particular, Singapore had 87 researchers per 10,000 persons in its 2006 labour force, higher than the OECD average 79 recorded for 2003 and higher than most of the industrialized economies, including Germany, France and Switzerland.

Comparably, Asian economies other than the Asian NIEs and Japan have fared less well. China's GERD/GDP ratio of 1.4% is, however, comparable to the lower end of the range observed among the small industrialized OECD economies. Malaysia and India had much lower R&D spending intensities, below 1% in both cases.

Scientific Publications Output & Intensity

Scientific publications, a means of diffusing and transferring knowledge, serve as a measure of the scientific output from R&D activities. On this score, **Table 2** shows that Asian economies have collectively achieved tremendous improvement in their publications output in the last 25 years. The absolute number of publications from ASEAN-4 remains quite low compared to the other Asian economies. While the growth in publications among the ASEAN-4 economies is admirable, particularly in the case of Malaysia and Thailand, it is overshadowed by the increase in publications recorded in the other Asian economies. The Asian NIEs have experienced large surges in publications in the 1990s and early 2000s, with Korea having the most impressive growth trend, almost tripling its publications output in the late 1990s. China has also recorded high growth in its publication figures, increasing more than ten-fold from the early 1980s to the mid 2000s. The other emerging economy of India has achieved less spectacular growth, but the number of publications has increased by almost 60% in this same period, a growth rate similar to that of the USA.

Table 2: Total no. of Scientific Publications, 1981-2005

	1981-1985	1986-1990	1991-1995	1996-2000	2001-2005
ASEAN-4					
Malaysia	1,345	1,670	2,648	4,081	6,535
Thailand	2,372	2,644	3,608	5,968	11,653
Indonesia	612	799	1,286	2,170	2,903
Philippines	1,177	1,241	1,403	1,888	2,462
Asian NIEs 3					
Singapore	1,575	3,492	7,397	15,091	28,117
South Korea	2,218	6,590	19,913	57,670	110,012
Taiwan	3,950	11,124	29,742	51,395	75,620
Emerging Economies					
China *	15,599	36,572	62,202	117,484	245,371
India	72,306	76,492	84,334	87,993	115,237
Advanced Economies					
Japan	162,482	218,011	292,863	365,434	400,479
US	1,031,771	1,180,515	1,351,540	1,410,620	1,512,217
Asia Pacific (Ex-Japan)	176,696	228,303	319,725	475,354	739,271
World	2,611,040	3,067,376	3,635,123	4,137,297	4,601,010

*China data includes Hong Kong for publications
Rough estimates from searching ISI Thomson shows HK publications to be 12-15% of total publications from PR China + HK combined
Source: Wong and Ho (2007b), computed from Thomson Reuters National Science Indicators

The Asia Pacific economies, excluding Japan, currently accounts for 16% of the world's total scientific publications, up from a 6.7% share in the period 1981-1985 (**Table 3**). Much of this gain in the global share has been accomplished in the last decade since the mid 1990s, attributed to growing shares by the emerging economies – especially China – as well as the 3 Asian NIEs – especially Korea. These trends are illustrated in **Figure 2**, which also highlights the decrease in the shares of the USA and other OECD nations as a counterpoint to the rising share witnessed in Asia. The contribution of the ASEAN-4 economies to this Asian phenomenon is unfortunately negligible, as shown

in both **Table 3** and **Figure 2**. While the share of global publications has increased over the years for both the ASEAN-4 collectively and Malaysia specifically, the figures attributable to these economies are very low (0.51% of world total publications for ASEAN-4 as a whole, 0.14% market share for Malaysia).

Table 3: Share in of World Total Publications/Patents (%)

	PUBLICATIONS				
	1981-1985	1986-1990	1991-1995	1996-2000	2001-2005
Asia Pacific (Ex-Japan)	6.77	7.44	8.80	11.49	16.07
Asian NIEs 3	**0.30**	**0.69**	**1.57**	**3.00**	**4.65**
Singapore	0.06	0.11	0.20	0.36	0.61
South Korea	0.08	0.21	0.55	1.39	2.39
Taiwan	0.15	0.36	0.82	1.24	1.64
Emerging Economies	**3.37**	**3.69**	**4.03**	**4.97**	**7.84**
China (incl HK)	0.60	1.19	1.71	2.84	5.33
India	2.77	2.49	2.32	2.13	2.50
ASEAN-4	**0.21**	**0.21**	**0.25**	**0.34**	**0.51**
Malaysia	0.05	0.05	0.07	0.10	0.14
Thailand	0.09	0.09	0.10	0.14	0.25
Indonesia	0.02	0.03	0.04	0.05	0.06
Philippines	0.05	0.04	0.04	0.05	0.05
Other Asia Pacific ex Jpn	**2.89**	**2.86**	**2.95**	**3.18**	**3.07**
Japan	6.22	7.11	8.06	8.83	8.70
US	39.52	38.49	37.18	34.10	32.87
World	100	100	100	100	100
N	2,188,812	2,589,316	3,144,518	3,612,976	3,942,141

	PATENTS				
	1981-1985	1986-1990	1991-1995	1996-2000	2001-2005
Asia Pacific (Ex-Japan)	**0.85**	**1.48**	**2.84**	**5.41**	**7.72**
Asian NIEs 3	0.21	0.73	2.11	4.49	6.26
Singapore	0.01	0.02	0.05	0.13	0.29
South Korea	0.04	0.15	0.79	2.03	2.53
Taiwan	0.16	0.57	1.27	2.33	3.43
Emerging Economies	**0.07**	**0.14**	**0.19**	**0.30**	**0.71**
China (incl HK)	0.05	0.11	0.15	0.21	0.47
India	0.02	0.03	0.04	0.09	0.24
ASEAN-4	0.02	0.02	0.03	0.06	0.11
Malaysia	0.00	0.00	0.01	0.03	0.06
Thailand	0.00	0.00	0.01	0.02	0.02
Indonesia	0.00	0.00	0.01	0.01	0.01
Philippines	0.01	0.01	0.01	0.01	0.02
Other Asia Pacific ex Jpn	**0.55**	**0.59**	**0.51**	**0.57**	**0.65**
Japan	15.45	20.59	22.26	20.77	21.18
US	57.76	53.03	54.81	55.67	53.27
World	100	100	100	100	100
N	315,306	412,796	487,805	660,562	776,799

Source: Wong and Ho (2007b)

Figure 2: Share in World Total Publications 1981-2005

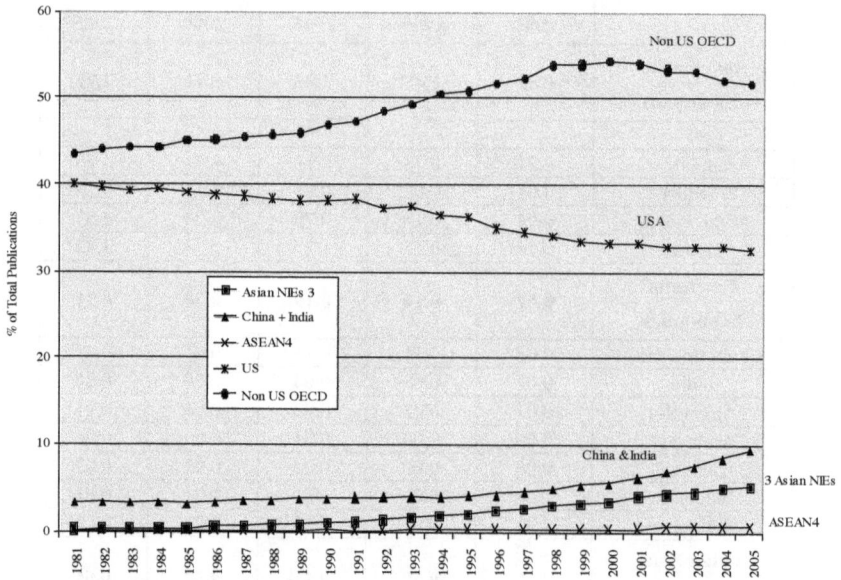

Source: Wong and Ho (2007b)
Note: China includes Hong Kong for publications. Rough estimates from searching ISI Thomson shows HK publications to be 12-15% of total publications from PR China + HK combined

A similar story is told by the figures on publication intensity, measured as the number of publications per million population. This allows for standardized comparisons across countries, regardless of population size. As seen in **Table 4**, publication intensity levels in the 3 Asian NIEs have multiplied manifold through the years, increasing at especially high rates in the 1990s and 2000s. By the early 1990s, publication intensity in the Asian NIEs had reached higher levels than the world average. Singapore had made the greatest stride in this regard, with publication intensity in the most recent period being higher than both the United States and Japan. Publication intensity has also increased significantly in China, but has shown little change over the last 25 years in India, although a slight increase was recorded in the last 5 years. The ASEAN-4 economies have collectively achieved improvement in publication intensity over the last 20 years; however, the level of intensity is very low compared to the Asian NIEs. Malaysia has consistently

achieved the highest publication intensity among the ASEAN-4 economies, and is more publication-intensive than both China and India.

Table 4: Publication/Patenting Intensity (Patents or publications per million population)

	PUBLICATIONS				
	1981-1985	1986-1990	1991-1995	1996-2000	2001-2005
Asia Pacific (Ex-Japan)	14.78	17.42	22.47	31.10	45.51
NIES3	**25.27**	**65.37**	**166.54**	**343.69**	**569.52**
Singapore	117.80	242.18	443.48	778.54	1315.45
South Korea	11.14	31.35	89.92	247.70	456.60
Taiwan	42.06	111.49	284.79	471.32	669.17
China + India	**9.99**	**11.77**	**14.09**	**18.51**	**30.81**
China	3.04	6.58	10.45	18.81	38.00
India	19.77	18.89	18.96	18.13	21.96
ASEAN-4	**3.88**	**4.06**	**5.21**	**7.52**	**11.61**
Malaysia	18.17	19.97	28.24	39.02	56.60
Thailand	9.55	9.85	12.57	19.64	36.84
Indonesia	0.74	0.88	1.30	2.00	2.47
Philippines	4.30	4.04	4.09	4.93	5.82
Japan	272.55	355.74	469.86	579.10	629.76
US	880.89	962.94	1039.14	1021.95	1041.61
World	111.52	120.30	131.70	139.83	146.11

	PATENTS				
	1981-1985	1986-1990	1991-1995	1996-2000	2001-2005
Asia Pacific (Ex-Japan)	0.23	0.47	0.99	2.41	3.85
NIES3	**2.24**	**9.45**	**30.49**	**84.49**	**135.12**
Singapore	2.54	4.58	15.29	43.95	111.11
South Korea	0.64	3.03	17.68	59.33	85.09
Taiwan	5.59	23.69	60.09	145.40	246.34
China + India	**0.01**	**0.03**	**0.05**	**0.11**	**0.37**
China	0.00	0.04	0.06	0.10	0.38
India	0.02	0.03	0.05	0.12	0.37
ASEAN-4	**0.04**	**0.05**	**0.10**	**0.22**	**0.44**
Malaysia	0.18	0.22	0.71	1.79	4.02
Thailand	0.03	0.05	0.13	0.37	0.64
Indonesia	0.01	0.02	0.03	0.04	0.05
Philippines	0.11	0.08	0.09	0.18	0.38
Japan	82.79	140.37	176.95	223.95	270.08
US	157.51	180.69	208.84	274.43	297.50
World	13.64	16.38	17.95	23.00	25.75

Source: Wong and Ho (2007b)
China includes Hong Kong for publications, excludes HK for patents.
Rough estimates from searching ISI Thomson shows HK publications to be 12-15% of total publications from PR China + HK combined

Patenting Output & Intensity

Patents serve as a useful indicator of innovation output with commercial potential and provide insights into the innovation performance of nations (Jaffe and Trajtenberg, 2002). In particular, utility patents as inventions with "usefulness", proxy the capability of an economy to produce innovations that have value as Intellectual Property (IP) assets that can be taken to market.

Table 5 reports trends in the number of patents invented in Asian economies and registered with the US Patents and Trademark Office (USPTO). As had been observed with publications, the Asian NIEs have experienced accelerated growth in patenting since the early 1990s. Particularly strong growth was achieved in the period 1996-2000, when the number of patents invented doubled (in Taiwan) and tripled (Korea and Singapore) within 5 years.

Table 5: Total no. of USPTO Utility Patents, 1981-2005

	1981-1985	1986-1990	1991-1995	1996-2000	2001-2005
ASEAN-4					
Malaysia	13	18	67	187	464
Thailand	7	13	36	111	201
Indonesia	7	18	34	44	59
Philippines	30	25	30	69	162
Asian NIEs 3					
Singapore	34	66	255	852	2375
South Korea	127	636	3916	13814	20501
Taiwan	525	2364	6275	15855	27838
Emerging Economies					
China	14	212	347	637	2453
India	73	119	218	590	1922
Advanced Economies					
Japan	49,358	86,024	110,295	141,322	171,751
US	184,487	221,516	271,621	378,808	431,905
Asia Pac (Ex-Japan)	2,727	6,196	14,088	36,826	62,617
World	319,390	417,757	495,544	680,437	810,733

Source: Wong and Ho (2007b)
Note: China data does not includes Hong Kong for patents

The two emerging economies of China and India also demonstrate a great increase in patenting (**Table 5**). In their case, the period of strong growth is more recent, in the five year period 2001-2005. **Table 6** provides more recent figures on the number of utility patents invented in Asia and further highlights the accelerated growth achieved in India and China in the last three years 2006-2008. Comparably, patenting activities in the Asian NIEs have stabilized in this recent 3 year period

with growth rates tapering off from the large increases seen in the 1990s till mid 2000s. On the whole, however, the absolute number of patents from these two large economies of India and China is still quite small in comparison to Korea's and Taiwan's output; however, the growth rates achieved are indicative of the potential for future expansion of innovation capacity. In contrast, the ASEAN-4 economies are producing very much smaller numbers of patents (in most cases, in the single or double digits annually), with Malaysia being the most prolific of this lagging grouping. On a more promising note, Malaysia's patenting has grown strongly in the last period. Malaysia's growth rate in USPTO utility patenting is in fact ranked 4th highest of 13 Asia Pacific economies, as reported in Wong and Ho's (2007a) Asia-Pacific IP Scorecard 2005.

Table 6: Patenting Output in Asia Pacific, 1978 - 2008 (Utility Patents)

	1978	1985	1995	2005	2006	2007	2008
Japan	6936	12,793	22,016	30,742	37,319	33,830	34,200
South Korea	5	41	1,185	4,452	6,012	6,421	7,678
Taiwan	12	175	1,667	5,249	6,594	6,332	6,601
Hong Kong	22	32	107	239	314	329	258
Singapore	3	13	71	433	520	483	515
Malaysia	1	4	10	117	162	212	200
Thailand	0	1	11	28	57	29	44
Indonesia	3	2	5	13	7	9	10
Philippines	3	6	5	26	44	33	29
Vietnam	0	0	0	6	2	1	4
China	0	2	89	685	1,079	1,198	1,757
India	18	13	63	498	672	743	848
Pakistan	0	1	1	5	5	3	4
Bangladesh	0	0	0	1	0	4	0
Sri Lanka	0	1	1	4	4	5	3
Australia	287	356	495	1,032	1,480	1,386	1,439
New Zealand	41	34	46	139	161	139	134
Asia Pacific	7,331	13,463	25,740	43,421	53,996	50,761	53,224
Asia Pacific ex Japan	395	670	3,724	12,680	16,809	17,044	19,151
WORLD	66087	71,668	101,431	143,806	173,771	157,282	157,774

	1978	1985	1995	2005	2006	2007	2008
Share of Asia Pacific (%)	11.1	18.8	25.4	30.2	31.1	32.3	33.7
Share of Asia Pac ex Jp (%)	0.6	0.9	3.7	8.8	9.7	10.8	12.1

Source: Computed from NUS Entrepreneurship Centre's US Patent Database
Note: National affiliations of patents are determined by the country of residency of their inventors. A patent is attributed to a country if at least one inventor is resident in that country

Given the above, it is unsurprising that the Asian NIEs have achieved an increasingly growing share of the world's total patenting output (**Table 3** and **Figure 3**). As a whole, the Asia Pacific region contributes more to global publications (16% in the most recent period) than to global patenting (7.7%). However, the three Asian NIEs have a higher global share of patents (6.3% in most recent period) than they do of publications (4.7%), suggesting some success in translating scientific knowledge into technological capability, as well as faster catching up in technology output (patenting) than in scientific output (publications), a feature of the NIE catch-up process (Wong and Ho, 2007b).

Figure 3: Share in World Total Patents 1981-2006

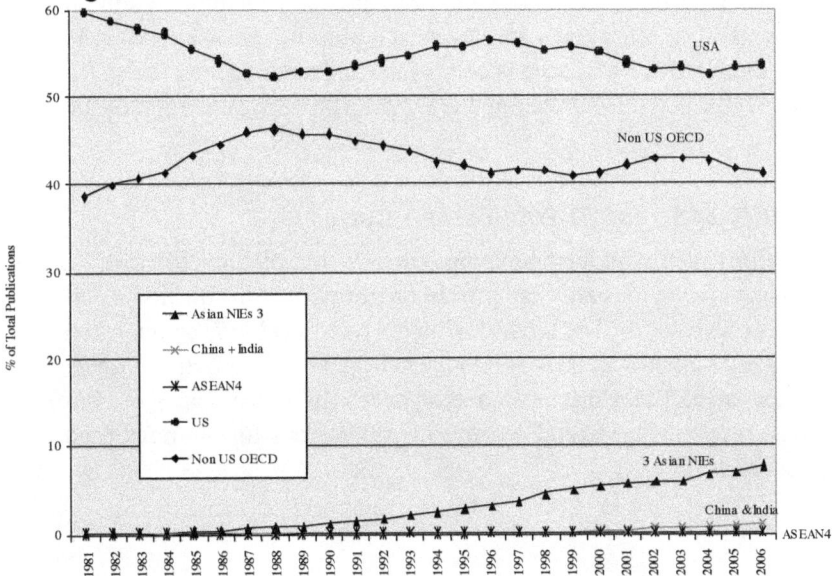

Source: Wong and Ho (2007b), computed from NUS Entrepreneurship Centre's US Patent Database   Note: China excludes HK for patents.

Outside of the Asian NIEs, the other Asian economies contribute very minor shares of global patenting (**Table 3** and **Figure 3**). Collectively, the ASEAN-4 economies only account for 0.11% of the world's total patents in the period 2001-2005. While this represents a large increase from 0.02% throughout the 1980s, the level of patenting is still very low and symptomatic of underdeveloped innovative capacity in this region.

Patenting intensity, as measured by the number of patents per million population, in the Asian NIEs has increased in tandem with the growth in patenting activities, particularly in the mid to late 1990s and continuing into the mid 2000s. While still somewhat lower than the intense levels recorded in the world's two most invention-intensive nations – the USA and Japan – patenting intensity in the Asian NIEs is in fact comparable to many OECD economies, which averages around 100 patents per million population (Wong and Ho, 2007a). Given the size of their populations, patenting intensity in China and India is still very low. Among the ASEAN-4 economies, Malaysia has the highest patenting intensity, at around 4 patents per million population, considerably higher than the average of 0.44 patents for the ASEAN-4 region as a whole. While this augurs well for Malaysia, the number is still far below the OECD average and levels achieved by the Asian NIEs. In fact, the figure for Malaysia is comparable to patenting intensity in the Asian NIEs in the 1980s, before the catch-up process gained significant pace.

Quality of Scientific Publications Output

Consistent with methodologies employed in bibliometric studies, publication citations are examined in order to assess the quality of scientific publications. The Relative Citation Index (**Table 7**) compares an economy's citation frequency relative to its publications output. Higher values of the Index are indicative of relatively higher shares of citations, hence higher overall quality of publications for the referenced economies.

Table 7: Relative Citation Index (Share in total citations/ share in total publications), 1981-2005

	1981-1985	1986-1990	1991-1995	1996-2000	2001-2005
ASEAN-4					
Malaysia	0.42	0.44	0.47	0.47	0.41
Thailand	0.56	0.68	0.83	0.74	0.63
Indonesia	0.63	0.55	0.84	0.67	0.63
Philippines	0.60	0.79	0.82	0.86	0.63
Asian NIEs 3					
Singapore	0.43	0.46	0.56	0.64	0.69
South Korea	0.61	0.53	0.55	0.59	0.64
Taiwan	0.65	0.56	0.54	0.57	0.58
Emerging Economies					
China *	0.40	0.41	0.45	0.51	0.56
India	0.27	0.28	0.33	0.41	0.48
Advanced Economies					
Japan	0.78	0.78	0.76	0.78	0.85
US	1.41	1.44	1.42	1.44	1.44
Asia Pacific(Ex-Japan)	0.61	0.60	0.61	0.65	0.66
World	1.00	1.00	1.00	1.00	1.00

Source: Wong and Ho (2007b)

As can be seen in **Table 7**, the Asian NIEs have consistently achieved the highest Index values among the non-Japan Asian economies. This testifies to the quality of scientific publications from the NIEs, in addition to the high level of quantitative output. Additionally, the Index values have gradually increased over the years, indicating that publications quality has improved. Publications from China and India are of relatively lower quality than those from the Asian NIEs. However, the Index values have been increasing slightly over the years, showing that qualitative improvements are being achieved.

Compared to the other Asian economies, Malaysia has scientific publications that are less frequently cited. Coupled with relatively low quantitative scientific output, this points towards a gap in Malaysia's scientific research community, potentially hampering the development of industrial and technological capability.

Malaysia's Performance on Innovation Indicators in Comparison with the Asian NIEs

A simple comparison of patenting trends in Malaysia versus its neighbour Singapore reveals the innovation gap that has emerged between the two economies since the 1990s (**Figure 4**). While patenting activity in Malaysia has picked up considerably in the early 2000s, the rate of growth does not match up to that of Singapore's during the mid to late 1990s, when Singapore was rapidly and successfully catching-up with more advanced economies.

Figure 4: Growth of Malaysian Utility Patents vs. Singaporean Utility Patents 1976-2008

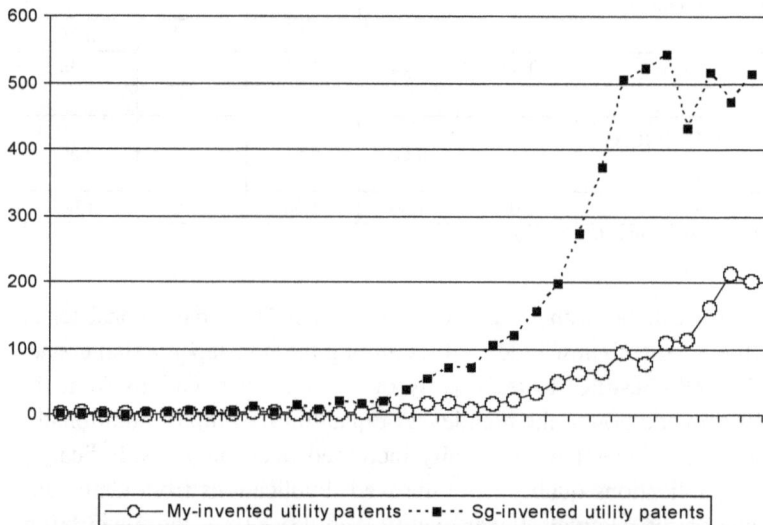

Source: Computed from NUS Entrepreneurship Centre's US Patent Database

The World Bank's Knowledge Economy Index (KEI) and Knowledge Index (KI), produced using its Knowledge Assessment Methodology (KAM) (World Bank Institute, 2008), provide further evidence of the gap between Malaysia and the Asian NIEs. **Table 8** reports the normalized performance scores for Malaysia compared to Singapore and South Korea on selected S&T indicators used in the computation of the KEI and KI (refer to World Bank Institute (2008) for further details on the KAM approach and methodology for normalization of variables measured on different scales and in different units). With a normalized scores range of 0 to 10, it is observed that Singapore and Korea score very highly on almost all the indicators, particularly those related to S&T education at the secondary school level. Malaysia, on the other hand, is in the middle of the normalized scale on most measures, and scores lower than both Singapore and Korea on all the indicators. This is clearly illustrated in **Figure 5**, which graphically reproduces the scores shown in **Table 8**. The gap between Malaysia and the two Asian NIEs is most pronounced for science education, R&D spending intensity, research manpower intensity and publications intensity.

Table 8: Normalized S&T Performance Score of Malaysia vs. Korea & Singapore

Selected S&T Indicators	Malaysia (Group: All)		Singapore (Group: All)		Korea, Rep. (Group: All)	
	actual	nor-mal-ized	actual	nor-mal-ized	actual	nor-mal-ized
Human Development Index, 2005	0.81	6.16	0.92	8.26	0.92	8.19
Researchers in R&D / Mil. People, 2006	508.93	4	5.479.14	9.67	3.723.28	8.56
Total Expenditure for R&D as % of GDP, 2006	0.63	5.26	2.36	8.87	2.99	9.59
Scientific and Technical Journal Articles / Mil. People, 2005	23.97	5.11	831.22	9.57	339.5	8.2

	Malaysia (Group: All)		Singapore (Group: All)		Korea, Rep. (Group: All)	
Selected S&T Indicators	actual	nor-mal-ized	actual	nor-mal-ized	actual	nor-mal-ized
Patents Granted by USPTO / Mil. People, avg 2002-2006	3.03	7.79	97.01	9.21	88.44	9
8th Grade Achievement in Mathematics, 2003	508	7.35	605	10	589	9.59
8th Grade Achievement in Science, 2003	510	5.51	578	10	558	9.59

Source: World Bank Knowledge Assessment Methodology (KAM) 2008.

Figure 5: Normalized S&T Performance Scores of Malaysia vs. Korea & Singapore

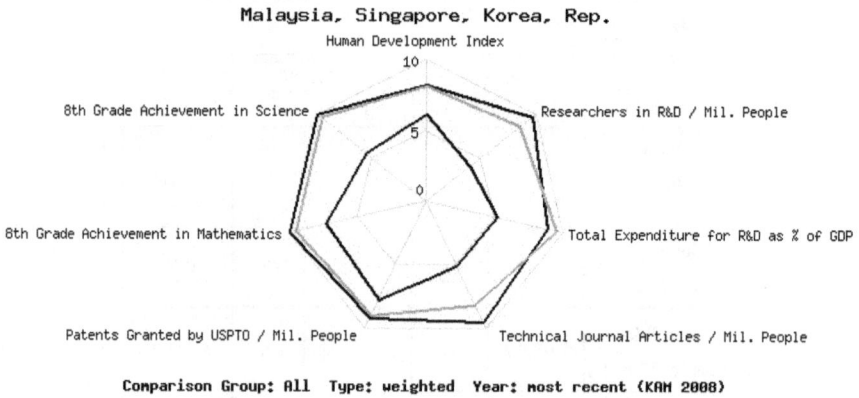

Malaysia, Singapore, Korea, Rep.

Comparison Group: All Type: weighted Year: most recent (KAM 2008)

Source: World Bank Knowledge Assessment Methodology (KAM) 2008.

Penang as a Source of Innovation in Malaysia

The key position Penang holds in Malaysia's national innovation system is evident in its share of Malaysian-invented patents granted by the USPTO (United States Patent and Trademark Office) (**Figure 6**). Overall, about one-third of Malaysian patents are invented by residents of Penang. Moreover, the region's role is growing, accounting for a consistently rising share of Malaysian patents, from 10.3% over 1976-85 to 37.2% over 2001-06. By this last period, Penang was responsible for a greater share of patents than Selangor (29.5%) or the rest of the country combined (33.3%).

Figure 6: Malaysian Patents by Region of Inventor, 1976-2006

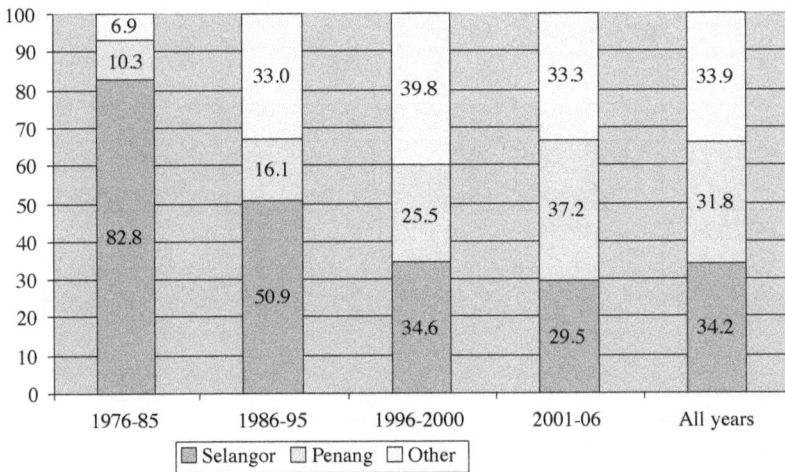

Source: Computed from NUS Entrepreneurship Centre's US Patent Database

However, closer inspection of the ownership of these patents shows that much of this is due to an increase in patenting by foreign-based MNCs. **Table 9** shows that three-quarters of patents invented in Penang are owned by foreign organizations. This is in fact an understatement of the true extent of foreign ownership of Penang's patents, since some MNCs extend ownership of patents to the local subsidiary where the

technology was invented rather than to the corporation's headquarters. Thus, almost half of Penang-invented locally-assigned patents are actually owned by German company Osram Opto Semiconductors and the Japanese Nikko Group. A comparison with Table 10 shows that the share of patents by foreign-based innovators in Penang is high even compared to national standards: during the period 1996-2006, when the bulk of the patents were issued, almost one-third of Malaysian patents were locally-assigned, whereas only 7% of Penang patents were locally assigned. Both in Penang specifically and Malaysia generally, there is a relatively high reliance on foreign-based MNCs generating local inventions. The proportion of locally invented patents that are owned by domestic entities is low compared to Singapore, where half of Singapore-invented patents are owned by Singaporean organizations.

Table 9: Local Assignment of Malaysian and Singaporean Patents, 1976-2006

	Percentage of patents which are locally assigned		
	Penang-invent-ed patents	Malaysia-invented patents	Singapore-invented patents
1976-85	66.7	65.5	57.7
1986-95	5.6	39.8	39.9
1996-06	6.8	29.8	50.9
TOTAL	24.9	31.8	50.0

Notes: Comprises patents with at least one inventor who is a Malaysia (Singapore) resident
Assignee location is based on the location of the 1st assignee.
Includes unassigned patents
Source: Computed from NUS Entrepreneurship Centre's US Patent Database

Table 10: Top 20 Organizations with Malaysia Patents[1]

No	Companies	Country	Patent Count			
			1986-1995	1996-2000	2001-2006	Cumulative Total as at end 2006
1	Motorola, Inc.	USA	30	51	49	130
2	Chartered Semiconductor Manufacturing Ltd.	Singapore	0	8	54	62
3	Intel Corporation	USA	1	9	51	61
4	CeramOptec Industries, Inc.	Taiwan	0	13	34	47
5	Agilent Technologies, Inc.	USA	0	0	43	43
6	Advanced Micro Devices, Inc.	USA	1	2	29	32
7	National Semiconductor, Corp.	USA	1	1	29	31
8	Sinorita Sendirian Berhad	Malaysia	0	4	24	28
9	Altera Corporation	USA	0	5	18	23
10	Avago Technologies, Ltd.	USA	0	0	18	18
11	Semiconductor Components Industries	USA	0	0	13	13
12	Grossman Products Services	Malaysia	0	0	10	10
13	Inventec Multimedia Telecom Corporation	Taiwan	0	0	9	9
13	Osram Opto Semiconductors GmbH	Germany	0	0	9	9
13	Texas Instruments Incorporated	USA	1	2	6	9
16	Artwright Marketing Sdn. Bhd.	Malaysia	7	1	0	8
16	Filplas Vacuum Technology Pte, Ltd.	Singapore	0	1	7	8
16	Nikko Electronics Bhd.	Japan	0	0	8	8
16	SilTerra Malaysia Sdn. Bhd.	Malaysia	0	0	8	8
20	Shin-Etsu	Japan	3	2	2	7

[1]*Patents where at least one inventor is a Malaysia resident. Jointly-assigned patents are allocated to the first-named assignee*
Source: Computed from NUS Entrepreneurship Centre's US Patent Database

Table 10 shows that the majority of the top patenting organizations in Malaysia are foreign electronics companies. This is also true of Penang, whose largest patent-holders are companies such as Motorola, Intel, AMD and Agilent, and reflects Malaysia's heavy reliance on foreign direct investment, particularly in the electronics sector. In this sense, its innovation pattern is closer to Singapore's a decade or more ago, but quite different from Korea and Taiwan, which have consistently placed greater emphasis on developing the innovative capabilities of local firms (large *chaebols* in the case of Korea and SMEs in

the case of Taiwan) (Wong and Ng 2001, Wong and Ho 2007b). While the recent growth in foreign MNC patenting in Penang is encouraging, Penang's very high proportion of foreign-owned patents also point to a dearth of innovation activities in local organizations, such as local firms or universities/public research institutes (PRIs). This will hinder Penang's shift towards a knowledge-based economy, which requires a significant increase in the indigenous capabilities of local enterprises to create and commercialize new knowledge, rather than just relying on knowledge transferred from foreign companies. This is particularly true given MNCs' reluctance to share technologies at the higher level of the technological spectrum (Wong, Ho and Singh 2007, Wong and Singh 2000). Singapore started this shift towards a more balanced pattern of innovation more than a decade ago.

Universities' Contribution To Innovation In Malaysia

Universities are playing an increasingly important role in Asia's innovation drive. In the Triple Helix model (Etzkowitz et al., 2000), universities are seen as key components of the national innovation system, shifting from their traditional primary roles of teaching and research to driving innovation and stimulating economic growth through commercializing knowledge and actively contributing to the development of private enterprises in the economy (Wong, Ho and Singh 2007). While this is a global trend, it is especially important for universities in latecomer Asian countries. Since many of the local firms that developed in the earlier industrialization phases tend to be laggards, rather than leaders, in engaging in R&D and innovation activities, local industries in latecomer countries often have less experience and lower capabilities to develop their own innovations, and to commercialize knowledge generated from local universities (Wong, Ho and Singh 2007). Moreover, while there is a great need for universities in these countries to take on this entrepreneurial role, they face hindrances that their counterparts in advanced countries do not. These include a more rigid bureaucratic control by the government which stifles competitive differentiation or development of an entrepreneurial culture in the universities, and an emphasis on absorbing and diffusing technological knowledge from advanced countries rather than on indigenous innovation, resulting in a lower base of research and inventive output coming from the university (Wong, Ho and Singh 2007).

Overall rankings show a significant gap between Malaysia's top universities and other leading Asian universities. The Times Higher Education-QS *World University Rankings* (WUR) for 2006 gave Universiti Sains Malaysia (USM) an overall ranking of 277th, while Universiti Kebangsaan Malaysia (UKM) and Universiti Malaya (UM) were ranked 185th, 192nd respectively (**Table 11**). This can be compared with other leading universities around Asia in **Table 11** – specifically, those from Hong Kong, Korea, Taiwan, China, Japan and Singapore - which generally ranked within the top 100.

Table 11: World University Rankings for Selected Malaysian Universities vs. other Leading Asian Universities, 2006

	Country	Overall Rank 2006	Rank for citations/faculty 2006
Universiti Sains Malaysia	*Malaysia*	*277*	*393*
Universiti Malaya	*Malaysia*	*192*	*376*
Universiti Kebangsaan Malaysia	*Malaysia*	*185*	*na*
Hong Kong Univ of Sci & Tech	Hong Kong	58	55
University of Hong Kong	Hong Kong	33	213
Seoul National University	Korea	63	291
KAIST	Korea	198	95
National Taiwan University	Taiwan	108	291
Peking University	China	14	350
Tsinghua University	China	28	376
University of Tokyo	Japan	19	15
Kyoto University	Japan	29	42
National University of Singapore	Singapore	19	170

Source: THES World University Rankings

One means of knowledge transfer from universities is through the publication of research papers. On this measure, there is a significant gap between the research output of USM and other top Malaysian universities on the one hand, and those of the leading Asian countries on the other. **Table 12** shows that the number of SCI and SSCI-indexed papers produced between 1999 and February 2009 by USM was 3250

- equivalent to UM's 3,440 and double UKM's 1,530. However USM's publication output was only about one-third of the output of the next closest university, the Hong Kong University of Science and Technology (HKUST), which published 10,400 papers over this period. The difference is all the greater when taking into account the size difference between the universities: HKUST has a faculty size of approximately 400, while USM has approximately 1,200 (websites of USM and HKUST).

Table 12: Publications and Citations of Selected Malaysian Universities vs. other Leading Asian Universities, Jan 1999-Feb 2009

	Country	No. of Papers	No. of Citations	Citations Per Paper
Universiti Sains Malaysia	Malaysia	3,250	13,257	4.08
Universiti Malaya	Malaysia	3,439	14,316	4.16
Universiti Kebangsaan Malaysia	Malaysia	1,528	5,624	3.68
Hong Kong Univ of Sci & Tech	Hong Kong	10,402	96,281	9.26
University of Hong Kong	Hong Kong	18,700	187,339	10.02
Seoul National University	Korea	33,779	271,702	8.04
KAIST	Korea	15,168	102,086	6.73
National Taiwan University	Taiwan	27,255	196,631	7.21
Peking University	China	22,857	148,132	6.48
Tsinghua University	China	23,182	121,584	5.24
University of Tokyo	Japan	67,864	882,361	13.00
Kyoto University	Japan	49,657	618,383	12.45
National University of Singapore	Singapore	28,602	236,388	8.26

Source: compiled from Thomson ISI's Essential Science Indicators

In terms of research quality, the Malaysian universities also fall somewhat behind the others, whether measured by citations per paper or citations per faculty. For the former, all three Malaysian universities received approx 4 citations per paper, whereas most of the comparison universities received more than 7 citations per paper (**Table 12**). For the latter, the WUR gave USM a ranking of 393rd for its citations/faculty in 2005, while UM was ranked 376th. This was lower than most of the comparison universities listed in **Table 12**.

As mentioned above, Asian universities play a particularly important role in commercializing their research output because the private sector often lacks the capabilities to absorb technology coming from the universities and develop them to the point where they can be utilized. One indicator then of the commercialization potential of universities is their patenting output, as it is a measure of the pool of innovations with the potential to be commercialized through licensing or spin-off formation. Generally, the patenting output of Malaysian universities is rather low, with USM having only three patents issued by the USPTO as of 2005, while UM had one and UKM none (**Table 13**). This is substantially lower than various leading Asian comparison universities, most of which had more than 20 patents, with the largest patenting universities (Korea Advanced Institute of Science and Technology and National University of Singapore) having 200 or more patents.

Table 13: Patents of Selected Malaysian Universities vs. other Leading Asian Universities, cumulative to 2005

	Country	No. of US patents cumulative to 2005
Universiti Sains Malaysia	*Malaysia*	*3*
Universiti Malaya	*Malaysia*	*1*
Universiti Kebangsaan Malaysia	*Malaysia*	*0*
Hong Kong Univ of Sci & Tech	Hong Kong	87
University of Hong Kong	Hong Kong	52
Seoul National University	Korea	22
KAIST	Korea	403
National Taiwan University	Taiwan	41
Peking University	China	7
Tsinghua University	China	53
University of Tokyo	Japan	73
Kyoto University	Japan	31
National University of Singapore	Singapore	200

Source: Computed from NUS Entrepreneurship Centre's US Patent Database

Cheng has argued that the low level of patenting by Malaysian universities may be partly an outcome of a government policy which clearly delineated the research roles played by universities and PRIs. The 5th Malaysia Plan, implemented from 1986 to 1990, stipulated that universities would give greater emphasis to basic research (40%) relative to PRIs (10%) (Cheng 2009). However, her assumption that a high emphasis on basic research does not generate commercializable research is not valid, because many of the leading universities in the world, including MIT and Stanford, that are highly focused on basic research have also been very prolific in generating patents. Likewise, the rapid rise in patenting among the leading Asian universities such as NUS and Tsinghua over the last ten years coincided with a growing emphasis on basic research. Rather than the basic vs. applied distinction, it is the quality of the research, and its strategic focus on economic significance (the so-called strategic basic research, or "Pasteur quadrant"), that matters.

In this regard, the fact that PRIs in Malaysia have generally focused on applied and developmental R&D, and yet have also produced relatively low patenting outputs, similarly suggests that the quality of its research has been low. As can be seen from **Table 14**, even among the top Malaysian PRIs, the number of US patents granted has been rather low (three for the Malaysian Palm Oil Board up to 2005, one each for the Rubber Research Institute of Malaysia and the Institute for Medical Research). By comparison, the top patenting PRIs in Singapore, Korea and Taiwan have produced at least ten times this number, with Singapore's Data Storage Institute producing 30 patents and the Institute of Microelectronics producing 80 patents. The gap is even higher in the other two NIEs, with their leading PRIs having at least 200 patents.

Table 14: Patenting by Selected PRIs in Asia, 1976-2005

	Total patents 1976 -2005	Location	1976-1995	1996-2000	2001-2005
Institute for Medical Research	1	Malaysia	0	0	1
Malaysian Palm Oil Board*	3	Malaysia	1	1	1
The Board of the Rubber Research Institute of Malaysia	1	Malaysia	1	0	0
Electronics and Telecommunications Research Institute (ETRI)	1025	Korea	71	480	474
Korea Institute of Science & Technology (KIST)	493	Korea	89	182	222
Korea Research Institute of Chemical Technology	241	Korea	41	103	97
Korea Atomic Energy Research Institute	92	Korea	3	35	54
Industrial Technology Research Institute	2471	Taiwan	554	899	1018
National Science Council	613	Taiwan	99	336	178
Institute of Microelectronics	83	Singapore	1	20	62
Data Storage Institute	31	Singapore	0	2	29
Agency for Science, Technology and Research (A*STAR)	30	Singapore	0	0	30

* Includes Palm Oil Research & Development Board
Source: Computed from NUS Entrepreneurship Centre's US Patent Database

Another way in which Asian universities can translate their research into technologies with commercialization potential and help build the technological capabilities of private firms is through collaborative research projects with industry (Wong et al., 2009). In the area of university-industry collaboration, Malaysia is again quite far behind most of the NIEs. The Global Competitiveness Report ranked Malaysia as 20th on this factor, whereas Singapore ranked fifth and Taiwan and Korea ranked 10th and 12th respectively.

Overall, it thus seems that there is much room for growth in both the quantity and quality of public research and its subsequent commercialization in Malaysia compared with not only Taiwan, Korea and Singapore, but also China. In terms of university research output, Razak and Saad (2007) note that Malaysian universities have made little progress in R&D of new and advanced technologies, such as fiber optic technology, partially because of a lack of adequate resources and equipment. In terms of technology transfer and commercialization, some progress has been made, as witnessed by the establishment of the technology transfer offices in the major public universities, and a commercial arm in USM in the form of USains Holdings (Razak and Saad 2007). However, the data shows that there is much further to go, not just in terms of building university culture and infrastructure, but also in the wider innovation system (Cheng, 2009).

Implications for Penang

Our analysis of available data indicates that Penang has significantly under-invested in innovation, despite being an economy that has achieved a relatively high level of manufacturing sophistication. In comparison to Korea, Taiwan and Singapore, innovation activity and output levels are low, suggesting weaknesses in the local innovation system. Unless greater public investment is channelled to innovative capability development, Penang risks falling further behind the Asian NIEs and being over-taken by China and India.

The success stories from the Asian NIEs reveal diverse strategies for technological development and economic catching-up (Wong and Ng, 2001, Wong and Ho, 2007b). This suggests the possibility and need for creative policy adaptation to the unique contexts of Penang. In particular, Penang can consider selectively adapting elements of the Korean, Taiwanese and Singaporean models that are more suited to her local context. This is indeed what China has done (in addition to adapting other models such as that of the Silicon Valley) in developing her own innovation strategies.

There is potentially a significant role that can be played by Penang's overseas diasporas, Both Taiwan and Korea have tapped their large overseas diasporas to speed up technological learning and catching-up. Apart from attracting back highly skilled and entrepreneurial returnees, they also leveraged those who stay overseas to access technology, capital, markets and network contacts. Increasingly, China and India are also drawing on this rich resource to establish business links and to facilitate knowledge and technology upgrading.

The three Asian NIEs have achieved their economic success through a rapid catching-up of industrial and technological capabilities in specific industrial clusters where they have now become globally competitive (Wong and Ng, 2001, Yusuf and Nabeshima, 2008). The experience of these NIEs suggests the importance of adopting an industrial cluster development strategy, which entails promoting investments into selected industrial clusters to achieve sufficient scale and agglomeration economies. The increasing globalization of production in recent years is likely to lead to even greater importance of scale and geographic concentration (e.g. the concentration of electronics manufacturing in Guandong, China, and souvenirs/gifts production in Zhejiang, China).

Penang and Malaysia are facing a situation of strong global competition for Direct Foreign Investments (DFI). The three Asian NIEs, Ireland, and more recently China and India, have established strong competitive positions as high tech DFI hubs. At the same time, other high tech hubs for DFI are emerging among the transition economies (e.g. Estonia) and Middle East (e.g. UAE). In addition, the continuing rapid rise of China, and more recently India, is threatening to cause an increasing range of high-tech DFI to bypass the ASEAN5 and other developing Asian economies, thus undermining the prospect of ASEAN5 to move up the technological ladder through attracting high-tech DFI. To compete for DFI effectively, Penang needs to target specific industrial clusters that leverage on the existing competencies of the state and the natural resources in its regional hinterland. While more in-depth research is obviously needed to identify the specific potential clusters that Penang can hope to excel in, example of possible industrial clusters that come to mind might include the Marine & Agro-technology sector, Opto-electronics and Precision Engineering, as these are sectors where Penang has already built some foundations over the years. To strengthen the chosen clusters, Penang must invest heavily in the relevant supporting applied R&D and technology development institutions to support the innovation activities of the existing firms in these clusters, as well as to attract new innovative firms into these clusters.

Last, but not least, Penang needs to recognize that an important element in the rapid industrial development of the Asian NIEs is *indigenous technology entrepreneurship*, or the formation of new technology enterprises that have the potential to grow through introducing innovative products or processes for both the domestic and international export markets. Ultimately, the creation of new high tech industries can only occur if there is a good supply of private sector entrepreneurs. Indeed, while public policies played a facilitating role, the many successful companies that have emerged from Taiwan and Korea such as Acer, Hong Hai, HTC, Hyundai, Samsung and LG owe their success primarily to the entrepreneurial drive and visionary leadership of their respective founders. Besides improving the technical contents of its educational system, Penang should also look into injecting an *entrepreneurial* dimension into its university research and education system, e.g. by offering educational programmes involving experiential learning of entrepreneurship among the science and engineering students, and by providing seed funding and mentoring of entrepreneurial start-ups by university professors and students.

References

Cheng, M.Y. "University technology transfer and commercialization: the case of Multimedia University, Malaysia". Forthcoming in P.K. Wong, Y.P Ho and A.A. Singh (eds) *The Role and Impact of Universities in a National Innovation System*. Singapore: Sasakawa Peace Foundation of Japan and Entrepreneurship Centre, National University of Singapore, 2009.

Etzkowitz, H., Webster, A., Gebhardt, C. and Terra, B.R.C. "The future of the university and the university of the future: Evolution of ivory tower to entrepreneurial paradigm", *Research Policy* 29, no. 2 (2000): 313-330.

Porter, M.E. *The Competitive Advantage of Nations*. London: Macmillan, 2000.

Razak, A.A. and Saad, M. "The role of universities in the evolution of the Triple Helix culture of innovation network: The case of Malaysia". *International Journal of Technology*

Management and Sustainable Development 6, no. 3 (2007): 211-225.

Wong, P.K. "Dynamics of S&T Catch-Up by Late-Industrializing Economies: The case of Singapore". Singapore: NUS Entrepreneurship Centre working paper, 2009.

Wong, P.K. "The role of global MNCs vs. indigenous firms in the rapid growth of Asian innovation: Evidence from US patent data". In *Greater China's Quest for Innovation*, edited by H.S. Rowen, M.G. Hancock and W.F. Miller. Brookings Institute, 2008, p. 281-308.

Wong, P.K. and Ng, C.Y. (eds.). *Industrial Policy, Innovation and Economic Growth: The Experience of Japan and the East Asian NIEs*. Singapore: Singapore University Press, 2001.

Wong, P.K. and Ho, Y.P. (2007a). *Asia Pacific Intellectual Property Scorecard 2005: Benchmarking IP Production and Quality in the Asia Pacific Economies*. NUS Entrepreneurship Centre Report for IP Academy of Singapore.

Wong, P.K. and Ho, Y.P. (2007b). "Dynamics of Science and Technology Catch Up by East Asian Economies: A Composite Analysis Combining Scientific Publications and Patenting Data." Paper presented at the 2007 Atlanta Conference on Science, Technology and Innovation Policy, October 19-20, 2007, Atlanta, USA.

Wong, P.K., Ho, Y.P. and Singh, A. (2007). "Towards an "Entrepreneurial University" Model to support knowledge-based economic development: The case of the National University of Singapore", *World Development* 35, no. 6 (2007): 941-958.

Wong, P.K., Ho, Y.P. and Singh, A. "Towards a 'Global Knowledge Enterprise': The entrepreneurial university model of the National University of Singapore". Forthcoming in P.K. Wong, Y.P Ho and A.A. Singh (eds) *The Role and Impact of Universities in a National Innovation System*. Singapore: Sasakawa Peace Foundation of Japan and Entrepreneurship Centre, National University of Singapore, 2009.

Wong, P.K. "From Using to Creating Technology: The Evolution of Singapore's National Innovation System and the Changing Role of Public Policy". In *Competitiveness, FDI and Technological Activity in East Asia*, edited by S. Lall and S.Urata. Edward Elgar Publishing, 2003: 191-238

Wong, P.K., and Singh, A. "The role of foreign MNCs in the technological development of Singaporean industries". In *Corporate Strategies for South East Asia After the Crisis: A Comparison of Multinational Firms from Japan and Europe*, edited by J. Legewie and H. Meyer-Ohle. Houndmills, Basingstoke, Hampshire: Macmillan Press, 2000: 40-54.

World Bank Institute. *KAM 2008 Booklet: Measuring Knowledge in the World's Economies*. Washington DC: World Bank Institute, 2008.

Yusuf, S. and K. Nabeshima (eds.), *Growing Industrial Clusters in Asia: Serendipity and Science*. World Bank, 2008

[3]

Shallow Pockets but Close to the Action: Industrial Policy at the Sub-national Level and the Case of Penang

Francis E. Hutchinson

Introduction

The challenges facing policy-makers responsible for sub-national governments are changing. Once acting as local representatives of the national government and content to let their larger counterparts do the 'heavy-lifting', sub-national governments are now increasingly expected to take a leading role in many areas.

Nowhere is this more evident than in the arena of economic policy-making. State governments in India now draw up their own plans for economic development, negotiate loans with international financial institutions like the World Bank, and establish highly-specialized research institutes in partnership with industry. Provincial leaders in China are playing key roles in fostering economic activity within their jurisdictions, receiving incentive payments from the central government in return for good performance.

Yet, while sub-national governments have acquired new visibility and additional responsibilities, they usually do not have a wide range of tools or a large quantity of resources at their disposal. Macroeconomic policy lies out of their purview and, usually, so do key responsibilities such as education and infrastructure. Often regarded as an 'add-on' or intermediate level of bureaucracy, sub-national governments sometimes struggle for relevance. This is particularly the case for Malaysia, which has a strong federal government and state governments with very limited responsibilities and few independent sources of income.

The challenges for successful policy-making at the sub-national level are accentuated by economic globalization. Increasingly mobile investment along with the heightened technological intensity of many manufacturing activities means that policy-makers must now, not only attract investment, but also work hard to retain it. Firms that have problems securing quality suppliers, sourcing appropriate labour, or obtaining permits will relocate to more amenable locations – often in a neighbouring state or province. Thus, competition between sub-national governments is also ratcheting up, as they strive to outdo each other by providing incentives and specialized infrastructure.

While technological changes have heightened competition and made investments more mobile, economic activity and, in particular, innovation have remained very sensitive to geography and their local institutional environments. This is because firms do not develop new products and processes in isolation, but rather through contact and communication with other firms, as well as institutions such as research institutes, technology centres, capital providers, and government agencies. This is particularly the case for smaller firms who, due to their size and limited in-house capabilities, need to be able to easily access external expertise and facilities.

Because of their deeper knowledge of the local environment and their proximity to local firms, sub-national governments are in a unique position to shape and mould the institutional environment in a way that supports economic activity in general, and innovation in particular. This can be achieved through strengthening regional innovation systems, which are comprised of firms and their networks and associations on one hand, and the surrounding supporting institutions such as research laboratories, universities and colleges, vocational training institutes, and credit agencies on the other. In some cases this may require establishing institutions to fill demand gaps, but in others the articulation of a locally-relevant development strategy or the creation of networks between existing institutions may be more appropriate.

The key is that by establishing and maintaining communication with relevant groups and constituencies in the private sector, local governments are in a privileged position to formulate 'enabling' policies. In addition, by strengthening the social 'fabric' that influences the way that firms relate to each other as well as their surrounding institutions, sub-national governments can help areas under their jurisdiction develop or strengthen their competitive advantage.

This paper will explore the issue of sub-national industrial policy with specific reference to Penang and its manufacturing sector. To this end, this paper will be structured as follows. The first section will review what is known about the relationship between economic activity, innovation, and location. It will also put forward a particular approach, Regional Innovation Systems, for analyzing how firms' potential for creativity and innovation is shaped by the local institutional context. Using this framework, the second section will look at Penang's manufacturing sector, specifically its firms and the institutional environment within which they operate. Using this as a base-line, the third section will make a series of policy suggestions with the aim of strengthening the state's regional innovation system. The fourth and final section will summarize the paper's main arguments.

Conceptual Framework - Economic Activity, Innovation, and Location

Mapping out a nation's economy reveals that its industries are not evenly spread throughout its territory, but rather concentrated in a small number of locations. For example, in the past Chicago and Detroit were synonymous with manufacturing, and Silicon Valley in California and Route 128 in Massachusetts are currently known for their IT industries. Regions in Northern Italy are reputed centres for high quality fashion-wear; and Tokyo, London, and Hong Kong are centres for international finance. Specific areas or regions[1] seem to be good at producing large numbers of new firms in certain sectors as well as attracting others from elsewhere.

The theory of comparative advantage argues that patterns of industry location are driven by the geographical distribution of factors of production. However, this framework is static and does not explain how regions with scarce endowments of capital and labour come to

---

1   A region is defined as 'a meso-level political unit set between the national or federal and local levels of government that might have some cultural or historical homogeneity but which at least ha[s] some statutory powers to intervene and support economic development, particularly innovation'. Philip Cooke, "Regional Innovation Systems, Clusters, and the Knowledge Economy". Industrial and Corporate Change, vol. 10, no. 4, (2001), p. 953.

host new, more complex types of production such as manufacturing and services. The more institutional approaches used to analyse the cases of successful 'upgraders' such as Japan, Korea, and Taiwan focus on the nation-state, and are ill-suited for looking at why industries locate in one part of a country and not another.

While economic geographers had been looking at this issue since the 1950s, the work of Piore and Sabel on industrial districts, Krugman on New Economic Geography, and Porter on clusters generated wider awareness about the local dimension of economic activity. Since then, the accelerating pace of economic globalization, exemplified by global production networks spanning across countries - yet rooted in specific locations within them - has underlined the local dimension of economic activity. Trends like the emergence of high-performing regional economies in developing countries as well as increasing inter-regional disparities within developed countries have prompted scholars to explore what causes economic activity to disperse on one hand, yet still remain rooted in a limited number of locations on the other – what Markusen terms 'sticky places in slippery space'[2].

Thus, the sub-national or regional dimension of economic activity has increasingly come to the fore as an arena for policy. Recent publications that explicitly look at the global and local dimensions of economic activity, and what enables specific 'regions' or 'clusters' of high-performing firms to pull ahead of others include the United Nations Industrial Development Organizations *Industrial Development Report* (2009), and the World Bank's *World Development Report: Reshaping Economic Geography* (2009).

What, then, do we know about economic activity, innovation, and location?

There are well-known reasons why firms tend to agglomerate or cluster together. They seek to benefit from externalities or spillover effects, which benefit all firms in the group. These externalities can be 'traded' or 'untraded'. Traded interdependencies refer to direct trans-

---

2   Ann Markusen, 'Sticky Places in Slippery Space: A Typology of Industrial Districts', *Economic Geography, 72(3), (1996), p. 293.*

actions between firms, and mean that firms in an established cluster[3] are more likely to benefit from a wider range of specialised suppliers, which will, through better quality inputs, quicker delivery times, and more competitive prices, increase the performance of all firms in the cluster. Furthermore, clusters also offer 'thicker' labour markets which have more workers with required technical competencies. Untraded interdependencies are less tangible, and include benefits such as more opportunities for the interchange of ideas, techniques, technology, and business opportunities that arise from proximity between firms. These benefits were first put forward by Marshall's work on industrial districts[4].

Other scholars have looked at the increased opportunities for learning offered by the collaboration between firms in the same cluster. Under certain circumstances, firms with similar levels of technological capability can group together and divide up discrete parts of the production process. This allows firms to specialize in their particular task – a process called 'speciation' – which results in deepened knowledge and capabilities which, in turn, allows the group as a whole to benefit from gains in efficiency. In addition, high levels of trust can also allow product and process technology to be transferred between subcontracting firms and their clients, as the latter benefit from the greater technological capabilities of the former. That said, these relationships are not found in every cluster, and only occur in specific locations that are characterized by high levels of trust, or what is termed 'social capital'[5].

Other work has looked at the role of the local institutional 'environment' and the role it can play in underpinning a region's economic advantage. Economic geographers such as Storper, Scott, and Saxenian have looked at how local customs, traditions, and attitudes can support economic growth and innovation through generating and maintaining

3   A cluster is defined as a spatial and sectoral concentration of firms. Timothy Bresnahan, Anthony Gambardella, and Annalee Saxenian, "'Old Economy' Inputs for 'New Economy' Outcomes: Cluster Formation in the New Silicon Valleys". Industrial and Corporate Change, vol. 10, no. 4 (2001), p. 836.

4   Peter Dicken, Global Shift: Transforming the World Economy, 4th Edition. London: Sage Publications, 2003, pp. 22-23.

5   Hubert Schmitz, "Small Shoemakers and Fordist Giants: Tales of a Supercluster", World Development, vol. 23, no. 1, (1995), p. 10.

Shallow Pockets but Close to the Action

collective attitudes on matters such as product quality, acceptable business practices, and openness to inter-firm collaboration. Some of the most developed institutional contexts include artisan associations that provide a range of business-relevant services to their members, local banks that offer loans to small firms based on their reputation in the community as opposed to collateral, and credit cooperatives that allow firms to guarantee each other's loans. Thus, these scholars have documented how the benefits of institutional environments contributed to the success of some regions in pulling ahead of their competitors.[6]

Despite advances in telecommunications and managerial processes and the tendency of productions tasks that rely on routine tasks and 'codified' knowledge to disperse, it is highly likely that tasks that rely on 'tacit' knowledge and that require large amounts of face-to-face contact will continue to cluster in specific locations. Leamer and Storper argue that while modern telecommunications allow simple routine functions to be carried out at cheaper and more distant locations, a great deal of economic activity involves complex concepts and interactions that cannot be simplified and managed from afar. Certain sectors or production processes that rely on familiarity, trust, and large amounts of knowledge that cannot be codified will cluster[7]. The archetypical examples of these include the financial services and fashion industries.

To summarize thus far, work from a variety of disciplines on the relationship between economic activity and location has argued convincingly that the latter can play an influential role for the former. Firms located in close proximity with other firms in the same or similar sectors benefit from well-developed supplier networks, thicker labour markets, and 'spillover' effects. In certain circumstances, firms can cooperate with each other, which offers additional opportunities for

---

6   For example: the IT industries in Silicon Valley and Route 128, and the entertainment industries in Hollywood and New York. See: Annalee Saxenian, Regional Advantage: Culture and Competition in Silicon Valley and Route 128 (Cambridge: Harvard University Press, 1994); Annalee Saxenian, "Regional Systems of Innovation and the Blurred Firm", in Local and Regional Systems of Innovation, edited by John De La Mothe and Gilles Paquet (Boston: Kluwer Academic Publishers, 1998); and Allen J. Scott, On Hollywood: the Place, the Industry (Princeton, N.J.: Princeton University Press, 2005).

7   Edward Leamer and Michael Storper, "The Economic Geography of the Internet Age", NBER Working Paper 8450 (Cambridge, MA: National Bureau of Economic Research, 2001), p. 25.

learning and improvements in production processes. In addition, the local 'institutional' environment surrounding firms can play a role in shaping and maintaining constructive attitudes to collaboration, quality and workmanship, as well as acceptable business practices. Last, while advances in managerial processes and technology have reconfigured the geographic distribution of production, different production processes have been affected differently. While routine processes can be more easily re-located and managed from afar, processes that rely on social exchange and large amounts of 'tacit' knowledge are increasingly dependent on clustering.

Regional Innovation Systems

While the abovementioned studies have demonstrated that there is a relationship between location and economic activity, the policy implications are less clear. Most studies on this issue have tended to centre on success stories, many of which are located in the United States and Europe. In many of these cases, much of the constructive clustering effects, collaborative efforts, and helpful local customs have arisen organically, rather than through deliberate policy-making.

However, the rapid pace of economic globalization and its potentially exclusionary nature has led policy-makers in emergent and declining regions to look for ways to strengthen or revitalize their economies. One comprehensive approach to systemically assessing a region's current and potential ability to provide an environment conducive to innovation, and hence economic growth, is the Regional Innovation Systems (RIS) school. Coming from an economic geographic standpoint and influenced by evolutionary economics, the RIS school analyzes the ways in which firms relate to each other on one hand, and with the surrounding institutional context on the other.

As its name would imply, the RIS school centres on innovation as the key to driving economic growth. Innovation is taken to mean the "commercialization of new knowledge in respect of products, processes, and organization". There are two particularities about this definition: a) the knowledge developed needs to be used in the market; and b) innovation is not limited to the development of entirely new

products, but also (often small) improvements in existing products or processes[8].

The RIS school starts from the assumption that firms do not possess all capabilities for effective creation or absorption of knowledge in-house. Rather much of their competitiveness relies on being able to access outside knowledge effectively, through contact with other firms or institutions such as research institutes, technology centres, business consultants, or collective facilities such as open labs. This establishes the need for a context conducive to constructive inter-dependencies. Figure 1 has a stylized depiction of a firm and its context.

Figure 1: A Firm and its Surrounding Context

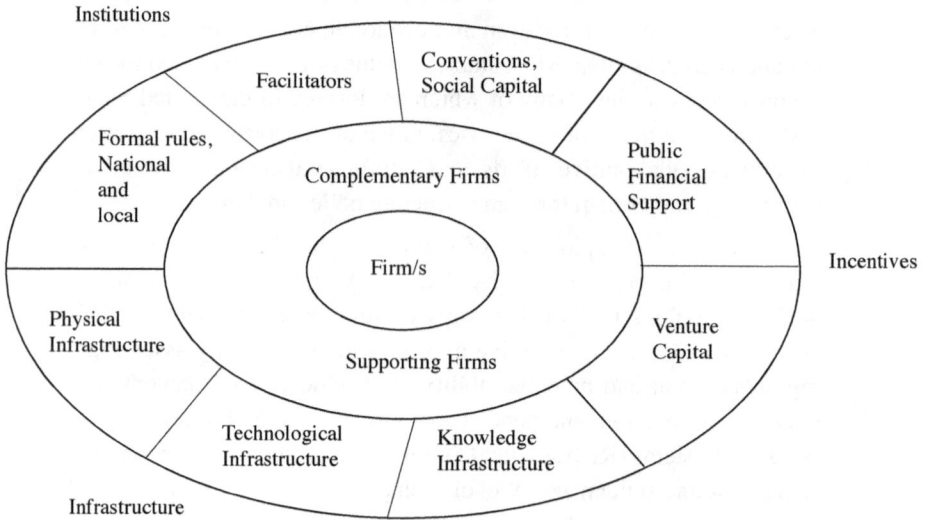

Institutions

Facilitators — Conventions, Social Capital

Formal rules, National and local — Complementary Firms — Public Financial Support

Firm/s — Incentives

Physical Infrastructure — Supporting Firms — Venture Capital

Technological Infrastructure — Knowledge Infrastructure

Infrastructure

Source: Martin Andersson and Charlie Karlsson, 'Regional Innovation Systems in Small & Medium-Sized Regions: A Critical Review and Assessment', CESIS Working Paper Series, No. 10 (Stockholm: Centre of Excellence for Science and Innovation Studies, 2004), p. 12.

---

8   Philip Cooke, "Regional Innovation Systems, Clusters, and the Knowledge Economy", *Industrial* **and** *Corporate Change, vol. 10, no. 4 (Oxford University Press, 2001), p. 953.*

Given this wider definition of 'innovation', the RIS approach does not focus exclusively on organizations such as research institutes and universities. While these are fundamental for certain types of knowledge, the RIS approach analyses all parts of a region's economic and institutional infrastructure and how it creates, absorbs, and diffuses knowledge. The RIS approach starts from the standpoint that an environment that has more opportunities to interface between firms and between firms and their surrounding institutions - which are themselves productive, well networked, and offer an extensive array of relevant supporting services - will be more conducive to innovation.

An RIS is comprised of two components[9].

- The regional production structure - comprised of individual firms and any networks that bind them together.

- The regional supportive infrastructure – comprised of all institutions that support economic activity and innovation such as government agencies, research institutes, technology centres, credit provision agencies and venture capitalists, universities and colleges, and business consultants.

The existence of these two parts is necessary, but not sufficient, for an RIS to work well, as there needs to be interaction, communication, and trust within each of the two parts of the system, as well as between them. The cluster as a whole benefits if firms are able to establish productive collaborative relationships with each other and also if they are able to readily access sources of new knowledge.

While the density and frequency of exchanges within a region makes an RIS approach appropriate for approaching local-level economies, this does not mean that firm clusters and local institutions exist in isolation from their national economic and institutional infrastructure, or that firms within an RIS are independent from international production networks. Rather, that it is at the regional level that firms, networks, and their surrounding institutions will tend to have more contact.

---

9   *Martin Andersson and Charlie Karlsson, 'Regional Innovation Systems in Small & Medium-Sized Regions: A Critical Review and Assessment', CESIS Working Paper Series, no. 10 (Stockholm: Centre of Excellence for Science and Innovation Studies, 2004), p. 10.*

Where the RIS approach differs from more market-centred approaches such as Porter's cluster theory[10], is that it does not assume that the more productive aspects of agglomeration such as collaboration, collective efficiency, and generalized diffusion of knowledge occur automatically. Rather, it starts from the stand-point that a variety of market failures may prevent firms from accessing knowledge and opportunities. Some of the more critical market failures are as follows:

First, many of the conditions that create positive externalities are under-developed if left to market forces alone. Non-excludable public goods such as a skilled workforce, basic research and development, collective facilities, and a regional 'brand name', will be under-developed due to the 'free-riding' problem – namely that individuals will seek to benefit from such goods without paying for them.

Second, negative aspects of agglomeration such as relationships characterised by low levels of trust, competition on price, or labour poaching can arise, undercutting the potential for collaboration. The successful resolution of many of these issues requires a mediator to overcome collective action failures, something the private sector is not always able to do. While organizations such as business associations can offer a partial response to some of these issues, they arise only in established sectors and benefits tend to be restricted to member organizations.

Third, the demand for 'knowledge-generating' services such as sector-specific research may be too incipient, dispersed, or unarticulated to warrant a private sector response. This is particularly the case for new or fledgling industries, where a market has yet to be created. In many cases, a private sector solution will emerge once the market is established and information on pricing is available, which may mean that the region's first-mover advantage has been lost. Research from regions in South Korea, Brazil, Northern Ireland, and Hungary shows that during the early stages of cluster formation, a public sector response may be more appropriate. However, over time, private sector offerings often surpass publicly-available services in quality and price[11].

---

10 Michael E. Porter, *The Competitive Advantage of Nations* (New York: The Free Press, 1990).

11 Philip Cooke, *"Strategies for Regional Innovation Systems: Learning Transfer and Applications"* (Cardiff: Centre for Advanced Studies, Cardiff University, 2001), p. 30.

Fourth, producers and consumers do not always have the necessary information regarding prices, products, markets, or technology in order to make informed decisions. Presence in a cluster of firms does not automatically guarantee access to information. Research from emergent clusters indicates that knowledge is distributed through networks of firms unevenly, with better-connected firms benefiting and other less-established ones being excluded[12]. Limited diffusion of industry-relevant knowledge can, in the long-term, affect a cluster's innovative potential.

Fifth, the acquisition and absorption of new technological information by firms is not straight-forward. Markets are good at giving signals for small changes in production and investment, but they are not good at providing information on returns that can accrue from the adoption of important technology. Therefore, existing prices may not be representative of potential profits, leading firms to abstain from investing in potentially lucrative activities or seeking to work collaboratively[13].

Thus, if not addressed, negative externalities, collective action failures, and information asymmetries can undercut a cluster's innovative potential. Symptoms of a 'fragmented' regional innovation include the following[14]:

- Small, closed, or unsophisticated markets for goods and services
- Firms in established industries with little appetite for innovation and weak links to local or international networks

---

12 Elisa Giuliani and Martin Bell, "Industrial Clusters and the Evolution of their Knowledge Networks: Revisiting a Chilean Case". SPRU Electronic Working Paper Series no. 171 (Brighton: Science Policy Research Unit, University of Sussex, 2008), pp. 21-22.

13 Helen Shapiro and Lance Taylor. "The State and Industrial Strategy", World Development, vol. 18 no. 6 (1990), p. 862.

14 Mikel Landabaso, Christine Oughton, and Kevin Morgan, 'Learning Regions in Europe: Theory, Policy, and Practice through the RIS Experience', in Systems and Policy for the Global Learning Economy, edited by David V. Gibson, Chandler Stolp, Pedro Conceicao, and Manuel V. Heitor (London: Praeger, 2003) p. 85. Arnoud Lagendijk, "Learning in Non-core Regions: Towards 'Intelligent Clusters'; Addressing Business and Regional Needs". In Knowledge, Innovation, and Economic Growth: the Theory and Practice of Learning Regions, edited by Frans Boekma, Kevin Morgan, Silvia Bakkers, Roel Rutten (Cheltenham: Edward Elgar, 2000), pp. 170-71.

- Lack of fora or intermediaries for firms, particularly small and medium enterprises to identify and articulate their needs regarding issues such as supporting services and research and development (R&D)
- Support schemes are not articulated with firm needs
- Financial systems with limited funding solutions for small firms ('patient capital', guarantor facilities, quick turnaround times)
- Communication gaps between universities, the government, and the private sector
- Research 'push' – the provision of research, funding, and facilities for which no demand has been made
- No articulation of 'regional needs' or overlaps and disjunctures between national and regional policy

Figure 2: A Fragmented Regional Innovation System

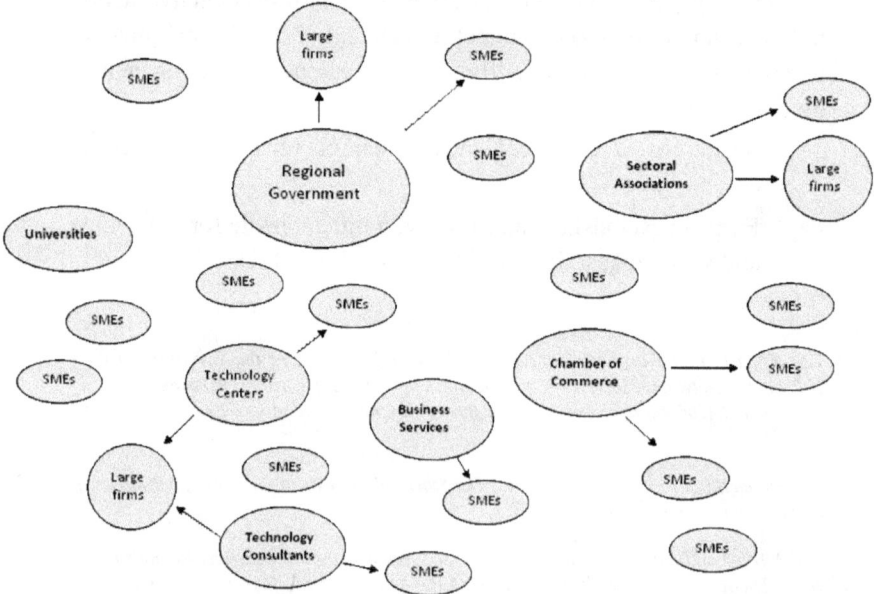

Source: Mikel Landabaso, Christine Oughton, and Kevin Morgan, 'Learning Regions in Europe: Theory, Policy, and Practice through the RIS Experience', in Systems and Policy for the Global Learning Economy, edited by David V. Gibson, Chandler Stolp, Pedro Conceicao, and Manuel V. Heitor (London: Praeger, 2003) p. 84.
about here

Figure 2 depicts what a fragmented regional innovation system could look like. In this scenario, firms have differing levels of access to information and services. In particular, a large number of firms are isolated and have little contact with the region's supportive institutions. Because of incomplete networks in the cluster and information asymmetries, they do not benefit from positive externalities or the opportunity of inter-firm learning. The supporting institutions are also not networked among themselves and are not able to share information and thus articulate a structured response to firm needs.

Thus, the end goal of a Regional Innovation System (RIS) is to increase the innovative potential of firms by correcting market failures, overcoming collective action dilemmas, and increasing the opportunities for collaboration and inter-firm learning. While the creation of an RIS is a long-term and piece-meal affair, it is very hard for competitors to emulate as, while infrastructure and financial capital can be provided relatively easy, human and, particularly, social capital take longer to build up.

Having put forward the concept of an RIS and the role it can play in underpinning regional competitiveness, the next section will look at the role for policy.

The Role for Policy

While economic activity may have a local dimension, it is worth asking whether the sub-national or regional level is the most appropriate for policy-making, as opposed to having decisions taken at the central level.

In many countries, the relationship between the central government and its sub-national counterparts is established in the constitution, which contains separate lists for unique responsibilities and a concurrent list for shared tasks. While the overall policy context is established by the central government, state governments have both formal and informal responsibilities that allow them to play a vital role in their region's economic development. Furthermore, elections at this

level are held much in the same mould as national ones, guaranteeing a minimum level of accountability to citizens.

While the scope of the responsibilities of state or provincial governments may differ in each country and their actions may be constrained by national-level institutions and initiatives, the key attribute is the authority to raise revenue - through taxation and other means - and spend[15].

In terms of relative power, the dice are clearly loaded in the national state's favour, as the resources under its control and, presumably, more territorially-extensive legitimacy put it in a unique position to provide certain public services and goods, particularly those associated with economic and political stability and sovereignty. However, on the other hand, decentralizing some economic decision-making responsibilities to the sub-national level offers considerable advantages.

First, the principle of subsidiarity argues that government institutions that are closer to their constituents are better-placed to deliver particular types of services. Abelson argues that central governments are in a better position to carry out stabilization tasks, such as managing aggregate employment and prices, as well as distribution tasks, such as fostering equity and ensuring minimum living standards. In contrast, the provision of goods that provide localized benefits like health and education can be more efficiently performed by sub-national governments, who will have more information as to their needs[16].

The second argument is that sub-national governments, due to their greater proximity to citizens, may be more responsive to citizen concerns and local priorities. In turn, due to this same proximity, citizens are better able to monitor government performance and ensure the effective delivery of services[17].

---

15   H. Peter Gray and John H. Dunning, "Towards a Theory of Regional Policy", in Regions, Globalization, and the Knowledge-Based Economy, edited by John H. Dunning (Oxford: Oxford University Press, 2002), pp. 10-11.

16   Peter, Abelson, Public Economics: Principles and Practice (Canberra: Applied Economics, 2003), pp. 346-47.

17   Omar S. Azfar, S. Kahkonen, A. Lanyi, and P. Meagher, "Decentralization, Governance, and Public Services: The Impact of Institutional Arrangements", University of Maryland Center for Institutional Reform and the Informal Sector, Working Paper no. 255 (1999), p.2.

In addition, greater knowledge of the local environment and more freedom in policy-making can enable policy-makers to more easily tailor measures to leverage their region's comparative advantage. This can enable regions to specialize in producing certain goods and services, which in turn can result in a more diversified and stable national economy. However, this autonomy needs to be accompanied by centrally-administered transfers to manage inter-regional inequality[18].

Furthermore, transferring some responsibility for revenue generation to the sub-national level can encourage 'creative' attempts to raise income. Competition between states for domestic and international investment can also have a similar effect, encouraging state and provincial governments to create and maintain a business-friendly environment. State-level analyses of policy-making in India following its 1991 reforms show the 'galvanizing' effect competition from neighbouring states can have on the ability of state governments to set priorities and address business concerns[19].

Last, while greater autonomy also encourages policy innovation and opportunities for the transfer of successful measures, it also limits the risks of such 'experimentation' to one component unit of a country, instead of its entirety. Measures that are successful at the local level can then be rolled out in other states or at the national level.

Using the logic of subsidiarity, Figure 3 sets out the appropriateness of different market complementing measures in relation to the level of governance.

---

18   Gareth Williams, Pierre Landell-Mills, and Alex Duncan, "Uneven Growth within Low-income Countries: Does it Matter and Can Governments Do Anything Effective?", The Policy Practice published papers (Oxford: The Policy Practice Limited, 2005), p. 18.

19   Lloyd Rudolph and Susan Hoeber Rudolph. "The Iconization of Chandrababu: Sharing Sovereignty in India's Federal Market Economy", Economic and Political Weekly. May 5, (2001), p. 1546. Francis E. Hutchinson, "Can Sub-national States be Developmental?: The Cases of Penang and Karnataka", PhD dissertation, Policy and Governance Program, Australian National University, Canberra (2006), p. 313.

Figure 3: The Appropriateness of Policies by Level of Governance

Market Complement- ing Interventions	Relative Appropriatenesss	
	National State	Sub-national State
Macroeconomic Policy	XXX	--
Foreign investment framework	XXX	X
Large-scale infrastructure	XXX	X
Access to finance	XXX	XX
R&D funding	XXX	XX
Reducing information asymmetries	XX	XXX
Reducing collective action failures	XX	XXX
Fostering inter-firm collaboration	XX	XXX
Providing skills training	XX	XXX
Providing specialized infrastructure	XX	XXX

Importance ranges from '--' to 'XXX'
Source: partially based on H. Peter Gray and John H. Dunning, 'Towards a Theory of Regional Policy', in Regions, Globalization, and the Knowledge-Based Economy, edited by John H. Dunning (Oxford: Oxford University Press 2002), p. 426.

However, allowing greater autonomy at the sub-national level will not automatically result in more responsive governance or innovative policy-making. Rather, reviews of decentralization experiences show that its success is contingent on state capacity at the sub-national level as well as the way in which it is implemented[20].

While there are certainly implementation issues involved in fomenting greater autonomy and responsibility for economic governance at the sub-national level, the awareness of the local dimension of eco-

---

20   Omar S. Azfar, S. Kahkonen, A. Lanyi, and P. Meagher, "Decentralization, Governance, and Public Services: The Impact of Institutional Arrangements", University of Maryland Center for Institutional Reform and the Informal Sector, Working Paper no. 255 (1999), p.4.

nomic development and the potential benefits of decentralizing some aspects of policy-making has led many countries such as the United Kingdom and Germany as well as international institutions such as the OECD and the European Union to include a regional component in their economic development strategies[21].

Having established that regional governments have a legitimate and productive role in seeking to foster and strengthen their economies, it is relevant to ask what can be done to create or strengthen a regional innovation system.

In general, the working of an RIS can be strengthened by policy measures aimed at achieving one of three ends: correcting market failures; overcoming collective action problems; and increasing the interaction with and between the region's production structure and supporting institutional structure. An indicative, but not exhaustive, list of potential measures includes the following:

Correcting Market Failures

- Improving access to information on business-relevant topics through compiling and disseminating material
- Improving access to finance for small and medium enterprises (SME) through, for example, the establishment of facilities for patient capital, adapting rules for guarantors and collateral, and re-weighting criteria for approval
- Investing in human resources, through institutions such as skills-training centres
- Providing access to business intelligence and marketing expertise
- Carrying out and disseminating results from basic research
- Providing publicly-available specialist facilities and equipment
- Providing technology-related services such as audits and forecasting, particularly where market supply is under-developed
- Overcoming Collective Action Problems

21   *See, for example: OECD. New Forms of Governance for Economic Development. Paris: Organization for Economic Cooperation and Development, 2004; European Commission. "Constructing Regional Advantage: Principles, Perspectives, Policies" (Brussels: Directorate-General for Research, European Commission, 2006).*

- Procuring inputs collectively to reap economies of scale and increase bargaining power
- Brokering agreements on labour standards, business practices, and poaching
- Facilitating joint-bids between groups of firms for large contracts
- 'Mapping' and pinpointing gaps in capabilities

Increasing the interaction between regional production structure and regional supporting structure

- Articulating a regional-level economic development strategy
- Intermediating between SMEs and relevant supporting services in the public and private sectors
- Acting as marriage-broker between SMEs and potential local and international clients
- Promoting interaction and collaboration between firms, knowledge institutions, and government agencies

However, while it is tempting to increase budgets for these and other related measures, policy-makers need to beware of the capacity of a set of institutions that are not well-articulated to successfully absorb additional funds. Experiences from Europe and elsewhere testify to the 'regional innovation paradox', which refers to the inability of lagging regions to usefully manage additional funding due to their under-developed networks and institutional infrastructure[22].

From this perspective, the aim of a regional government is to articulate a local economic development strategy. More than assuming responsibility for vast amounts of additional services, the role of the government is to act as an 'intelligent cell' that compiles information, establishes development priorities, makes use of existing national institutions and policies, promotes communication between the different parts of the RIS, and, where necessary, tackles market failures directly. Figure 4 depicts how an idealized RIS could look, with the regional government carrying out the abovementioned functions.

---

22 *Christine Oughton, Mikel Landabaso, and Kevin Morgan. "The Regional Innovation Paradox: Innovation Policy and Industrial Policy", Journal of Technology Transfer, 27 (2002), p. 97.*

Figure 4: A Well-Articulated Regional Innovation System

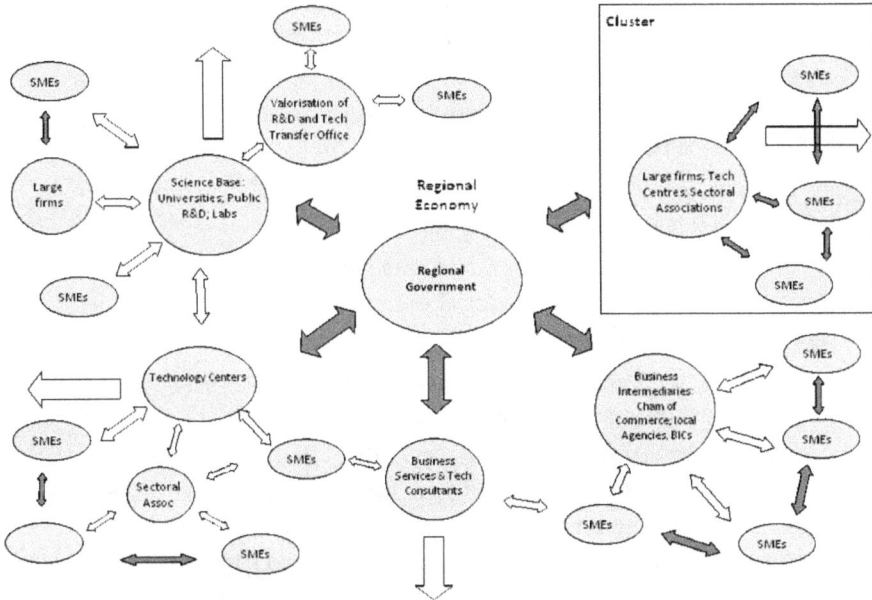

Source: Mikel Landabaso, Christine Oughton, and Kevin Morgan, 'Learning Regions in Europe: Theory, Policy, and Practice through the RIS Experience', in Systems and Policy for the Global Learning Economy, edited by David V. Gibson, Chandler Stolp, Pedro Conceicao, and Manuel V. Heitor (London: Praeger, 2003) p. 88.

The creation or strengthening of an RIS is a long-term process. Available experience from studies of regional development in the European Union, the United States, and Korea and elsewhere offer the following lessons learned[23]:

It is constructive to gather a wide range of stakeholders in the development of a strategy to ensure up-to-date information, consensus, and support

---

23 Bresnahan, Timothy, Anthony Gambardella, and Annalee Saxenian. "'Old Economy' Inputs for 'New Economy' Outcomes: Cluster Formation in the New Silicon Valleys", pp. 856-8; Choi, Ji-Sun. "Potential and Limitation of New Industrial Policy in Korea: Fostering Innovative Clusters", New Economic Spaces: New Economic Geographies, edited by Richard Le Heron and James W. Harrington (London: Ashgate, 2005), p. 216; Gray, H. Peter and John H. Dunning. "Towards a Theory of Regional Policy", p. 422; European Commission. "Constructing Regional Advantage: Principles, Perspectives, Policies" (Brussels: Directorate-General for Research, European Commission, 2006), p 19-21.

Decision-makers should be wary of importing a 'model' from elsewhere, rather policy-making must be organic and reflect local realities

Regional governments should be wary of relying on financial incentives and easily-replicable infrastructure as the core of their competitive advantage, as this can result in an unproductive race to the bottom between competitors

Economic development plans should be made in reference to neighbouring regions to avoid over-lap

There is a tendency to prioritize attracting high-tech and promising industries, rather than rooting the decision in an analysis of the region's strength and capabilities

The priority should be the long-term development of the cluster, rather than the fortunes of a select group of 'babies'

Policy frameworks must evolve over time, as the policies needed to start a new industry are different from those needed to make it grow. Thus, policy-making must be based on detailed and constant communication between the private sector, government, and supporting institutions.

This section has: put forward the Regional Innovation Concept and explained how it can help regions further construct or develop their competitive advantage; explored the advantages of decentralized policy-making; and looked at how regional governments can go about creating or strengthening an RIS. Using this framework, the next section will look at Penang's current Regional Innovation System.

Penang's Regional Innovation System Today: A Snapshot

Following the framework set out in the previous section, this section will provide a snap-shot of Penang's Regional Innovation System. It will be divided into two parts. The first will look at what is known about firms in the manufacturing sector in Penang, including how many there are, what they do, how they relate to each other, and what issues they face. The second will look at the supportive institutional infrastructure in the state, namely all institutions that relate to the creation and diffusion of knowledge. The discussion in both sections will make specific reference to what can be established about the extent and quality of interaction within and between the two aspects of Penang's RIS.

The Regional Production Structure

Penang is a leading centre for manufacturing in Malaysia, particularly for the electrical and electronics sector (E&E). What sets Penang apart from other regions in Malaysia, such as the Klang Valley and Johor Bahru is not so much the size of its manufacturing sector, but rather the quality of its operations. Penang has attracted considerable investment in the semi-conductor and hard disk drive sectors. In contrast, the other two regions have specialized in less technologically-intensive sectors. In addition, more than the other two states, multinational corporations have relocated more value-added tasks to their Penang affiliates such as research and development, supply chain management, and customer care.

At present, the manufacturing sector in Penang is comprised of approximately 1,400 registered firms that employ some 200,000 people. Figure 5 displays the results of a survey of approximately half of the known firms in the sector. The electrical and electronics sector is by far the most important and accounts for almost 60% percent of all activity. There is a relatively large group of unrelated activities that account for some 30% of the total, of which food processing and chemical/petrochemical production are the most important. There are also small information and communication technologies (ICT) and biotech/agro sectors.

Figure 5: Manufacturing Activities in Penang by Sector and Sub-Sector

Manufacturing Sector	Percentage of total	Subsectors
Electrical and Electronics	58%	E&E (16%) Automation/machinery/ Precision-tooling/ equipment (13%) Fabricated Metal (13%) Plastic and Plastic Products (8.9%) Manufacturing related services (6.5%)

Manufacturing Sector	Percentage of total	Subsectors
ICT	2%	Multimedia
Biotech and Agro	3.2%	Biotech Medical Equipment Agro-based Production
Others	32%	Food processing (6.1%) Chemical/petro (5%) Paper Metal Publishing Gold and jewellery

Note: N=626
Source: InvestPenang, "2007 Penang Industrial Survey Report" (Penang: InvestPenang, 2008), p. 13.

Figure 6 depicts the revenue and contribution to the workforce of registered firms broken down by size and ownership. As can be seen, multinationals and large foreign firms represent about ten percent of the number of firms, but account for more than 80% of revenue and almost 70% of the workforce. There are a similar number of foreign SMEs, which account for a small proportion of revenue and jobs in the sector. Local large firms account for slightly less than ten percent of firms, a similar proportion of revenue, and about 13% of the workforce. Local SMEs are the largest group of firms, accounting for about 2/3 of the total. While they are the second employer at 15% of the total workforce, they account for a mere 5% of total revenue.

Figure 6: Manufacturing Activities in Penang by Firm Size and Ownership

Firm Type*	Proportion	Total Revenue	Workforce
MNC and foreign large firms	11%	82%	68%
Foreign SMEs	11%	4%	4%
Local Large Firms	9%	9%	13%
Local SMEs	67%	5%	15%

Note: N=629
Source: InvestPenang, "2007 Penang Industrial Survey Report" (Penang: InvestPenang, 2008), p. 11.

* *Small and medium enterprises (SMEs) are companies with less than RM 25 million annual sales turnover or less than 150 full-time employees. Large Firms are companies with more than RM 25 million annual sales turnover and more than 150 full-time employees. MNCs are 'corporations based in one country that maintain manufacturing facilities or operations offices in other countries and that market their products or services on an international basis' InvestPenang, "2007 Penang Industrial Survey Report", p. 8.*

In addition to these firms, many of which are on Penang Development Corporation (PDC) land or other recognized industrial parks, there is an unknown quantity of backyard firms. Estimates of their number range from 1,000-3,000. These firms are found in Georgetown as well as the mainland, in areas such as Bayang Bay, Sungai Ara, Sungai Nibal, and Bukit Jambul[24]. There are few records of these companies, as many of them are operating in residential areas and do not have all requisite permits. While these firms are not registered with local authorities, they are well-known in the E&E sector, as they perform routine services for larger firms, including those that do not comply with established ISO 9000 practices[25].

---

24 Interviews with industry observers BA, BB, and BD (Penang, 15/04/2009, 21/04/2009, and 22/04/2009).

25 There could well be many more firms than this number, particularly in sectors such as software that are very hard to track. Interviews with industry observer BA (Penang, 15/04/2009), and industry observers BB and BC (Penang, 21/04/2009).

What are the recent trends in the manufacturing sector in Penang[26]?

- Despite recent high investment levels, manufacturing is losing ground to the service sector.

- There is a narrowing of the state's industrial structure, as over the last five years growth has largely been limited to the E&E sector.

- There is a slow-down in the growth of new firms, particularly over the last 10 years. There are less than 10 new firms being created per year – compared to nearly 20 per year being established 15 years ago.

- Most technological capabilities that local firms possess have come from multinational corporations (MNC), through client-supplier relations.

- Due to this mechanism, a group of local firms has grown over time and acquired deep technical capabilities.

- However, the majority of SMEs are relatively small operations, with less than 50 workers and little working capital. Many are also family-owned affairs.

- Backyard firms are even smaller operations, usually sole-proprietorships, with some 4-5 additional workers.

- R&D and product development expenditure of firms is low and is carried out by a small group of MNCs and even fewer established SMEs (less than 5%).

- However, while there are established competencies among local firms in specific areas, they are dispersed, making it hard to construct complete value chains.

- Most SMEs still rely on product definitions coming from customers.

- Efforts by SMEs to find markets beyond the Penang-based economy have met with limited success.

---

26 InvestPenang, "2007 Penang Industrial Survey Report" (Penang: InvestPenang, 2008), pp. 1-3; PSDC. "Technology Roadmap for the Electrical and Electronics Industry of Penang" (Penang: Penang Skills Development Corporation, 2007), pp. 1-6. Interviews with: senior state government officials, Penang (20/04/2009) and (24/02/2004), and industry observer BD, Penang (22/04/2009).

There is some evidence that SMEs are moving out of manufacturing into other sectors such as trading.

Thus, while recent trends in the manufacturing sector are positive, there are indications that the manufacturing sector is becoming narrower, less successful at generating new firms, and does not display significant inter-firm collaboration.

The reluctance of firms to cooperate or divulge information is historic, and dates back at least to the early 1970s[27]. In part, this is due to the structure of the industry and how it developed. Before the advent of the electronics industry, Penang had a core of largely Chinese-owned manufacturing firms in the metalwork and fabricated metalwork sectors[28]. Over time, some of them came to offer services to MNCs. Initial relationships with MNCs were long-running, permitting the gradual acquisition of capabilities, and tended to be one-on-one. As competition and technical requirements increased, firms became more hermetic[29]. Even today, many established SMEs do not publicize their services, preferring to rely on reputation and word-of mouth for business. This is even more the case for backyard firms, who seek to maintain a low profile. Notwithstanding the structural difficulties in creating value chains mentioned above, this local cultural context is not conducive to the creation of inter-firm linkages and collective learning.

Available evidence suggests that SMEs have limited access to collective facilities and necessary information to help encourage innovation. While conventional wisdom posits that small firms' most frequent complaint is the lack of access to capital, according to Penang's Technology Roadmap, the three most frequently voiced complaints were the following[30]:

- A shortage of skilled workers

---

27   A review of local firms in the early 1970s found that most avoided contact with government bodies or other firms. F.R. Von der Mehden, "Industrial Policy in Malaysa: A Penang Micro-study", Program for Development Studies Monograph, Rice University, Houston (1973) p. 13.

28   Yii Tan Chang, "Penang Island Structure Plan: Technical Report" (Penang: Majlis Perbandaran Pulau Pinang, 1984), p.3.51.

29   Interview with senior state government official, Penang (24/02/2004).

30   PSDC. "Technology Roadmap for the Electrical and Electronics Industry of Penang", p. 55.

- A weak government research structure
- A lack of public technical services

With regard to skilled labour, recent survey data indicates that multinational corporations are able to recruit the best local graduates and overseas returnees, leaving local firms short of skilled labour. In actual fact, there are indications that smaller firms need to pay more for labour of a similar quality. In part, this is due to a cultural stigma against local firms, who are seen as less prestigious and sophisticated. As a result, graduates' first choice of employment is with MNCs, and they are reluctant to leave the stable confines of employment with them to work in an SME or start their own company[31]. These skills shortages have been ameliorated somewhat by the expansion of private education providers, through universities such as Multimedia University, as well as colleges offering engineering courses. However, structural shortages in crucial areas remain.

With regard to government-funded research, there could be several factors at work. Comparisons with other countries in the region show a relative under-investment in R&D, with Malaysia investing USD 37 per capita in R&D as compared to USD 206 in Hong Kong, USD 412 in Taiwan, and USD 593 in Korea[32]. In addition, there are questions as to whether R&D expenditure is appropriately targeted. At present, government funding is oriented to academic research, rather than private sector-led industry-specific research. In addition, there has been little take-up of what funding for private sector R&D there is available[33]. As will be discussed in the next section, there have also been structural difficulties in establishing linkages with the local university. The expansion of the private higher education sector has provided some response to the shortage of workers, but has not really addressed the need for industry-relevant R&D.

At present, there is very little in the way of publicly accessible technical facilities to help firms upgrade. There are no specialist li-

---

31 Interview with industry observer AA, Penang (04/02/2004).

32 IMD, World Competitiveness Yearbook 2008 (Lausanne: International Institute for Management Development, 2008), table 4.3.03.

33 Tham, S.Y. and Rugayah, H.M.Z. "Moving towards High-Tech Industrialisation: The Case of Malaysia", The East Asian High-Tech Drive, edited by Y.P. Chu and H. Hill (Cheltenham: Edward Elgar, 2006), p. 199.

braries for SMEs to consult[34], there are no facilities to access market information, and there are no publicly-available laboratories to test prototypes[35]. In addition to limiting their technical potential, the lack of these facilities also has an impact on the ability of SMEs to procure grants and access loans. Venture capitalists often claim that SME owners lack knowledge of the markets they tend to enter. Banks tend to be even more risk-averse[36].

This aggravates already existing information asymmetries and market failures in the supply of capital. SMEs find it hard to get funds from the banking sector or government agencies, due to their rather onerous requirements[37]. Many of these procedures take too long for SMEs, which do not have large stocks of working capital[38]. Furthermore, many of the grants that are available are geared towards high-technology, rather than more shop-floor level issues such as incremental improvements in products or processes. While these issues are serious enough for registered SMEs, they are prohibitive for those working in the informal economy.

This 'disconnect' is exacerbated by communication issues between supporting institutions and local SMEs. On one hand, many of the older and smaller operations do not use the internet for publicity

---

34 One interviewee became a member of the British Council to access their library. Another uses personal connections to access books in USM's library. Interview with industry observer BA Penang (14/04/2009) and AB, Penang (18/03/2004).

35 Interviews with industry observers BA and BD (Penang, 15/04/2009 and 22/04/2009).

36 Interviews with Industry Observer AC, Penang (08/03/2004) and Venture Capitalist, Penang (19/03/2004).

37 In many cases, firms need to have an established track record, formal accounting systems, all relevant building permits, and collateral. Yet, most manufacturing firms are family-owned and lacking in modern management and accounting techniques, and many do not operate in appropriate areas.

38 Interviews with a MIDA official, Penang (06/04/2004) and a MIDF official, Penang (19/03/2004). Interview with industry observer AB, Penang (03/18/2004). In 2004, only 10 per cent of applications that agencies such as the Malaysian Industrial Development Fund received were funded. One venture capitalist I spoke to in 2004 approved six projects in 2 years, out of more than 150 applications. Interview, Penang (19/03/2004).

and information-gathering[39]. As in many traditional firm clusters, information travels by word-of-mouth, rather than through established means of communication. Furthermore, there are linguistic issues, as a significant number of firm owners are not fluent enough in either English or Bahasa Melayu to deal with many of the technical questions necessary to fill in the forms[40].

This 'gap' in communication has been addressed, in part, by intermediate associations that have emerged in Penang.

The Free Industrial Zone, Penang, Companies' Association (FREPENCA) represents some 60 of the largest firms in the states' industrial parks. It has acted to reduce information asymmetries among firms regarding security, customs clearances, and infrastructure issues, as well as lobbying the Penang State Government for more investment in various areas, better incentives, and more skilled workers. However, FREPENCA, along with associations like the Malaysian International Chamber of Commerce and the Malaysian-American Electronics Association, represent the large firms and MNCs, most of who have the legal and technical expertise to obtain concessions directly from the state and federal governments[41]. That said, these associations do benefit SMEs through voicing general issues that affect the sector as a whole.

The ethnic-based associations, such as the Indian, Malay, and Chinese Chambers of Commerce, for their part, have limited membership among firms in the manufacturing sector[42]. The Federation of Malaysian Manufacturers (FMM) is the most visible and proactive business association in the manufacturing sector in Penang. Originally drawing most of its members from large domestic companies, it has now turned to aggressively recruiting SMEs. The FMM chairs the only forum that brings together state and federal institutions to discuss technical issues

---

39 *According to the representative of one of the more-established industry associations, less than half of their members had websites. Interview with industry association representative, Bukit Minyak (23/04/2009).*

40 *Interview with industry observer BD, Penang (22/04/2009).*

41 *Interviews with senior MNC managers, Penang (04/03/2004, 09/04/2004).*

42 *Interviews with representatives from the Malay Chamber of Commerce, Malaysian Indian Chamber of Commerce, and the Chinese Chamber of Commerce, Penang (25/03/2004, 10/03/2004, 24/02/2004).*

facing SMEs[43]. It also carries out surveys of the manufacturing sector, has produced a comprehensive business guide for SMEs, and also offers a range of courses on human resource and management topics. In addition, the Federation has proven adept at handling the media to pressure the state government on particular issues. However, the Federation only has about 200 SME members in the Northern Region, and not all are from Penang or in the electronics sector[44].

Other business associations in Penang's eco-system include the Small and Medium Enterprises Association (SAMENTA), whose membership is comprised of some 200 firms in the manufacturing and services sector, and the Penang Foundry and Engineering Industries Association (PENFEIA) which also has some 200 members in the foundry and engineering sectors[45].

Business associations carry out vital services for firms. However, while they can articulate concerns facing their membership, offer technical and educational services, and act as mediators in some circumstances, they cannot be relied on exclusively to energize and direct an innovation system. First, business associations are not public organizations and need to restrict their services to their membership. Second, they may not enjoy sufficient economies of a scale that is able to provide extensive collective facilities. In addition, business associations emerge once sufficient demand exists, which means smaller firms or those in new industries may not be represented. Proof of this is that most of the associations consulted have few members from the informal sector.

The Regional Supportive Infrastructure

The previous section looked at the regional production structure, namely firms as well as their networks and associations. This section, in contrast, will look at the regional supportive infrastructure, which consists of institutions in Penang that create and diffuse information and/or help firms to do so. This will entail a brief analysis of institu-

---

43   *Interview with a FMM representative, Penang (15/04/2004).*

44   *Interview with a FMM representative, Penang (15/04/2009).*

45   *Interview with a PENFEIA representative, Penang (23/04/2009).*

tions such as state and federal agencies concerned with economic development[46], as well as universities and colleges.

Penang State Government Institutions

The Penang State Government is, and has been, one of Malaysia's most proactive and entrepreneurial sub-national governments. It has a reputation for effective administration, proactive liaising with international investors, and innovative policy-making. During the 1970s and 1980s, in particular, it resembled a 'sub-national' development state, as it: had a capable bureaucracy; prioritized economic growth; and developed close relations with the private sector to attain that end[47].

The roots of Penang's economic success can be found in the events of 1969, when state elections in the wake of a deep recession led to an over-haul of the state's economic model. Overcoming severe resource constraints and limited governmental responsibilities, the government was able to launch an investment drive and diversify its economy. Through capitalizing on its constitutional mandate to buy and sell land, the state government was able to raise funds to build industrial parks for investors, as well as engage in a variety of self-discovery experiments designed to create jobs and widen the state's economic base.

---

46 It is worth noting the way that responsibilities and income are apportioned between the federal and state governments. Malaysia has a federal system of government. The 1957 Constitution lays out the responsibilities for each level of governance, with a list each for the federal and state governments and a concurrent list with shared responsibilities. The federal government is responsible for public goods such as defence, internal security, external affairs, and finance, as well as services such as education, health, and transport. The states are given residual responsibilities, consisting of land, forestry, Islamic affairs, and local government, and the federal government has precedence of state governments in the event of a dispute. (Ninth Schedule, Constitution of Malaysia) This division of power is correspondingly matched by access to resources. The Constitution assigns the bulk of revenues to the federal government and establishes fixed formulas for the transfer of funds from the federal to the state governments. The federal government has power to receive trade duties and levy taxes on income, companies, and capital gains. The states have smaller, less flexible sources of income such as revenue from land sales, natural resources such as mines and forests, an Islamic tax, and duty on entertainment. Abdul R. Anuar, "Fiscal Decentralization in Malaysia", Hitotsubashi Journal of Economics, no. 2, (2000), p. 87. Chong Hui Wee, "Fiscal federalism", Malaysia's Economic Development: Policy and Reform, edited by Kwame Sundaram Jomo and S.K. Ng (Kuala Lumpur: Pelanduk Publications, 1996), p. 284.

47 Francis E. Hutchinson, "Developmental States and Economic Growth at the Sub-National Level: The Case of Penang", Southeast Asian Affairs 2008, edited by D. Singh and M.M.T. Tin (Singapore: Institute of Southeast Asian Studies, 2008), pp. 240-41.

The Penang Development Corporation (PDC) has traditionally been the State Government's implementing arm. Established in 1971, the PDC was a semi-autonomous government body charged with overseeing economic growth in the state. The Chief Minister of Penang, Lim Chong Eu, hand-picked key staff members and used the agency to spearhead the state's industrialization drive.

During the 1970s and 1980s, the PDC undertook a variety of strategies to achieve this end. First, it bought and sold land to raise revenue. Second, it marketed Penang aggressively to overseas investors. Third, it provided infrastructure for investors including industrial parks and housing for workers. Fourth, it made strategic investments in a variety of sectors such as ship-building, agribusiness, electronics, furniture production, and high quality glass fabrication, among others. Fifth, it helped reduce information asymmetries through fostering links between international investors and local SMEs. Sixth, it created mechanisms for targeted skills provision[48].

Over time, these strategies paid off, particularly with international investors. The manufacturing sector grew consistently over the 1970 and 1980s, generating more employment for Penang and people from surrounding states. In addition, through personal connections, the Chief Minister was able to broker relationships between a small group of SMEs and MNCs, who were encouraged to source components locally. This worked with an initial group, and subcontracting ties with MNCs were later expanded to other firms.

That said, it is important to note that communication between local firms and the PDC was not institutionalized. While there was a Small-Scale Industries Unit within the PDC in the 1980s, it lasted only two years. Consistent with the thinking of the day, policy-makers in the state government thought that once a core of local firms were established, learning and technology would spread from the larger firms

48   PDC. 1977 Annual Report (Penang: Penang Development Corporation, 1977), p.13. PDC. 1980 Annual Report, (Penang: Penang Development Corporation, 1980), p.25. Francis E. Hutchinson, "Developmental States and Economic Growth at the Sub-National Level: The Case of Penang", Southeast Asian Affairs, 2009 (Singapore: Institute of Southeast Asian Studies), pp. 227-28.

downwards to smaller ones, and the group as a whole would grow over time[49].

During the 1980s, greater centralization at the federal level, particularly in the area of staffing, saw some of the PDC's autonomy erode[50]. In the 1990s, under a new state leadership, its activities and investments began to move away from manufacturing towards more lucrative operations in real estate, leisure facility management, and construction. The biggest area for new activity in the manufacturing sector was in supporting industries such as air cargo handling, warehousing, and information technology. In addition, the PDC made investments in private colleges and hospitals to diversify the economy. Despite education being a federal responsibility, the state government was very active in the education and training sector. It established the Penang Skills Development Corporation and fostered the growth of the private education sector – often through joint ventures[51].

Notwithstanding greater federal involvement at the state level, the Penang State Government has proactively sought to articulate its own developmental needs. The state government has commissioned various strategic plans to provide a blueprint for development. The first Penang Strategic Development Plan (PSDP) came out in 1991, to be followed by the Second Penang Strategic Development Plan (PSDP2) in 2001. Other notable development plans include the Knowledge ICT Blueprint (2002), which envisioned the state's transition from a production to a knowledge-economy, and the Technology Road-Map for the Electrical and Electronics Industry of Penang (2007).

The Development Plans set out broad-ranging strategic frameworks for the state in the economic, social, environmental, and governance areas. They provide very good analyses of the structural issues that the state faces. That said, attempts to ensure that their recommen-

---

49 *Interview with a former senior state government official, Penang (22/04/2009).*

50 *Chet Singh, 1991. "Learning from the Malaysian Experience: A Case Study of the Penang Development Corporation (PDC)", Public Enterprise Management: Strategies for Success (London: Commonwealth Secretariat, 1989), p. 108.*

51 *In 2001, more than 1,800 students were enrolled in engineering courses in private colleges. This compares to 1000-1,200 enrolled in similar subjects in 2000-01 in the federally-funded university in Penang, Universiti Sains Malaysia. SERI. "A Study on Penang's Private Institutions of Higher Learning". Penang: Socio-economic and Environmental Research Institute, 2002, p. xi.*

dations are followed up have been less successful. This is due, in part, to the fact that the Penang State Government has limited resources for development expenditure and federal agencies in Penang are not beholden to it. During 1999-2003, the state government's development budget amounted to only 16 per cent of the federal government's budget for projects in Penang[52]. Furthermore, this planning mechanism is superceded by federal procedures for the Malaysia Plans, which federal agencies are tasked with following.

During the 1990s and the early part of this decade, communication with international investors and large local firms continued to be good. In addition to periodic meetings with business associations, the State Government had constant contact with private sector 'leaders' and 'captains' through fora such as the Penang Economic Council, the Penang Industrial Council, and the Penang Competitiveness Committee. However, communication with smaller firms in the manufacturing sector began to decrease[53]. The Penang State Government created the Small and Medium Industry Centre in 1992 to broker contacts between MNCs and local companies as well as provide information on government initiatives. At its height, it had two full-time staff and 180 member companies in the metals, electric, and plastics sectors[54]. However, its resources and staffing decreased over time and it ceased operations in late 2004.

In 2004, the Penang State Government underwent a large-scale restructuring. A new organization, InvestPenang, was created, and became the peak agency charged with facilitating investment and fostering industrial development in the state. Down from its previous staff strength of 360 in 2004, the PDC now has a staff complement of some 200 people and today focuses on land development, managing invest-

52 <http://www.penang.net.y/index.cfm> (accessed 29/04/2005).

53 Interviews with a senior state government official, Penang (24/02/2004), industry observer AD, Penang (25/02/2004), and a venture capitalist, Kuala Lumpur (10/05/2004).

54 JICA. "Study on Strengthening Supporting Industries Through Technology Transfer in Malaysia", Penang: Japanese International Cooperation Agency/Penang Development Corporation, 2001, 7.11.

ments, tourism, as well as entrepreneur development among the Bumiputera community[55].

InvestPenang is now Penang's premier agency for investment promotion. As the PDC used to be, it is an autonomous organization. It has some 20 people and deals with all investment to Penang, including in the education, health, manufacturing, and hospitality sectors. This involves acting as a resource centre, as well as liaising with investors and helping them with state and federal government agencies. InvestPenang also has links to firms through a series of consortia that were established with State Government seed funding.

These are the Radio Frequency Cluster, the Software Consortium of Penang (SCoPe), the Penang Automation Cluster (PAC), and Techbiz, a cluster for Bumiputera businessmen in the ICT sector. These clusters were created with the aim of generating contacts and synergy between firm owners, as well as serving as a collective means of marketing Penang talent to MNCs. Some of these consortia, such as SCoPe, are very active and organize a range of technical and promotion events[56]. The consortia have been good mechanisms for member firms to articulate their concerns and exchange industry information. However, interest from MNCs has been limited. And, success at creating collaborative relations has not met with much success due to the fact that most members are, in fact, competitors[57].

The Socio-economic and Environmental Research Institute was set up in 1997, upon the recommendation of the first PSDP. It has served as the state government's think-tank, contributing technical and policy information on a wide range of economic, social, and environmental topics, including the formulation of the Second Penang Strategic Development Plan and the K-ICT Blueprint. The Institute has been very active in the higher education sector, trying to monitor and improve the quality of private colleges. It tracks national and international economic developments, and seeks to foment policy-learning and transfer. As a

---

55   <http://www.pdc.gov.my/article.cfm?id=814> (accessed 21/05/2009), interview with a PDC representative, Penang (21/04/2009).

56   Interview with industry observers BB and BC, Penang (18/03/2009).

57   PSDC. "Technology Roadmap for the Electrical and Electronics Industry of Penang", p.49.

result, it has become a source of considerable institutional capacity that has helped bolster the state government's planning machinery.

The state government institution that is the most involved in the generation and diffusion of knowledge is the Penang Skills Development Corporation (PSDC). Established in 1989 by the Penang State Government with a mandate to provide technical training to high-school graduates, it was set up after extensive consultation with MNC managers. Twenty-six founder companies employing some 44,000 workers had input into the eventual structure of the Centre. As a result the PSDC is largely industry-driven and client companies pool their resources, including equipment, and provide training on industry-specific issues[58]. The Corporation thus acts to reduce collective action problems by providing a forum for identifying training needs for the manufacturing sector as a whole.

The PSDC has also contributed significantly to planning at the state level through spearheading the Technology Roadmap for the Electrical and Electronics Sector. It also made attempts to address the shortage of skilled workers through providing pathways for its graduates to pursue university degrees. It has established twinning arrangements with a variety of universities overseas, and offers Masters in areas such as Micro-electronics and Photonics[59]. The PSDC also provides training in very specialized areas with institutions such as the Semiconductor Manufacturing Institute in Singapore. In addition, it has worked to correct some of the deficiencies of the formal education system through its Graduate Re-skilling Program, which works to make unemployed graduates more industry-ready through a series of improvement programs.

The Corporation has proactively moved to cater to SMEs. The PSDC works closely with the federal agency for small firms, SMIDEC, which has appointed the Corporation as the approved training provider for the Northern Region. SMIDEC thus underwrites part of the costs of training programs that SME owners and employees attend, which benefited almost 900 people in 2008. The PSDC also has an SME Intervention Program, which is a series of 2-day workshops for SME

58   <http://www.psdc.com.my/> (accessed 18/04/2005 and 22/05/2009).

59   <http://www.psdc.com.my/page.cfm?name=Consultancy> (accessed 23/05/2009), and interview with a PSDC representative, Bayan Lepas (23/04/2009).

owners covering managerial, technical, marketing, and technical topics. In 2007, it established a business coaching program, which works with SMEs and larger, sponsor firms over a period of 12 months to help them improve their technical and managerial capabilities. The initial results from the four firms that have participated have been promising. In addition, there are indications that the PSDC could house testing equipment which could be made publicly available. If so, this would prove of immense utility to the local E&E industry[60].

To conclude thus far, the Penang State Government has a high level of bureaucratic capacity, and has shown remarkable innovative capacity at various moments in its history. During the 1970s, through astute managing of its ability to acquire and develop land, the State Government was able to spearhead its industrialization drive through aggressive investment, proactive liaising with investors, and 'self-discovery' attempts. During the 1990s, it was able to develop the skill-base of its workforce through providing industry-relevant training and fostering the development of the private education sector.

That said, the state has not had a consistent approach to working with its local SMEs. The State Government played a catalytic role in the 1970s and 1980s by mediating between MNCs and a local group of firms. However, this function was personality-based and not institutionalized. In part, this was due to the mind-set that once local entrepreneurship had taken root in the manufacturing sector it would grow by itself. Communication also tended to favour more established firms, who were thought to be representative of the entire SME community. This limited the amount of 'shop-floor' information feeding into policy-making.

Federal Government Institutions

This section will apply the same RIS framework to federal institutions located in Penang.

During the 1970s, the Federal Government had relatively little presence in Penang. However, after the mid-1980s, federal government institutions began to establish branches in the state. By 1991, there were 150 government agencies in Penang: of these 36 belonged

---

60   Interview with industry observer BD, Penang (22/03/2009).

to the state government and 114 to the federal government[61]. This institutional presence has been matched by resources. During 1985-99, federal government expenditure was 4.5 times the expenditure of all state governments put together[62].

Given the sheer amount of resources that the federal government controls as well as its more extensive array of constitutional responsibilities, it is the de facto development agency in any state. National planning processes in Malaysia are very well-developed and the machinery geared towards developing and monitoring the Malaysia Plans is prodigious. However, plans are articulated and organized along sectoral lines, rather than on a state-by-state basis.

In recent years, there has been some recognition of regional specificities through incorporating the concept of growth corridors in planning. In Penang's case, it is grouped with Perlis, Kedah, and the northern part of Perak into the Northern Economic Growth Corridor. While comprehensive, the Malaysia Plans do not dovetail with state-level initiatives such as Penang's Strategic Development Plans. There are quarterly meetings of federal agencies at the Penang branch of the Economic Planning Unit, the Unit's main emphasis is on physical infrastructure projects and preparations for submissions to the Malaysia Plans[63]. In addition, local branches of federal government agencies have little autonomy to depart from national policy thrusts, and com-

---

61 ISIS/PDC. *"Penang Strategic Development Plan"*, *Penang: Institute of Strategic and International Studies/Penang Development Corporation, 1991, p. 17-1.*

62 Kwame Sundaram Jomo and Chong Hui Wee. *"The Political Economy of Malaysian Federalism: Economic Development, Public Policy and Conflict Containment"*, *Journal of International Development, 15, (2003), p. 445.*

63 SERI. *"The Second Penang Strategic Development Plan 2001-2010 (Technical Report)"*, *(Penang: Socioeconomic and Environmental Research Institute, 2001), p. 25.15.*

munication between federal agencies in Penang takes place in Kuala Lumpur rather than at a state level[64].

From a state-level perspective, 'prestige' projects such as Kuala Lumpur International Airport, the Petronas Towers, and the Multi-Media Super-Corridor seemed to be concentrated in the capital region. Conversely, long-standing requests to upgrade the airport or extend Multimedia Super Corridor (MSC) status to industrial parks in Penang were not heeded. It was only in 2005 that MSC status was granted to Penang, nearly a decade after its roll-out in Cyberjaya.

While industry-relevant agencies such as the Ministry of Trade and Industry (MITI), the Malaysian Industrial Development Authority (MIDA), and the Malaysia Productivity Corporation (MPC) were founded in the 1960s, their Penang-based offices were not set up until after 1990. By this time, the electronics sector had been in existence for nearly 25 years, and for smaller Penang-based firms, what little contact there had been with the government was through the state government.

In 2002, the Small and Medium Industry Development Corporation (SMIDEC) established an office in Penang, providing the first local, centralized contact point for SMEs to access a wide range of federal initiatives. SMIDEC's remit includes: providing technical and advisory services to SMEs; forging industrial linkages between SMEs and large corporations; and managing and coordinating financial assistance initiatives for SMEs.

This was much needed, as prior to this, SME initiatives had been widely dispersed across a range of agencies and focused largely on Kuala Lumpur[65], and firms wanting assistance or contact with federal initiatives had to travel to the capital. SMIDEC certainly has played a

---

64 *The officials that I interviewed had implementation, but not-decision-making, responsibilities as projects and applications were approved at headquarters in Kuala Lumpur. Rather, their roles were predominantly to facilitate and provide information to potential clients at the local level. The officials confirmed that they did not discuss policy issues directly with their colleagues from other federal institutions in the state. Rather, they channelled information back to their headquarters, which would then be discussed in meetings between agencies in Kuala Lumpur. Interviews with officials from MIDA, MIDF, SMIDEC, SIRIM, and the Human Resource Development Council (Penang, February-April 2004).*

65 *Interview with an SME expert, USM, Penang (20/02/2004).*

role in building capabilities among SMEs, particularly through underwriting many training initiatives. It also has a range of grants and loans for market feasibility and technology feasibility studies, product and process improvements, and factory relocation. However, at a sectoral level, it may not be fully linked into Penang's priorities as, at least up until recently, its focus was largely handicrafts and food processing, rather than electronics-based activities[66].

The many federal agencies present in Penang have become part of the regional innovation system. MIDA plays a central role in liaising with investors, the state government, and the top levels of the federal government. Other relevant agencies include: the Human Resource Development Council, which handles tax rebates to firms for investing in worker training; Malaysian Industrial Development Finance, which provides loans to SMES in the manufacturing sector; the Standards and Industrial Research Institute of Malaysia (SIRIM) which provides services such as contract R&D for the industrial sector as well as help with ISO certification, training on quality management, and an array of measurement and calibration services; and the Malaysian Institute of Microelectronic Systems (MIMOS), which has a branch in nearby Kulim High-Tech Park that provides research facilities for the ICT and microelectronics sector and possesses facilities to pilot test new circuit designs. In addition, the federal government has moved decisively in the area of technical training, setting up a polytechnic and a joint Japanese-Malaysian Technical Institute in Penang.

While these agencies provide facilities, access to capital, and training facilities for workers, the work of many of them appears to be hampered by a relationship of distrust. SME programs in Malaysia have a history of being geared exclusively to Bumiputera entrepreneurs. While this is changing with the introduction of a wide range schemes open to all ethnic groups, this perception has meant that many non-Bumiputera-owned companies are hesitant to use government-provid-

Shallow Pockets but Close to the Action

---

66 *Interview with a SMIDEC official, Bukit Minyak (05/03/2004).*

ed support services[67]. Officials from MIDA, HDRC, and SMIDEC all confirmed difficulties in approaching and working with SMEs[68]. This may also be complicated by communication problems between Chinese firm owners and Malay government officials[69]. One indication of this communication gap is a well-developed consulting 'industry' that offers to liaise between SMEs and grant and loan-disbursing industries in return for a portion of the grant/loan amount[70].

Furthermore, many of these agencies are involved in the creation and promotion of 'high-tech' industries, which may not target the activities of many Penang-based firms. A study team, sponsored by the Japanese International Cooperation Agency (JICA), conducted an in-depth analysis of the electronics sector, including interviews and site-visits with some 100 local SMEs. The most serious issue that the study found was the need for institutional support to help companies upgrade. Its review of SME support programs found that: local entrepreneurs did not adequately understand the aims of various initiatives; there was an overlap between federal and state government programs; and initiatives were too oriented to high-technology ventures such as IT and biotechnology and not enough to dealing with technical production issues[71].

The federally-funded Universiti Sains Malaysia (USM) is the centre-piece of knowledge creation in Penang. Given that the E&E sector is the most important for Penang's manufacturing sector, it is

---

67   JICA. "Study on Strengthening Supporting Industries Through Technology Transfer in Malaysia", p.3-32; Leo van Grunsven, "Development of Local SMEs Through Supply Linkages with MNC Transplants", in Small and Medium Enterprises in Asia-Pacific Countries, vol I, edited by M.A. Abdullah and M.I.B. Bakar. (Huntington N.Y.: Nova Science Publishers, 2000), p. 63; Abdullah, Moha A., "Myths and Realities of SMEs in Malaysia", in Small and Medium Enterprises in Asia-Pacific Countries, vol I, edited by M.A. Abdullah and M.I.B. Bakar (Huntington N.Y.: Nova Science Publishers, 2000), p. 66.

68   The HDRC official I interviewed stated that their biggest challenge was getting SMEs in Penang to cooperate. The SMIDEC official lamented 'there are so many seminars and workshops that we organize, but still they don't come'.

69   Interview with industry observer AD, Penang (25/02/2004).

70   Interview with a state government employee, Bayan Lepas (23/04/2009).

71   JICA. "Study on Strengthening Supporting Industries Through Technology Transfer in Malaysia", p.S-2.

interesting to note that USM has traditionally specialized in research for the pharmaceutical industry[72]. In addition, its engineering school was relocated from Penang to Perak in 1986. This geographical separation impeded early attempts to create university-industry linkages, such as those attempted by the Innovation and Consultancy Centre. In 2001, the engineering faculty was moved back to Penang, but to Nibong Tebal, which is on the outer edges of the state and difficult to access from the island[73]. While contact between the electronics sector and the university has been helped by the creation of the University's corporate arm, UniSAINS, it appears that R&D collaboration between research institutions, MNCs, and local companies is quite limited[74]. Until recently, the existing links between the faculty of engineering and the electronics industry were geared towards MNCs, as opposed to local firms[75].

What does the snapshot tell us?

With regard to the regional production structure, while the manufacturing sector is well-established and has deep capabilities in particular areas, it faces various structural issues. Innovative work, particularly in research and development, as well as design and development tends to be the preserve of MNCs. Some local firms have, through established relationships with MNCs, acquired deep technological capabilities. However, the majority of SMEs are small firms lower down on the value-add chain that operate in relative isolation from other parts of the RIS. The dispersed nature of firm capabilities as well as the structure of industry - which is characterized by a high degree of competition for locally-present demand - makes the creation of collaborative networks difficult.

---

72 *Interview with an education expert, USM, Penang (17/02/2004).*

73 *Personal observation – my trip to the faculty in 2004 took 90 minutes from downtown Georgetown.*

74 *PSDC. "Technology Roadmap for the Electrical and Electronics Industry of Penang", p. 50.*

75 *Interview with a faculty member of the School of Electrical and Electronic Engineering, Nibong Tebal (30/03/2004).*

Business associations have emerged to provide an answer to some of these issues. However, it is the larger, more established firms that have organizations to voice their collective concerns. They benefit the sector as a whole by bringing sectoral issues to light, but are less able to feed information to policy-makers on operational matters that affect smaller firms as well as those in fledgling industries.

This is communication gap is exacerbated by the dearth of publicly accessible facilities for firms to improve their capabilities on their own. Knowledge gaps in areas such as technical and marketing issues further hamper the ability to access grants, loans, and other forms of finance.

The regional supportive infrastructure is comprised of significant number of institutions with quite a comprehensive array of supporting services.

Despite legal and financial constraints on its operation, the state government has played an enormously influential role in fostering economic growth. It was very resourceful in raising and deploying funds to kick-start its industrialization drive. The state government invested in different activities to diversify the state's economic base and had very well-developed marketing and liaison competencies for dealing with international investors. It also has well-developed planning capabilities and has articulated a number of significant 'visions' for the state as a whole.

Over time, the state government also created a core of institutions, many of whom have become fundamental parts of the state's RIS. In particular, the Penang Skills Development Corporation provides a wide array of training services. And, the state government has been particularly aggressive in fostering investment in supporting sectors for the manufacturing sector as well as private education.

However, the state government has not had a consistent approach to small and medium enterprises. Intermediation efforts carried out by the government between MNCs and a group of local manufacturers in the 1970s and 1980s were key to creating the first linkages. However, this approach was not institutionalized. In addition, after 1990, communication with local firms tended to be through fora whose membership was comprised of larger, more established firms.

The federal government has also made a major contribution to Penang's RIS. Over time, the state has come to host a formidable array of institutions with a wide range of supporting services. That said, there is evidence of a mis-match between supply and demand. This could be due to the national, as opposed to state-level, focus of planning procedures. Thus, many initiatives prioritize 'high-tech' or, indeed, more artisanal activities than those in Penang's manufacturing sector. In addition, outreach and communication activities are hampered by issues of communication and trust. Interactions with the local university, which possesses formidable research capabilities in engineering, have been curtailed by the latter's physical isolation.

Figure 7: Penang's Regional Innovation System

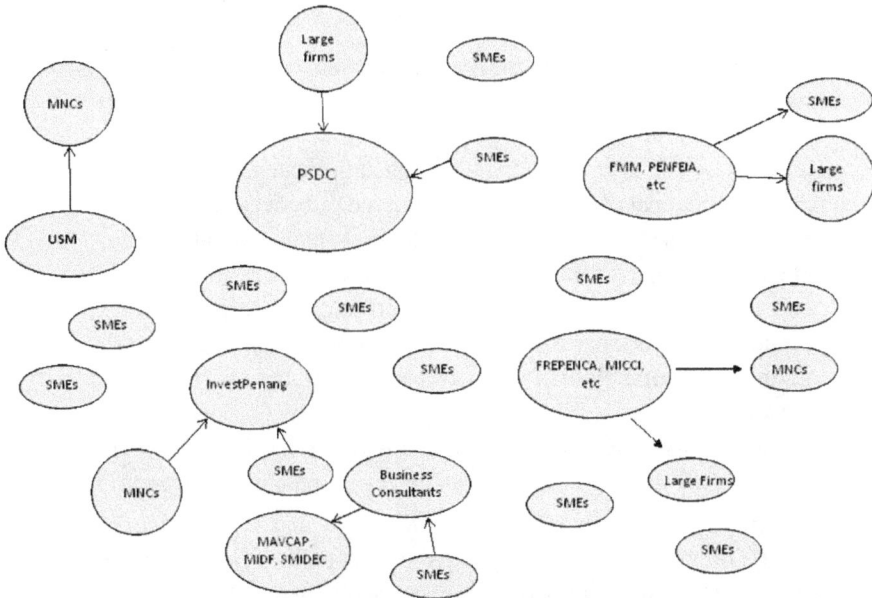

Figure 7 depicts a stylized vision of Penang's regional innovation system. While the system has quite a comprehensive array of supporting services, the circulation of knowledge among firms, among supporting institutions, and between the regional production system and the regional supporting infrastructure is impeded. This, in turn, limits the innovative potential of Penang's manufacturing sector.

Strengthening Penang's Regional Innovation System: Some Ideas

The previous paragraphs have used the RIS framework to analyse Penang's regional innovation system. This section will put forward some ideas for steering the state's firms and supporting institutions in this direction. It must be borne in mind that the creation and strengthening of social capital is a long-term and continuing process.

The Penang State Government has demonstrated formidable planning processes, which it has used to develop a comprehensive range of strategies and blueprints. These capabilities can be used to generate a vision of Penang as a regional economy, with local entrepreneurship at its centre, as opposed to as a complement to investment from outside the state.

Following the tradition of the Penang Strategic Development Plans, the state government should place itself at the centre of development efforts, in recognition of its closer proximity to local actors and institutions as well as the need for planning at the state level. This need not imply functional over-lap with existing federal government institutions. Rather, based on a long-term development plan, the state government can map Penang's current and future needs. In recognition of the federal government's greater resources and range of responsibilities, it can utilize existing machinery where appropriate, concentrating instead on information dissemination and mediation. In other cases, and where feasible, it can provide these services directly. The key aspect is for the state government to strengthen its RIS through facilitating and encouraging the flow of information between all parts of the system.

Outreach and communication with SMEs and backyard firms should be improved. To date, participation has tended to privilege the 'captains' of industry, as opposed to the 'foot-soldiers'. This deprives policy-makers of detailed, up-to-date information on problems and issues faced by the bulk of firms. Available research shows that firm capabilities and needs change over time, requiring constant communication for policy-makers to adapt policies and measures appropriately.

Much of the resulting ideas from this planning process could be carried out by an 'intelligent cell' housed within an existing state government institution or as a stand-alone institution. The idea is not for it to duplicate services already offered by national level institutions, but rather to implement the regional development strategy, reduce information asymmetries, leverage existing facilities where possible, and offer services directly where needed. Figure 8 depicts what the RIS could look like.

Figure 8: Penang's Regional Innovation System Tomorrow?

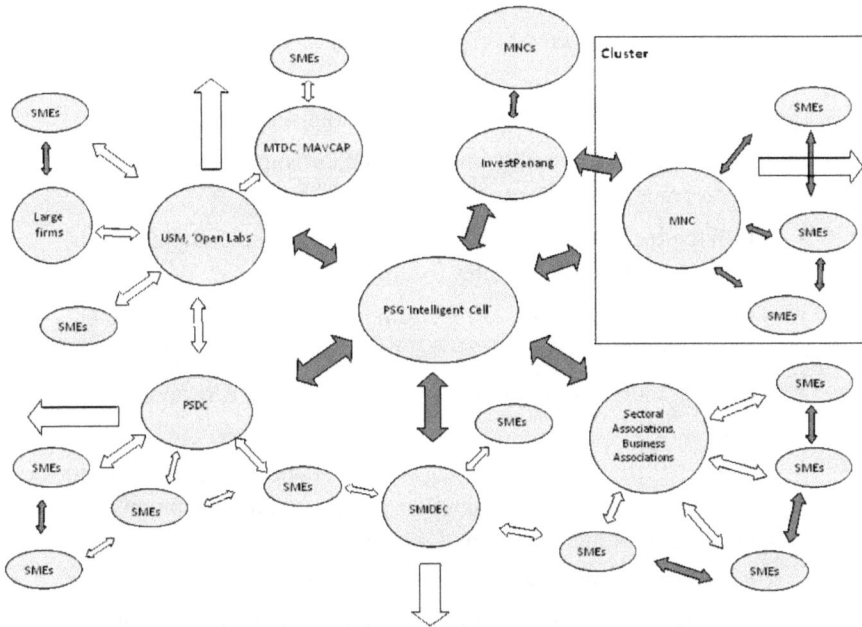

Based on available information, an indicative list of services the 'cell' could offer - or refer firms to as appropriate - is:

- Carry out a survey to find (and reach out to) 'backyard' firms to establish how many there are, where they are located, and what needs they have
- Provide access to legal advisers to help firms obtain permits and approvals where necessary, perhaps accompanied by grants to help firms relocate

- Centralize information on all permits and approvals for manufacturing firms in hard copy and on the website (in English, Malay, and Chinese to ensure maximum dissemination)

- Track applications for grants and loans made by local firms to gather data on success rates as well as the most common problems encountered

- Provide publicly-accessible key reference works covering the various sub-sectors of manufacturing activities in Penang, as well as those targeted for future growth

- Provide subscriptions to market intelligence services and key technical journals in current and potential sectors

- Provide access to multi-lingual technical support to help firms write grant applications

- Provide technical support on marketing issues, including establishing and hosting websites for firms

- Provide open labs with test instrumentation on a pay-per-use basis to allow entrepreneurs to test the viability of their prototypes

- Broker collective sourcing of inputs to achieve economies of scale

- House a 'travelling guidance unit' available to local firms to monitor and evaluate production processes on their premises – thus encouraging incremental innovations

- Establish a small portfolio for 'self-discovery' activities – seed funding for carrying out activities that could diversify the state's economy. These grants are once-off, and only for projects in activities that are new to the state

- Broker internships and research projects between universities and local SMEs to: improve graduates' industry readiness; lessen the social stigma facing SMEs; and create linkages between firms

- Co-locate educational facilities within industrial parks to improve interaction with industry

- Facilitate the emergence of 'local communities' in industrial parks through providing spaces, more conducive architecture, and activities for socialization and interaction

In-depth planning carried out in consultation with SMEs and backyard firms may well yield a demand for services that are different from those listed above. However, the planning process itself will yield an intangible yet no less important result – a consultative process will be initiated where a desired end-state is articulated and future initiatives are measured against this vision in an open and participatory manner.

Conclusions

This article has looked at industrial policy at the sub-national level with reference to the case of Penang. In order to do so, it has looked at the link between economic activity, innovation, and location, and argued that there is a relationship between economic activity and the local institutional environment.

From there, the article put forward a framework for analysing how information is created, diffused, and absorbed, and how this affects the potential for innovative activity. This framework, the Regional Innovation System, stresses the importance of communication within and between the regional production structure, comprised of firms, and the regional supportive infrastructure, comprised of institutions that create and diffuse knowledge. This section also examined the rationale for sub-national governments to take a central role in articulating development strategies for their territories and what advantages decentralized policy-making offers above exclusively centralized policy-making.

Using this framework, the article then examined Penang's Regional Innovation System. Regarding the regional production structure, it argued that there are communication gaps between firms, which are due to the local structure of demand in the electronics industry, as well as cultural issues. These are compounded by a lack of publicly-accessible facilities for firms to augment their capabilities. Regarding the regional supportive infrastructure, the article argued that while there is an extensive array of supporting institutions, there are also significant bottlenecks in the flow of information. Communication between firms and the surrounding institutional infrastructure has tended to work better for larger, more established companies. Smaller firms have not benefited from a consistent policy approach and have also been reluctant to engage with federal government agencies.

The last section of this article put forward some ideas for strengthening Penang's regional innovation system. Given the state government's proximity to the range of institutions in Penang, it should take the lead in articulating a strategy for strengthening its RIS in consultation with a full range of stakeholders. The key aspect of any attempt to strengthen the RIS should be to focus on fostering flows of information between the existing institutions in the state. Only when the parts of the system work together and diffuse information effectively will additional resources be of maximum benefit.

Notes:
I would like to thank Y.B. Liew Chin-Tong, Dato' Leong Yueh Kwong., Lim Wei Seong, and Fatimah Hassan for their kind hospitality and assistance during my time in Penang. Fieldwork in April 2009 was made possible through support from SERI. Dr. Lorraine Salazar provided valuable feedback. Responsibility for the content of this article is mine alone.

Bibliography

Abelson, Peter, *Public Economics: Principles and Practice*. Canberra: Applied Economics, 2003.

Abdullah, Moha A., "Myths and Realities of SMEs in Malaysia", in *Small and Medium Enterprises in Asia-Pacific Countries*, vol. I, edited by M.A. Abdullah and M.I.B. Bakar. Huntington N.Y.: Nova Science Publishers, 2000.

Andersson, Martin and Charlie Karlsson, "Regional Innovation Systems in Small & Medium-Sized Regions: A Critical Review and Assessment", CESIS Working Paper Series, no. 10, Stockholm: Centre of Excellence for Science and Innovation Studies, 2004.

Anuar, Abdul R. "Fiscal Decentralization in Malaysia", *Hitotsubashi Journal of Economics*, no. 2, (2000): 85-95.

Azfar, Omar, S. Kahkonen, A. Lanyi, and P. Meagher, "Decentralization, Governance, and Public Services: The Impact of Institutional Arrangements", University of Maryland Center for Institutional Reform and the Informal Sector, Working Paper no. 255, 1999.

Bresnahan, Timothy, Anthony Gambardella, and Annalee Saxenian. "'Old Economy' Inputs for 'New Economy' Outcomes: Cluster Formation in the New Silicon Valleys". *Industrial and Corporate Change*, vol. 10, no. 4 (2001): 835-859.

Chang, Yii Tan, "Penang Island Structure Plan: Technical Report", Penang: Majlis Perbandaran Pulau Pinang, 1984.

Choi, Ji-Sun. "Potential and Limitation of New Industrial Policy in Korea: Fostering Innovative Clusters", in *New Economic Spaces: New Economic Geographies*, edited by Richard Le Heron and James W. Harrington. London: Ashgate, 2005.

Cooke, Philip. "Regional Innovation Systems, Clusters, and the Knowledge Economy". *Industrial and Corporate Change*, vol. 10, no. 4, (2001): 945-973.

Cooke, Philip. "Strategies for Regional Innovation Systems: Learning Transfer and Applications". Cardiff: Centre for Advanced Studies, Cardiff University, 2001.

Crouch., Colin, Patrick Le Gales, Carlo Trigilia, and Helmut Voelzkow. *Local Production Systems in Europe*. Oxford: Oxford University Press, 2001.

Dicken, Peter. *Global Shift: Transforming the World Economy*, 4th Edition. London: Sage Publications, 2003.

European Commission. "Constructing Regional Advantage: Principles, Perspectives, Policies". Brussels: Directorate-General for Research, European Commission, 2006.

Giuliani, Elisa and Martin Bell. "Industrial Clusters and the Evolution of their Knowledge Networks: Revisiting a Chilean Case". SPRU Electronic Working Paper Series no. 171. Brighton: Science Policy Research Unit, University of Sussex, 2008.

Gray, H. Peter and John H. Dunning. "Towards a Theory of Regional Policy", in *Regions, Globalization, and the Knowledge-Based Economy*, edited by John H. Dunning. Oxford: Oxford University Press, 2002.

Hutchinson, Francis E. "Developmental States and Economic Growth at the Sub-National Level: The Case of Penang" in *Southeast Asian Affairs 2008*, edited by D. Singh and M.M.T. Tin. Singapore: Institute of Southeast Asian Studies, 2008.

Hutchinson, Francis E. "Can Sub-national States be Developmental: The Cases of Penang and Karnataka", PhD dissertation, Policy and Governance Program, Australian National University, Canberra, 2006.

IMD. *World Competitiveness Yearbook 2008*. Lausanne: International Institute for Management Development, 2008.

InvestPenang. "2007 Penang Industrial Survey Report". Penang: InvestPenang, 2008.

JICA. "Study on Strengthening Supporting Industries Through Technology Transfer in Malaysia", Penang: Japanese International Cooperation Agency/Penang Development Corporation, 2001.

ISIS/PDC. "Penang Strategic Development Plan". Penang: Institute of Strategic and International Studies/Penang Development Corporation, 1991.

Jomo, Kwame Sundaram and Chong Hui Wee. "The Political Economy of Malaysian Federalism: Economic Development, Public Policy and Conflict Containment". *Journal of International Development,* 15, (2003): 441-56.

Lagendijk, A. "Learning in Non-core Regions: Towards 'Intelligent Clusters'; Addressing Business and Regional Needs". In Knowledge, Innovation, and Economic Growth: the Theory and Practice of Learning Regions, edited by Frans Boekma, Kevin Morgan, Silvia Bakkers, Roel Rutten. Cheltenham: Edward Elgar, 2000.

Landabaso, M., Christine Oughton, and Kevin Morgan, 'Learning Regions in Europe: Theory, Policy, and Practice through the RIS Experience'. In *Systems and Policy for the Global Learning Economy,* edited by David V. Gibson, Chandler Stolp, Pedro Conceicao, and Manuel V. Heitor. London: Praeger, 2003.

Leamer, Edward and Michael Storper. "The Economic Geography of the Internet Age". NBER Working Paper 8450. Cambridge, MA: National Bureau of Economic Research, 2001.

Markusen, Ann R. "Sticky Places in Slippery Space: A Typology of Industrial Districts". *Economic Geography,* 72 no. 3, (1996): 293-313.

OECD. *New Forms of Governance for Economic Development.* Paris: Organization for Economic Cooperation and Development, 2004.

Oughton, C., Mikel Landabaso, and Kevin Morgan. "The Regional Innovation Paradox: Innovation Policy and Industrial Policy". *Journal of Technology Transfer,* 27 (2002):97-110.

Porter, Michael E. *The Competitive Advantage of Nations.* New York: The Free Press, 1990.

PDC. *1977 Annual Report*. Penang: Penang Development Corporation, 1977.

PDC. *1980 Annual Report*. Penang: Penang Development Corporation, 1980.

PSDC. "Technology Roadmap for the Electrical and Electronics Industry of Penang". Penang: Penang Skills Development Corporation, 2007.

Rodriguez- Pose, Andres, and Nicholas Gill. "On the 'Economic Dividend' of Devolution", *Regional Studies*, 39 no. 4 (2005): 405-20.

Rudolph, Lloyd and Susan Hoeber Rudolph. "The Iconization of Chandrababu: Sharing Sovereignty in India's Federal Market Economy", *Economic and Political Weekly*. May 5, (2001): 1546-60.

Saxenian, Annalee. *Regional Advantage: Culture and Competition in Silicon Valley and Route 128,* Cambridge: Harvard University Press, 1994.

Saxenian, Annalee. "Regional Systems of Innovation and the Blurred Firm". In *Local and Regional Systems of Innovation* edited by John De La Mothe and Gilles Paquet. Boston: Kluwer Academic Publishers, 1998.

Schmitz, Hubert. "Small Shoemakers and Fordist Giants: Tales of a Supercluster", *World Development*, vol. 23, no. 1, (1995): 9-28.

Scott, Allen J. *On Hollywood: the Place, the Industry*. Princeton, N.J.: Princeton University Press, 2005.

SERI. "A Study on Penang's Private Institutions of Higher Learning". Penang: Socio-economic and Environmental Research Institute, 2002.

SERI. "The Second Penang Strategic Development Plan 2001-2010 (Technical Report)". Penang: Socioeconomic and Environmental Research Institute, 2001.

Shapiro, Helen and Lance Taylor. "The State and Industrial Strategy", *World Development,* 18 no. 6, (1990): 861-78.

Singh, Chet. "Learning from the Malaysian Experience: A Case Study of the Penang Development Corporation (PDC)" in *Public Enterprise Management: Strategies for Success*. London: Commonwealth Secretariat, 1991.

Tham, S.Y. and Rugayah, H.M.Z. "Moving towards High-Tech Industrialisation: The Case of Malaysia". In *The East Asian High-Tech Drive*, edited by Y.-P. Chu and H. Hill. Cheltenham: Edward Elgar, 2006.

UNIDO. *Industrial Development Report 2009: Breaking In and Moving Up: New Industrial Challenges for the Bottom Billion and Middle-Income Countries*. Vienna: UNIDO, 2009.

Van Grunsven, Leo. "Development of Local SMEs Through Supply Linkages with MNC Transplants". In *Small and Medium Enterprises in Asia-Pacific Countries,* vol. I, edited by M.A. Abdullah and M.I.B. Bakar. Huntington N.Y.: Nova Science Publishers, 2000.

Von der Mehden, F.R. "Industrial Policy in Malaysa: A Penang Micro-study", Program for Development Studies Monograph, Rice University, Houston, 1973.

Wee, Chong Hui. "Fiscal federalism", in *Malaysia's Economic Development: Policy and Reform*, edited by Kwame Sundaram Jomo and S.K. Ng. Kuala Lumpur: Pelanduk Publications, 1996.

Williams, Gareth, Pierre Landell-Mills, and Alex Duncan. "Uneven Growth within Low-income Countries: Does it Matter and Can Governments Do Anything Effective?". Oxford: The Policy Practice Limited, 2005.

World Bank. *World Development Report 2009: Reshaping Economic Geography*. Washington D.C.: World Bank, 2009.

[4]

Implementing Pro-Employment Policies at the Sub-national Level

Liew Chin Tong & Francis E. Hutchinson

Introduction

In the 21st century, the test of a government is its ability to ensure the social and economic well-being of its citizens. The creation and provision of employment is a central part of this challenge as - through its economic, social, and psychological impact - it affects the welfare of individuals, families, and communities.

At a national level, mass unemployment or underemployment can lead to a decline in consumer spending, which, in turn, affects business confidence and economic resilience. In addition, high unemployment can have serious implications for poverty and inequality. At an individual level, joblessness is keenly felt by those directly affected and their families.

While indicators such as low inflation and high growth-rates are often seen as the goal of economic policy, the link between economic growth and employment is not as direct nor as strong as commonly perceived. An economy's structure, its labour markets, and policy frameworks also have important implications for the level and quality of employment. This implies a role for government that goes beyond simply striving to keep inflation down and exports up. A pro-active role in seeking to foster job creation encompasses policies such as training, labour market legislation, unemployment insurance and, in some cases, directly employing people.

At the national level in Malaysia, the issue of job creation has not been addressed adequately. The lack of importance attached to generating decent, fairly-remunerated jobs for our citizens can be seen in

various areas of state policy, such as: economic stimulus packages that prioritize growth as opposed to employment; an immigration policy which, through allowing large-scale importation of cheap foreign labour, discourages investments to foster innovation and increase productivity; and the lack of a coordinated approach to encourage greater female participation in the workforce.

While aspects of economic policy such as interest rates, migration, and education policy are federal government responsibilities, this does not preclude state governments from playing a role in shaping their local labour markets. Given their importance as consumers of goods and services, state governments can have an indirect effect on labour markets through decisions on issues such as procurement, employment policies in government departments, and expenditure levels. In addition, they can have a direct impact on labour markets through policies to reduce information asymmetries, provide skills training, and establish public work programs. At the international level, one area that has seen a considerable amount of policy innovation and learning is public work programs. Run by both national and sub-national governments in a range of countries, they play an important role in providing a safety net for otherwise vulnerable populations.

This article will look at labour market policy options open to state governments in Malaysia, with specific reference to Penang. To this end, it will be comprised of five sections. The first will look at job creation and state policy. The second will look at public work - or workfare - programs, with reference to international best practice. The third section will look at labour market issues in Malaysia. The fourth will put forward a range of policy options relevant to Penang. The fifth and final section provides some conclusions.

Job Creation: A Government Responsibility?

Following the Second World War, it was common practice for governments in the United States and Europe to engage in counter-cyclical spending to smooth peaks and troughs in economic trends and keep unemployment low. During the post-war economic boom, social welfare systems expanded quickly and came to encompass services such as pensions, unemployment, and disability. While many of these services were not affordable for developing countries, a belief in a role for the state in managing the economy led to a range of state-led development strategies.[1]

During the economic turmoil of the 1970s, the viability of this 'Keynesian' model was questioned. In the decades that followed, state controls were wound back with the aim of reducing waste, increasing efficiency, and freeing individual creativity. One of the casualties of this trend was a commitment to full employment. Rather, attention turned to maintaining a good environment for investment and economic growth, usually consisting of keeping inflation down and interest rates high, with ensuing negative implications for employment.[2]

Following the 2008 financial crisis, the tide seems to have turned. Instead of merely providing an enabling environment for business, states are now increasingly being called upon to strengthen regulations, boost aggregate demand when needed, and foster job creation. This sea change can be witnessed in US President Barack Obama's 2009 stimulus package, which was influenced by the work of James Tobin, a notable proponent of active state involvement to smooth demand levels and encourage full employment.[3]

While the explicit recognition of the importance of job creation in advanced capitalist countries is welcome, it is even more pressing in countries that are characterised by lower income levels, greater vulnerability to economic downturns, and little in the way of social insurance or other forms of safety net.

Fostering economic growth is one way of encouraging the creation of jobs. However, in many countries, high growth rates coincide with high unemployment levels, as the jobs and wealth created may be the preserve of specific groups rather than the economy as a whole. In addition, many of the economic changes wrought by globalization entail the demise of some sectors and the birth and growth of others, with ensuing implications for the labour market. This calls for some

1   Ha-Joon Chang, *Globalization, Economic Development and the Role of the State* (Penang: Third World Network, 2003), p. 47.

2   Gerald Epstein, "Central Banks as Agents of Employment Creation" *Towards Full and Decent Employment*, edited by Jose Antonio Ocampo and K.S. Jomo (Penang: Third World Network, 2007), p. 99.

3   Oliver Staley and Michael McKee, "Yale's Tobin Guides Obama From Grave as Friedman Is Eclipsed", *Bloomberg*. February 27, 2000.

form of social protection to help workers cope with higher levels of instability.

According to McCord, governments seeking to foster job creation tend to adopt one of three approaches[4]. The first focuses on the formal sector and relies on economic growth to generate jobs. While this does not require any specific policy measures, it has several disadvantages: it relies on constant growth at a rate sufficient to absorb available labour; it does not address structural issues that impede certain groups from entering the labour market; and it does not afford protection in cyclical downturns.

The second method is to seek to expand the informal sector. This approach holds promise for industrialising countries, many of which have large and dynamic informal sectors. This can be done through the provision of: training for SME owners and workers; help to obtain relevant permits and approvals; and micro-credit. While this approach is promising, it also suffers from two shortcomings: it is likely to only be effective for the more established and dynamic SMEs; and it is unlikely to generate enough jobs to significantly reduce the number of unemployed.

The third is the establishment of public works programs, which involves the provision of income support, usually in the form of cash or food, by the government in return for work. These programs can be permanent, seeking to provide a safety net guaranteeing work for the poor, or they can be temporary, put in place to help economically vulnerable people cope with crises. These programs have the virtue of directly creating jobs. That said, in order to be effective, initiatives of this sort require considerable care regarding targeting and design.

In addition to the approaches outlined above, which seek to increase the total number of jobs, governments can also improve aggregate citizen welfare by helping workers who are excluded from the labour market to access opportunities. While markets are presumed to operate in a vacuum, in reality they are governed by institutions, which are 'rules of the game' that constrain and incentivise action. Thus, a market is an array of institutions that regulates and decides what goods

---

4   Anna McCord, *"Public Works as a Response to Labour Market Failure in South Africa", Centre for Social Science Research Working Paper No. 19 (Cape Town: University of Cape Town, 2002), p. 23-24.*

and services can be traded, who can participate, how transactions should be carried out, and to what extent prices can vary.[5]

Due to their composition as a group of institutions, markets are not entirely 'free' and are easier to enter for some groups as opposed to others. As a result, certain groups suffer disproportionately and are more vulnerable than others. Younger workers, possessing less experience, often find it hard to join labour-markets. Many spend years looking for their first job or are on temporary contracts. In addition, in times of crisis, younger workers are usually the first to be laid off. Similarly, female workers often work in occupations that are not legally recognised or remunerated. They are more likely to assume the burden of care for children, family members, and the aged; and are also more likely to enter and exit the labour market frequently – to the detriment of their careers and earning capacity. Older workers are also vulnerable as once they are laid off, they are less likely to find another job. These categories of workers are, in turn, likely to form the ranks of 'discouraged' workers - those who have stopped looking for employment out of frustration.[6]

Therefore, in addition to seeking to create more jobs, governments can also implement a range of policies to help marginalized groups access a wider variety of opportunities in the labour market. This involves drafting new legislation to eliminate discrimination, extending existing legislation to cater to firms and workers operating in the informal sector, as well as providing skills training, guidance counselling, and facilities for job-seekers. A key aspect is legislation for women on issues such as maternity leave, access to day-care, and equal opportunities.

Having looked at job creation and the role of public policy, the next section will proceed to look at the logic behind work creation programs that are currently being implemented.

---

5   Ha-Joon Chang, "The Role of Institutions in Asian Development", Asian Development Review, 16(2) (1998), p. 67.

6   Diane Elson, "Macroeconomic Policy, Employment, Unemployment, and Gender Equality", Towards Full and Decent Employment, edited by Jose Antonio Ocampo and K.S. Jomo (Penang: Third World Network, 2007), p. 74-75.

Work Creation Initiatives: A Review of International Experiences

Publicly-funded work creation, or workfare, programs provide income in the form of money or food in exchange for participants' labour on specific initiatives. Usually encompassing public goods such as roads, bridges, and other types of infrastructure, workfare programs have been in existence for many years. Variants were used in the United States in the wake of the Great Depression, in Europe after the Second World War, and in South Korea after the 1997 Financial Crisis. Since the 1970s, public employment programs have gained in popularity and are now used in a range of countries in South Asia, Sub-Saharan Africa, and Latin America.[7]

Workfare programs usually involve remuneration in cash or in kind for work in one or more of the following areas.[8]

a) Infrastructure – construction, maintenance, and repair of basic infrastructure such as roads, bridges and canals

b) Environmental and agricultural projects – planting, harvesting, and tending to crops for food purposes or forest cover to combat erosion and minimize disasters such as flash-floods or land-slides

c) Social services – food preparation, domestic help, and care-giving

In some cases, these tasks can be combined with training and/or job placement activities to enhance the employability of workers and help them access opportunities in the labour market. In lower-income countries, public works programs tend to focus on building infrastructure and environmental mitigation works. In middle income countries, such as Argentina and South Africa, such programs also include pay-

---

7   Kalanidhi Subbarao, "Systemic Shocks and Social Protection: Role and Effectiveness of Public Works Programs", Social Protection Discussion Paper Series No. 0302 (Washington D.C.: World Bank, 2003), p.1-2.

8   Carlo del Ninno, Kalanidhi Subbarao, and Annamaria Milazzo, "How to Make Public Works Work: A Review of the Experiences", SPD Discussion Paper No. 0905 (Washington D.C.: World Bank, 2009), p. 8.

ment for social services such as care-giving and early childhood development.[9]

Workfare programs can have one or more aims. The first is to provide a safety net for the poor in the absence of unemployment insurance programs. One example of this is the Indian state of Maharashtra's Employment Guarantee Scheme (EGS), which has been running since the 1970s. Focusing largely on basic infrastructure, the EGS provides guaranteed work to adults in rural areas at a stipulated daily rate. While wages are low to limit the participation to the most needy, the Scheme provides a much-needed guaranteed minimum level of income to rural families and has contributed to reducing rural poverty in the state.[10]

Workfare programs can also be established for a specified period time to attain particular objectives before being dissolved. In these cases, they are usually used to help populations cope with external shocks such as natural catastrophes or massive economic contractions. They can also be used in the after-math of civil wars as a way of generating income and livelihoods. Once the crisis period has passed, these programs can then be phased out. The Food for Work program in Bangladesh has been in operation since the mid-1970s. It operates only during the country's dry season, and provides workers with employment opportunities on a range of public works projects such as constructing river embankments, irrigation channels, and roads in rural areas. Evaluations of the program have found important benefits for communities in areas where the program is present, including higher income levels and higher levels of agricultural production.[11]

Public works programs can also have a range of other benefits. On the one hand, the facilities and services that participants build or offer can benefit the wider community. On the other, these programs generate a 'multiplier' effect by generating money within the community, they can also exert an upward wage pressure on lowly-paid jobs, and can contribute to increasing the employability of participants. These

9   Carlo del Ninno, Kalanidhi Subbarao, and Annamaria Milazzo, "How to Make Public Works Work: A Review of the Experiences", Ibid., p. 13.

10   Jenny Kimmis. "Public Works: An Effective Safety Net for the Poor". 3ie Enduring Questions Brief #1. International Initiative for Impact Evaluation: New Delhi, March 2009, p. 1.

11   Jenny Kimmis, "Public Works: An Effective Safety Net for the Poor", p. 2.

benefits are not usually included in traditional cost-benefit analyses and can lower the apparent advantages of such programs.[12]

What are Some of the Lessons Learned from the Implementation of These Projects?

Available international evidence shows that for public works programs to be successful, they must have clear objectives regarding their aim and desired target group. They must also be managed with the goal of producing public goods of acceptable quality. Funding needs to be predictable and regular, and a good monitoring program must be in place to troubleshoot and direct efforts.[13]

Discerning the ultimate goal of a public works program is not always easy. Devereux argues that public works programs can be placed in one of two categories according to their ultimate objective.[14] The first category consists of labour-intensive employment programs that seek to generate a substantial number of short-term jobs as a way of tackling poverty. The second category is comprised of employment programs that emphasise the creation of assets. In this case, the focus is on the quality of the jobs created and their outputs. The first type of public works programs are more suited to having a broad-based, but short-term impact on job creation and poverty. The second type is better suited for having a long-term poverty alleviation impact, but for fewer people. The ultimate aim of a given public works program will influence its design and ensuing impact.

Having reviewed the aims of workfare programs, signalled their key principles, and discussed relevant lessons learned from international experiences, the next section will look at labour market issues in Malaysia.

---

12 Subbarao, Kalanidhi, "Systemic Shocks and Social Protection: Role and Effectiveness of Public Works Programs", p. ii.

13 Carlo del Ninno, Kalanidhi Subbarao, and Annamaria Milazzo, "How to Make Public Works Work: A Review of the Experiences", p. 60.

14 Stephen Devereux, "From Workfare to Fair Work: The Contribution of Public Works and other Labour-Based Infrastructure Programmes to Poverty Alleviation", Issues in Employment and Poverty Discussion Paper No. 5 (Geneva: International Labour Organization, 2002), p. 7.

Labour Market Issues in Malaysia: Some Points of Departure

During the 1980s and 1990s, the unemployment rate in Malaysia remained in the 2-2.5% range. Given the country's solid economic growth during this period, little active policy-making was needed to foster job creation. However, in recent years, growth has slowed and the economy has undergone structural changes, away from labour-intensive manufacturing towards services. The impact of these changes has been exacerbated by the Financial Crisis. In 2009, the economy is expected to shrink and the unemployment rate is forecast to reach 4.5%.[15]

On the one hand, this raises the need for a more active approach to labour market policy to help workers cope. On the other, it also draws much-needed attention to the opportunity cost of existing policies that introduce distortions in the labour market. While affordable in a time of plenty, these policies have a deleterious economic and social effect in a time of need.

The first and most obvious distortion is Malaysia's dependence on low-skill foreign labour. Of the country's labour-force of 11.3 million workers, 2.2 million are documented foreign workers.[16] While there is no conclusive figure for undocumented foreign workers, available estimates range from 500,000 to 3 million. These workers are concentrated in labour-intensive industries such as manufacturing, construction, and domestic help. While foreign workers do perform important tasks for the country, an excessive reliance on cheap, unskilled labour has long-term implications for economic growth, as this will discourage employers from investing in training and equipment to boost productivity. According to the Ministry of Labour, at present some 45% of new jobs created in the country are taken by foreign workers,[17] signalling the economy's structural reliance on labour-intensive processes.

15 Najib Tun Abdul Razak, "Speech introducing the Supplementary Supply Bill 2009", Kuala Lumpur, Dewan Rakyat, March 10, 2009.

16 Bernama (Kuala Lumpur), One in Five Workers in Malaysia is a Foreigner, Oct 20, 2008.

17 Bernama (Kuala Lumpur), One in Five Workers in Malaysia is a Foreigner, Oct 20, 2008.

Federal and state government agencies also contribute to this situation through their procurement decisions. The practice of outsourcing construction, maintenance, and upgrading of public works has further aggravated the demand for low-skill and poorly-remunerated jobs. Rather than generating fairly-remunerated jobs for local workers, private sector contractors recruit foreign workers, whose rapid turnover precludes the acquisition of necessary skills to the detriment of quality. In recent years, federal expenditure for 'supplies and services' has escalated from around RM 12 billion in 2003 to RM 26.5 billion for 2009, with little improvement in quality or extent of services.[18] Furthermore, many of these contracts are directly allocated with little transparency as to process, quality considerations, or reasonable profit margins. Thus, attempting to stimulate the economy through increased public spending often does not translate into a commensurate number of new jobs.

Another area requiring attention is the level of female participation in the labour force. The female labour force participation rate in Malaysia has been under 50% for the past two decades. This rate is significantly below that of other countries in the region, including Hong Kong, the Philippines, and Indonesia.[19] This is due to a mixture of 'pull' and 'push' factors. On one hand, wages for women tend to be lower than for their male counterparts. On the other, women must reconcile the multiple expectations placed upon them as care-givers, mothers, and wives. In addition, many of the valuable roles that women play in the community are not remunerated.

Having looked at some national level issues affecting the labour market, the next section will look at implementing a pro-active employment policy at the state level in Penang.

---

18   Ministry of Finance, *Economic Report 2003/4*, Putrajaya: Ministry of Finance, 2004, Table 4.4. Ministry of Finance, *Economic Report 2008/9*, Putrajaya: Ministry of Finance, 2009, Table 4.4.

19   UNESCAP, *Economic and Social Survey of the Asia Pacific: Surging Ahead in Uncertain Times*, Bangkok: United Nations Economic and Social Commission for the Asia-Pacific, 2007, p. 104.

Implementing a Pro-Employment Policy in Penang

In Malaysia, state governments have very limited powers, which are essentially restricted to land, forestry, Islamic affairs, and local government. Regarding income, state governments receive revenue from land sales, natural resources such as mines and forests, an Islamic tax, and a duty on entertainment. In theory, this means a circumscribed range of action.

However, the key attribute for governing is the authority to raise revenue – through taxation and other means – and to spend.[20] As it has been able to do in the past, the Penang State Government has innovated, raising funds through entrepreneurial initiatives and using the proceeds to move into new policy areas. In addition, the State Governments' responsibility for local government entails managing local public services such as water supply, waste collection and disposal, basic public infrastructure, and parks. At the local level, the State Government is thus a significant consumer of goods and services.

The State Government has taken a direct role in shaping Penang's labour market in the past. During the late 1960s, Penang's unemployment rate reached 15 percent, nearly twice the national average.[21] After the 1969 elections, the new State Government of Penang took the Nathan Report as a blueprint for action and embarked on an industrialization drive that would transform the state's economic and social structure.

The State Government sought to promote tourism and labour-intensive manufacturing to diversify the economy and reduce unemployment. This was to be done by inviting foreign firms to invest in the state and encouraging the production of produce for export. This was accompanied by subsequent measures to encourage foreign firms to development linkages with the local economy.[22]

---

20   H. Peter Gray and John H. Dunning, "Towards a Theory of Regional Policy", Regions, Globalization, and the Knowledge-Based Economy, edited by John H. Dunning (Oxford: Oxford University Press, 2002), pp. 10-11.

21   Chairman of the Penang Branch of the States of Malaya Chamber of Commerce. "Notes on the Economic Situation in the State of Penang", (Penang: States of Malaya Chamber of Commerce, 1968), p. 10.

22   Nathan Associates, "Penang Master Plan", Penang: Robert R. Nathan Associates Inc, 1970, p. 218.

These policies were complemented by direct measures to create jobs and provide relevant skills training to prepare workers to staff new sectors. One such initiative started by then-Chief Minister Tun Lim Chong Eu was to employ unemployed youth as parking attendants, requiring that they spent four hours per day on the streets and the other four in a skill-training centre at 57 Macalister Road.[23] These youths were among the first to be employed by the electronics sector. The City Council also employed young educated school-leavers to work as data collectors or assistant surveyors to compile statistics and information to support policy-making.

Direct and Indirect Pro-Employment Policies

Given the current economic situation, it is timely to contemplate a more pro-active employment policy at state level, entailing an expansionary budget if necessary. This would encompass a range of 'asset-creating' initiatives that would generate a considerable number of good quality jobs for Penangites. These policies could encompass direct employment creation in a variety of public service areas coupled with capacity-building measures to enable more people to access opportunities in the labour market.

Regarding direct measures, the state government could implement one or more of the following:

Construction and Maintenance of Basic Infrastructure:

At present in Penang, a considerable proportion of services in this area is provided by private sector firms who rely on low-cost foreign labour. Opacity in procurement means that there is little transparency regarding the cost or quality of services. This has been a contributing factor to the rapid increase in the Penang Island Municipal Council's budget from RM 72.2 million in 1991 to RM 224 million in 2009. Were the Council's maintenance departments expanded to undertake construction and maintenance tasks directly, formal sector jobs for Malaysian citizens would be generated and greater transparency would be brought to this sector. In more complex areas, where specialist exper-

---

23 Lim Chong Eu, "Party Crisis: Speech to Gerakan Party Members, Penang, 16th July 1971", Selected Speeches and Statements of Lim Chong Eu 1970-1989, edited by Lim, C.S. (Penang: Oon Chin Seang, 1990), p. 11.

tise is needed, procurement can be carried out via publicly-accessible e-systems. In addition to ensuring that public monies remain in the local economy, these measures would bring some order, structure, and transparency to the fragmented and opaque outsourcing sector.

Expanding Penang's Public Park and Garden System:

The state has benefited immensely from its natural heritage in the form of Penang Hill and the Botanic Gardens. In addition to helping reduce greenhouse gases, these facilities have constituted a source of recreation for citizens as well as adding to Penang's attractiveness for tourists. Previous urban development initiatives such as the Penang Global City Centre have relied on private sector initiatives and have focused on complex, expensive and high-end facilities. While there is space for this, the State Government can capitalize on its control over the allocation and zoning of land to create more green and public spaces for residents to use. Embarking on a 'green development drive' would also enable more formal, public sector jobs to be created with ensuing multiplier effects for the local economy. In addition, increasing the quality of Penang's urban environment would help attract and retain skilled workers, and support initiatives such as Malaysia My Second Home.

Expanding and Diversifying the State's Public Transport System:

Given its population and income level, Penang has a woefully under-developed public transport system. The success of recent public transport initiatives such as RapidPenang testifies to the unmet demand for public services of acceptable quality and price. Through investing in a multi-modal transport system to link major suburbs, as well as the island and the mainland, the State Government can create jobs and decrease the economic burden on low-income families who are forced to purchase cars and motorcycles due to the absence of a functioning public transport system. Through investing in an articulated, low-cost network of articulated buses and ferries, the state government can similarly create demand for more formal sector jobs which will be economically self-sustaining.

Piloting a Care-Giver Programme:

At present, many women provide essential services in the community by taking care of elderly, sick, or disabled people. However, these vital tasks lie outside the formal sector and are not remunerated. By formalizing these positions, an income stream would be generated for these women. In addition, by ensuring a certain standard of quality through a licensing system, these services could be made available to the public. This, in turn, could free up other women who are currently acting as care-givers to take up formal sector employment.

Establishing a State Government Statistics, Survey, and Valuation Department:

Malaysia's planning processes are geared to federal priorities. As a result, there is a dearth of statistics and information for state-level issues, particularly with regard to the take-up of federal government grants and loans by Penang-based individuals and groups. The State Government, through establishing a Department to track Penang-related issues, would create a source of demand for local skilled labour and could also provide a means for young graduates to access the labour market.

In addition to resulting in a wider range of public services for Penang's citizens, the above-mentioned measures would have an important effect on the local job market and the local economy through constituting a source of demand in the formal sector. In addition, through quotas for women, young graduates, and older workers, these groups could be helped to access the labour market.

In addition to the direct job creation measures mentioned above, the following indirect policies could also be contemplated.

Establishing a Local Employment Office:

A local employment office catering to Penang's job-seekers would play a key role in reducing information asymmetries. A database or Job Portal centralizing information on current job opportunities with the State Government and local firms would help local job-seekers. This office could also disseminate information on skill providers as well as help Penangites prepare applications to access federal government initiatives, scholarships, and grants.

Creating a Job Portal for Care-givers:

This Job Portal would encourage and facilitate the exchange of care services for children, aged people, and the disabled, as well as domestic help. A consolidation of this fragmented sector would reduce information asymmetries, and help more care-givers, most of whom are women, access the labour market. This Portal could either be placed under the Workfare Department or the Women's portfolio in the State Executive Council.

Costing a Pro-Employment Policy Framework

How much could implementing the above-mentioned policies cost and what reach would this have? Assuming an average family size of five people, creating 5,000 jobs would affect 25,000 people directly. If standard remuneration levels, including benefits, were an average of RM 1,000 per month per job, the total annual cost would be in the order of RM 60 million.

To put this in perspective, in 2008, the Penang State Government's annual budget was RM 450 million.[24] This does not include the budgets of Penang Island Municipal Council and Seberang Perai Municipal Council. Thus, the total cost of creating 5,000 jobs would constitute some 13% of the State Government's budget.

However, this assumes that these jobs would represent additional expenditure for the State Government. In reality, the cost could be substantially lower as a good proportion of these funds would be generated by the initiatives themselves – in the case of the public transport system – or funded from re-oriented expenditure – in the case of public works.

Furthermore, the citizens of Penang would benefit from an extensive range of new 'assets' in the form of a more extensive transport system, additional parks and gardens, better maintained infrastructure, as well as a more capable and well-informed state government.

---

24 *Suresh Narayanan, Lim Mah Hui, and Ong Wooi Leng, "Re-examining State Finance and Governance: The Challenge for Penang", paper prepared for the Penang Outlook Forum 2009, June 1&2, 2009, p. 4.*

Conclusions

This article has looked at the relationship between state policy and employment, in particular how governments can encourage the creation of jobs and increase access to the labour market through a range of direct and indirect policies. One method of direct job creation, workfare programs, has been analysed and lessons drawn from international experience. From there, the general employment situation in Malaysia has been assessed, before examining a range of policy options available to the Penang State Government.

This article has advocated a pro-active employment policy for the Penang State Government. While labour policy has not traditionally been perceived as the responsibility of state governments in Malaysia, this level of government can have, and has had in the past, an important effect on local labour markets. Through indirect policies such as procurement and hiring practices, the state government and its local counterparts can generate employment as well as lower barriers to entry for disadvantaged workers. In addition, a range of options has been put forward to generate a significant number of formal sector jobs as well as develop a range of public goods for the benefit of Penang's citizens. A simple budget calculation has shown that many of these initiatives could be undertaken at a reasonable cost. In addition, the potential for income generation and increased efficiency of many of these initiatives could entail substantially lower public outlays.

Given the Penang State Government's history of successful policy innovation, the development of a pro-active employment policy would be of direct benefit to its citizens, both through the jobs created as well as through the improvements in the quality and range of public services offered.

Bibliography

Bernama (Kuala Lumpur), "One in Five Workers in Malaysia is a Foreigner", Oct 20, 2008.

Chang, Ha-Joon. *Globalization, Economic Development and the Role of the State*. Penang: Third World Network, 2003.

Chang, Ha-Joon. "The Role of Institutions in Asian Development", *Asian Development Review*, 16(2) (1998): 64-95.

Chairman of the Penang Branch of the States of Malaya Chamber of Commerce. "Notes on the Economic Situation in the State of Penang". Penang: States of Malaya Chamber of Commerce, 1968.

del Ninno, Carlo, Kalanidhi Subbarao, and Annamaria Milazzo. "How to Make Public Works Work: A Review of the Experiences". SPD Discussion Paper No. 0905, Washington D.C.: World Bank, 2009.

Devereux S. "From Workfare to Fair Work: The Contribution of Public Works and other Labour-Based Infrastructure Programmes to Poverty Alleviation", Issues in Employment and Poverty Discussion Paper No. 5, Geneva: International Labour Organization, 2002.

Elson, Diane. "Macroeconomic Policy, Employment, Unemployment, and Gender Equality". in *Towards Full and Decent Employment*, edited by Jose Antonio Ocampo and K.S. Jomo. Penang: Third World Network, 2007.

Epstein, Gerald. "Central Banks as Agents of Employment Creation". in *Towards Full and Decent Employment,* edited by Jose Antonio Ocampo and K.S. Jomo. Penang: Third World Network, 2007.

Gray, H.P. and John H. Dunning, "Towards a Theory of Regional Policy", in *Regions, Globalization, and the Knowledge-Based Economy*, edited by John H. Dunning. Oxford: Oxford University Press, 2002, pp. 10-11.

Kimmis, Jenny. "Public Works: An Effective Safety Net for the Poor". 3ie Enduring Questions Brief #1. International Initiative for Impact Evaluation: New Delhi, March 2009.

Lim Chong Eu. "Party Crisis: Speech to Gerakan Party Members, Penang, 16th July 1971". In *Selected Speeches and Statements of Lim Chong Eu 1970-1989*, edited by Lim, C.S. Penang: Oon Chin Seang, 1990.

Lim Chong Eu. "National Economic Policy: Speech at the Gerakan National Delegates' Conference, Port Dickson, 16-17th

August, 1980". In Selected Speeches and Statements of Lim Chong Eu 1970-1989, edited by Lim, C.S. Penang: Oon Chin Seang, 1990.

McCord, Anna. "Public Works as a Response to Labour Market Failure in South Africa". Centre for Social Science Research Working Paper No. 19. Cape Town: University of Cape Town, 2002.

Ministry of Finance, *Economic Report 2003/4*, Putrajaya: Ministry of Finance, 2004, Table 4.4.

Ministry of Finance, *Economic Report 2008/9*, Putrajaya: Ministry of Finance, 2009, Table 4.4.

Najib Tun Abdul Razak, "Speech introducing the Supplementary Supply Bill 2009", Kuala Lumpur, Dewan Rakyat, March 10, 2009.

Narayanan Suresh, Lim Mah Hui, and Ong Wooi Leng, "Re-examining State Finance and Governance: The Challenge for Penang", paper prepared for the Penang Outlook Forum 2009, June 1&2, 2009.

Nathan Associates. "Penang Master Plan". Penang: Robert R. Nathan Associates Inc, 1970.

Staley, Oliver and Michael McKee. 'Yale's Tobin Guides Obama From Grave as Friedman Is Eclipsed'. Bloomberg. February 27, 2000. <http://www.bloomberg.com/apps/news?pid=20601109&refer=home&sid=ajz1hV_afuSQ>, accessed July 6th, 2009.

Subbarao, Kalanidhi. "Systemic Shocks and Social Protection: Role and Effectiveness of Public

Works Programs". Social Protection Discussion Paper Series No. 0302. Washington D.C.: World Bank, 2003.

UNESCAP. *Economic and Social Survey of the Asia Pacific: Surging Ahead in Uncertain* Times. Bangkok: United Nations Economic and Social Commission for the Asia-Pacific, 2007.

[5]

Re-thinking State and Health Care in Penang

Chan Chee Khoon

Malaysia: A Federal-Unitary State?

Malaysia as a polity exhibits a very highly centralised federal structure which in practice makes it more like a unitary state.[1] The Federal Constitution decrees that with the notable exceptions of land matters and matters pertaining to Islam, all other areas which are subject to governmental jurisdiction fall under the federal purview[2].

In particular, state governments are not empowered to directly collect income taxes and corporate taxes, nor export, import and excise duties, and they are also largely restricted from borrowing internationally. They have to depend on revenues from forests, lands, territorial

---

1   *Conversely, one could argue that Malaysia in 2009 has a surfeit (multiplicity) of state governments. Not as dramatic as in the case of the state of Perak where a constitutional crisis continues to simmer as rival claimants to governmental power pursue their options through legal and political channels, Penang is "blessed" with an unelected parallel "shadow government" which unashamedly receives federal allocations (e.g., for tourism development) which should properly be channeled to the legitimately constituted state government elected in March 2008. A federal allocation of RM25 million for instance, promised to Penang after its listing as a Unesco World Heritage Site in 2008, has been diverted to Khazanah Nasional Berhad instead (The Star, 20 September 2009).*

2   *Sabah (North Borneo at the time), upon attaining self-government as part of the decolonization process, negotiated a 20-point agreement as a basis for its entry into what would be the Federation of Malaysia on September 16, 1963. An analogous 18-point agreement provided the basis for Sarawak's concurrent entry into the federation. Both agreements allowed for considerable autonomy for the two territories in the areas of immigration, the civil service, education, and development and finance, but this autonomy has been eroded over the years.*

waters, mines, petroleum and gas royalties, the entertainment industry, and most importantly, transfer payments from the central government. Along with this centralised financial control, the federal government has authority over external affairs, defence, internal security, justice (except civil law cases among Malays or other Muslims and other indigenous peoples which are adjudicated under Islamic and traditional law), federal citizenship, commerce, industry, labour matters, communications, transportation, health, education and other matters.

Such being the case, it is commonly held that state governments in Malaysia have such limited jurisdiction and responsibilities (and in most cases, such limited independent sources of revenue)[3] that Dr Toh Kin Woon (Penang state executive councillor, 1995-2008) has often remarked that "you could shut down the Penang state government and not many people would notice it".

Indeed, the recent trend in the federal-state balance of jurisdiction has been towards greater federalisation rather than devolution, as indicated by instances such as:

- municipal clinics being absorbed into the Ministry of Health

- nationalisation of petroleum and gas resources, and assertion of federal discretionary powers over the royalties due to state governments (Terengganu's "*wang ehsan*"[4])

- erosion of the state autonomy agreed to as part of the terms of accession of Sabah and Sarawak into the Federation of Malaysia

- sewage disposal services, traditionally a function of local authorities, which went through a process of centralisation, privatisation, nationalisation over the period 1996-2004, after a failed attempt at centralisation-cum-privatisation by Indah Water Konsortium (IWK[5])

---

3   The annual operating budget of Universiti Sains Malaysia for instance was double that of the Penang state government in 2008.

4   Terengganu was ruled by PAS from 1999-2004 when the federal government controversially re-designated Terengganu's oil and gas royalties as "wang ehsan" ("goodwill money") subject to federal discretion and control. Meanwhile, the PAS-led state government in Kelantan is currently pressing its claims for RM1 billion in royalties from oil production 150km off the coast of Kelantan, which began in 2004.

5   IWK took over the sewerage services from all local authorities in Malaysia except for those in Kelantan, Sabah, Sarawak and the Majlis Perbandaran Johor Bahru.

- the National Water Council proposing to rebalance the jurisdiction over water management away from the states, as one response towards mismanagement by some state water authorities and their privatised counterparts.

The Johor Corporation and Kumpulan Perubatan Johor

Against this backdrop, we nonetheless have the striking instance of the Johor state government which operates through its corporate arm, the Johor Corporation, a diversified healthcare conglomerate which includes the largest proprietary chain of private hospitals distributed throughout the country *(Kumpulan Perubatan Johor, KPJ)*, a veritable mini-Ministry of Health but operated along largely commercial lines[6].

In 1979, the Johor State Economic Development Corporation (the corporate arm of the Johor state government, later renamed as the Johor Corporation) marked its entry into the private healthcare industry with the incorporation of the Johor Specialist Hospital. Over the next 25 years, KPJ Healthcare Berhad grew into the largest chain of private hospitals in Malaysia (nineteen hospitals wholly or partially owned or managed by KPJ, with another six in Indonesia, Bangladesh, and the Middle East), and along the way was listed on the main board of the Kuala Lumpur Stock Exchange on 29 November 1994. With paid-up capital of RM 191 million and assets of RM1,021 million (plus shareholders' funds in excess of RM430 million), KPJ has expanded into a publicly-listed health conglomerate which offers not just medical and specialist inpatient care, but a diversified portfolio of services including hospital management, hospital development and commissioning, nursing training, health sciences and continuing education for healthcare professionals, pathology and other technical services, central procurement and retailing of pharmaceutical products.

Meanwhile, at the federal level, Khazanah Nasional Berhad, the investment holding arm of the Government of Malaysia, acquired on 28 August 2006 a 30.68 percent controlling share of Pantai Holdings Berhad [7], the largest healthcare conglomerate in Malaysia with interests in private hospitals (8 in number, 1,086 beds and 368 physicians - the

6   C. K. Chan, *"Re-inventing the Welfarist State? The Malaysian Health System in Transition"*, *Journal of Contemporary Asia (in press, 2010)*.

7   *Khazanah Nasional Berhad media statement, 28 August 2006*

second largest private hospital chain in Malaysia), clinical waste management, cleaning and maintenance services for government hospitals in the southern states of Negri Sembilan, Malacca and Johor (Tongkah Medivest), management, administration and consultancy services for hospitals and medical centres, medical diagnostic services (medical laboratory services, imaging, etc), radiotherapy services, educational and training programs in healthcare and related fields, managed care, geriatric, rehabilitation and convalescent care, supervision of medical screening and registration of foreign workers in Malaysia (Fomema), telemedicine services, cardiac catheterization services, and lithotripter services[8].

In April 2001, chief executive officer of Pantai Holdings Bhd. Mokhzani Mahathir, a son of the serving Prime Minister at the time (Dr Mahathir Mohammad), disposed of his 32.9 percent stake to Lim Tong Yong who succeeded him as CEO. On September 13, 2005, Parkway Holdings Ltd of Singapore in turn acquired a 31 percent stake in Pantai, making it the largest single shareholder in Pantai. Parkway, which became Southeast Asia's largest private healthcare provider, also has controlling stakes in three hospitals in Singapore (East Shore Hospital, Gleneagles Hospital, and Mount Elizabeth Hospital), two in Malaysia (Gleneagles Medical Centre, Penang, and Gleneagles Intan Medical Centre, Kuala Lumpur) and a cardiac centre in Brunei besides operating a hospital in Kolkata in joint venture with Apollo Hospitals Enterprise Ltd[9]. Following this acquisition, Parkway changed five of the seven board members of Pantai, replacing them with nominees of

---

8   *Pantai Holdings Berhad (Company No. 11832-K, incorporated in Malaysia) and its Subsidiary Companies: Financial statements for the year ended June 30, 2003. Kuala Lumpur Stock Exchange annual audited accounts, 2003. In April 2001, two and a half years before Dr Mahathir stepped down as Prime Minister, Mokhzani Mahathir disposed of his entire stakes in Tongkah and Pantai. Mirzan Mahathir, another son of Prime Minister Mahathir Mohamad, had a 25.8% stake in the Lion Group, another conglomerate which operated the Mahkota Medical Center in Malacca state. The Lion Group also has plans to build hospitals in Kuala Lumpur, Ipoh and Seremban, and eventually, possibly in China.*

9   *The Singapore Stock Exchange-listed health conglomerate also includes Parkway Shenton Pte Ltd, one of Singapore's biggest general practice, Medi-Rad Associates Ltd, a radiology service provider; Parkway Laboratory Services Ltd, a major provider of laboratory services, as well as Gleneagles CRC Pte. Ltd., which offers clinical research services (e.g., drug trials) on a contract basis.*

Parkway and those of its largest shareholder, Newbridge Capital Inc.[10], a US-based fund manager which had acquired a 26 percent stake in Parkway on 26 May 2005[11].

It was this acquisition by the Singapore-listed company (in turn, controlled by a US-based fund manager) which set off alarm bells and provided the political opposition in Malaysia with an opportunity to castigate the Malaysian authorities for their regulatory and strategic oversight[12]. Amidst the red faces and embarrassment of allowing the largest health care conglomerate in the country (a beneficiary of major outsourcing concessions for government hospital support services and foreign worker medical registration, not to mention the second largest private hospital chain in the country) to slip into foreign hands, a compromise was eventually struck which entailed Khazanah's intervention to acquire a 51 percent stake in Pantai Irama Ventures Sdn Bhd, with the remaining 49 percent going to Parkway in a reshuffling of corporate equity which would see Pantai Irama holding a 35 percent controlling stake of Pantai Holdings Bhd. Aside from a lucrative margin accruing to Parkway from the share swaps, operational and management control of the hospitals would remain with Parkway for fifteen years[13].

This may have been an unplanned purchase and contingency forced upon the Malaysian government (as far as timing), but Khazanah has nonetheless emerged in the last four years as a major shareholder in private health enterprises in Malaysia, allegedly with strategic and synergistic considerations in mind, but possibly also preferential support for government-linked companies benefiting from major outsourcing concessions. At the present time, Khazanah has interests in Fomema, Pantai Holdings Bhd., Pharmaniaga (fifteen year concession for supplying pharmaceuticals and medical disposables to government hospitals and health facilities), a 13.2 percent stake in Apollo Hospitals En-

---

10 Established in 1994 by Texas Pacific Group and Blum Capital Partners.

11 Business Week, 13 June, 2005.

12 "Gov't concedes mistake, says Husam", Malaysiakini.com (accessed on 30 August 2006).

13 Khazanah Nasional Berhad media statement, 28 August 2006, Malaysiakini.com (30 August 2006).

Re-thinking State and Health Care in Penang

terprise Ltd (India)[14], as well as a recently-acquired 67.5 percent stake in the International Medical University (IMU), Malaysia's first private medical university[15]. On April 30, 2008, the Pantai-Parkway saga came full circle when Khazanah announced that it had paid RM1.23 billion for an additional 16.41 percent stake in Parkway[16], thereby raising its total stake in Parkway to 20.79 percent.

Indeed, it appears that the Malaysian government in concert with GLCs (government-linked companies) at both federal and state levels in effect owns and operates three parallel systems of healthcare providers:

- the regular Health Ministry facilities (as well the health facilities of the Ministry of Defence)

- corporatized hospitals (Institut Jantung Negara, university teaching hospitals of Universiti Malaya, Universiti Kebangsaan Malaysia, Universiti Sains Malaysia)

- a huge "private wing": the Pantai chain of hospitals, operated as commercial hospitals with Khazanah as a controlling shareholder, similarly with the Kumpulan Perubatan Johor (KPJ) chain of hospitals, controlled by the Johor state government through its corporate arm, the Johor Corporation.

Are the KPJ and Pantai hospitals *public* or *private*? Is this a "nationalization" of private enterprise space, or an extension of the logic of capital into strategic adjuncts of the state? What contending interests and policy conflicts are being engendered, exacerbated, or attenuated

---

14 *Khazanah Nasional Berhad media statement, 3 August 2005.*

15 *Khazanah Nasional Berhad media statement, 30 November 2006. Founded by a team of academicians in 1992, IMU today has an enrolment of over 1,800 students in medicine, pharmacy, nursing, and postgraduate programs in medical sciences and community health, in partnership with 25 medical schools in Australia, Canada, Ireland, New Zealand, United Kingdom and United States of America.*

16 *Khazanah Nasional Berhad media statement, 30 April 2008.*

by these developments?[17] What balance between social vs. economic (profit maximising) objectives is desirable on the part of public owners?

It is worth emphasizing that even if the profits and returns accruing to the KPJ and Pantai hospitals are redistributed via cross-subsidies to poorer patients (not much evidence of this), or through corporate taxes and more diffuse channels of the Johor Corporation (Amanah Saham Johor?) and Khazanah (the various Amanah Saham schemes?), there are still concerns arising from the well-known market failures of private health care markets which introduce distortions and inefficiencies (not to mention inequities) into the healthcare subsector as a whole.

An Efficient Market in Healthcare?

The arguments in favour of healthcare privatization rest on the allocative efficiency of the market. Remarkably, this persists despite repeated market failures and the fact that important pre-requisites for efficient markets are often not met for the microeconomics of health care:

- the health care consumer is often disadvantaged relative to the healthcare provider (*information asymmetry*[18]), further compounded by imperfect information and uncertainty (*stochastic occurrences, treatment efficacy*) in healthcare markets[19]

---

17 *The Malaysian health ministry's hospitals as well as the teaching hospitals of medical schools are plagued with a perennial outflow of senior experienced staff to the private sector as well as to foreign emigration, due to push and pull factors. This chronic understaffing in the public sector, which has compelled the Health Ministry to resort to foreign hires, will undoubtedly be worsened by stepped-up efforts to develop the medical tourism subsector, and by continued poaching of public sector staff trained at public expense. On the other hand, the emergence of private hospital chains may allow for some degree of rationalization in the acquisition and use of expensive medical equipment. In the early 1990s for instance, there were reportedly more MRI scanners in the Klang Valley area (metropolitan KL) than in all of Australia.*

18 *U. E. Reinhardt, "Can efficiency in health care be left to the market?", Journal of Health Politics, Policy and Law 26 (5)) (2001), pp. 967-992.*

19 *K. J. Arrow, "Uncertainty and the welfare economics of medical care", American Economic Revue, vol. 53, no.5 (1963), pp. 941-73.*

- there is often no alternative provider in sparsely populated areas[20]

- low patient volume (in small or medium-sized facilities) can lead to degraded skills of medical specialists and poorer patient outcomes (*medical equivalent of economies of scale*) [21]

- wasteful or inappropriate use of resources (*over-treatment and under-treatment*)[22], depending on the payment incentives in healthcare financing

- reduced access for poor patients (*more an issue of equity[23]*)

Beyond theoretical considerations, the peer reviewed literature also reports many instances where profit-driven healthcare empirically falls short in comparison with not-for-profit healthcare, across a range

---

20 See for example, K. J. Khoo, "Health Care in Sarawak: Model of a Public System", *Health Care in Malaysia: The Dynamics of Provision, Financing, and Access*, edited by H. L. Chee & S. Barraclough (London: Routledge, 2007).

21 See for example, E. L. Hannan, M. Racz, T. J. Ryan, et al., "Coronary angioplasty volume-outcome relationships for hospitals and cardiologists", *The Journal of the American Medical Association*, vol. 277 (1997), pp. 892-898.

22 Abu Bakar Suleiman, Wong Swee Lan, A. Jai Mohan, et al., "Utilisation of Specialist Medical Manpower", *Report from a collaborative study by the Ministry of Health and the Academy of Medicine, Malaysia, 1992 - 1993 (1993)*.

23 H. Wadee & L. Gilson, "The Search for Cross Subsidy in Segmented Health Systems: Can Private Wards in Public Hospitals Secure Equity Gains?" in *Commercialization of Health Care: Global and Local Dynamics and Policy Responses*, edited by Maureen Mackintosh and Meri Koivusalo (Basingstoke: Palgrave Macmillan, 2005).

of outcome measures[24]. Public sector healthcare of course is not without problems and may not always outperform the private sector, but the reverse is demonstrably false, and to continue dismantling the public healthcare sector out of an obsessive faith that market-based solutions will invariably deliver higher efficiency and lower unit costs, is clearly unwarranted.

Public-Private Interactions: IJN as Price Bulwark

When the *Institut Jantung Negara* (IJN, National Heart Institute) was hived off from the Kuala Lumpur Hospital in 1992 and corporatized as a government-owned referral heart centre, one of its explicit missions was to provide high quality services in cardiovascular and thoracic medicine to Malaysian citizens at medium cost. Civil servants and government pensioners would continue to receive treatment for heart ailments at IJN at government expense, as an employment health benefit.

For Malaysian citizens who were not civil servants, patient charges at the corporatized IJN would be increased from the hitherto highly-subsidised rates, and IJN staff would be paid salaries markedly above the corresponding Ministry of Health scales. The IJN however would continue to be subsidised by public funds although not to the extent of 90-95 percent as was commonly the case for the regular Ministry of Health facilities.

The intention was that IJN should also act as a *price bulwark*, i.e. a fallback option which would serve as a *competitive price check* against

24 S. Woolhandler & D Himmelstein, "When Money is the Mission: The High Costs of Investor-Owned Care", New England Journal of Medicine, vol. 341(1999), pp. 444-446; P. Devereaux, P. Choi, C. Lacchett, et al., "A systematic review and meta-analysis of studies comparing mortality rates of private for-profit and private not-for-profit hospitals", The Canadian Medical Association Journal, vol. 166 (2002),pp. 1399-1406; S. Woolhandler, T. Campbell, and D. Himmelstein,"Costs of Health Care Administration in the United States and Canada", New England Journal of Medicine, vol. 349 (2003), pp. 768-775; Donald Light (editor), "Comparative Studies of Competition Policy", Social Science & Medicine, vol. 52, no. 8 (special issue, April 2001); The PLoS Medicine Debate: Is Private Health Care the Answer to the Health Problems of the World's Poor? (Kara Hanson, Lucy Gilson, Catherine Goodman, Anne Mills, Richard Smith, Richard Feachem, Neelam Sekhri Feachem, Tracey Perez Koehlmoos, Heather Kinlaw). PLoS Medicine November issue, vol.5 (2008), pp. 1528-1532;
P. S. Heller, "A Model of the Demand for Medical and Health Services in Peninsular Malaysia", Social Science & Medicine, vol.16 (1982), pp.267-284.

steep price increases in the private healthcare sector (such as the Sime Darby Medical Center in Subang Jaya).

We do not have systematic, disaggregated data to evaluate whether the IJN is in fact exerting such a price restraining effect, but we do note that the Star (December 18, 2008) for instance included the figures below as part of its investigative reporting into the attempted acquisition of a controlling share of IJN by Sime Darby in December 2008:

Medical Charges Comparison

in '000	SDMCSJ*	IJN
Single by pass	RM 40 ~ 50	RM 25 ~ 30
Angioplasty	RM 35 ~ 45	RM 18 ~ 35

* Sime Darby Medical Centre Subang Jaya
Sources: SDMCSJ and IJN

If these figures are comparable between the two institutions and are not seriously misleading, one might even ask, going beyond IJN, if this bulwark function could be generalised as a strategic role that subsidised, publicly-provided healthcare could play in the Malaysian healthcare system, as a price brake against ever-escalating fees and charges levied by a profit-driven private healthcare sector, and as a benchmark for quality?

It is for this reason that the continued existence of well-funded, widely accessible quality healthcare provided by the public sector is in the interests of *all Malaysian citizens*, regardless of whether they patronise the public or the private healthcare sector. Good quality, no frills, needs-based healthcare - funded and provided by the public sector - should therefore be supported by all, not just by those who cannot afford the charges of the private healthcare market.

In Singapore, the government's strategically located and well-equipped polyclinics account for only 20% of primary healthcare on the island, but their subsidised outpatient services seem to provide sufficient price competition to help restrain fee increases amongst the private clinics. In Hong Kong, well-remunerated and adequately-staffed public sector healthcare achieves a similar effect. It is noteworthy that both territories enjoy among the highest levels of population health indices worldwide, at quite modest levels of national health expenditures (Singapore 3.5% GDP; Hong Kong 5.5% GDP) which bracket Malaysian expenditures (4.2% GDP).

Questions for Brainstorming, or Further Inquiry:

In re-thinking the role of the state in healthcare in Penang, I would like to propose the following for further reflection and deliberation:

- Can we reconceptualise the role of the Penang state government in health development as going beyond that of facilitator, i.e. creating the enabling environment for market-driven healthcare? The Johor state government has given us one answer to that question – the state government itself becoming an economic actor in the form of a profit-seeking health entrepreneur.

- Should the Penang state government (or the Penang Development Corporation) explore the feasibility of a non-profit, publicly-owned version of the *Kumpulan Perubatan Johor* for Penang? A modest chain of state-owned (and operated?) medium-sized hospitals which could provide medium-cost healthcare and at the same time serve as a price bulwark against even steeper price increases in the for-profit private sector?

- Financing: can the state government leverage on its jurisdiction over land matters to generate the necessary financing for a realistic business plan, within the existing (and foreseeable) political, economic and jurisdictional contingencies? What can we learn from other financially viable and successful state enterprises such as *Perbadanan Bekalan Air*?

- What are other potential (non-land) sources of financing which the state government might be able to tap for such an enterprise? A state-operated health insurance scheme to generate the cash flow for a business plan to seek project financing? What can we learn from the Selangor state government's *takaful* (insurance) scheme which was launched in October 2008 which also promised free medical care worth RM3500 for Selangor citizens aged 60 years and above[25]? In terms of a learning curve, does it make sense to begin with a health insurance scheme, with a later con-

---

25 *"Basket of goodies for Selangor folk", The Malaysian Insider (25 July2008).*

sideration of a healthcare provider role for the state government? Are there potential synergies in the form of a teaching hospital in partnership with the Penang Medical College?

- What are the *pros* and *cons* of using political parties, rather than state governments as the institutional bases for non-profit private ventures in health care (and education?). For instance, we see many more party-based initiatives in tertiary education, rather than concerted efforts to establish state universities in the mould of, say, US state (land grant) universities. What can we learn from the existing (or past) engagements of state governments with (tertiary) educational ventures, ranging from equity partici- pation to a role as owner-operator?

- Should we explore the possibilities and feasibility of a *consortium of state governments* – pooling resources, land and resource-based revenues, royalties, and educated and skilled human resources (such as Penang loyalists, retired professionals with accumulated experience, who have hands-on experience in managing hospi- tals, who are knowledgeable about the local healthcare market, who have experience running health insurance schemes, social and professional and business networks, etc) as expanded insti- tutional bases for collaborative regional ventures in educational, health and other services?

- Hospitals aside[26], what are other potential interventions that the state government could consider to improve population health in Penang within the existing (and foreseeable) political, economic and jurisdictional contingencies? An example might be the im- proved urban management of the (social) ecology of dengue propagation and transmission?

- How should efforts in this direction and at this level be balanced against efforts to turn things around at the federal level, i.e. to rehabilitate educational and other service institutions within the

---

26 *In this paper, we have adopted a relatively restricted scope for the definition of healthcare, largely confined to medical and health facilities and the care provided by their personnel. Social and environmental determinants of health however remind us that there is only a modest overlap between health and healthcare (in the narrow sense). Health interventions therefore should be guided by a social ecological perspective of health and disease and should not be unduly restricted to immediately antecedent deter- minants.*

federal public sector? What degree of duplication at federal, state, and other levels might be acceptable or desirable in any subsequent effort to de-centralise, de-federalise, or devolve jurisdiction over these (public) service sectors?

Concluding Remarks: Pathways towards Decentralisation?

The existing lopsided balance of federal vs. state jurisdiction has been an effective tool of central control thus far, sustained by the uninterrupted incumbency of a ruling federal coalition anchored by its dominant partner, UMNO. Whether by design or otherwise, the periodic rotation and redistribution of UMNO's top leadership positions among its regional support bases have blunted what might otherwise have been more pronounced centrifugal tendencies in federal-state power configurations.

In the aftermath of the March 2008 general elections, some realignments were anticipated, between KL and the states ruled by the Pakatan Rakyat coalition, but were also discernible in BN-ruled states.

In Terengganu state, where the control over royalties from petroleum and gas seems to have inflamed factional infighting within UMNO Terengganu, the royal house stepped in with a proposal for a sovereign wealth fund to receive and to manage these revenues and accumulated assets.

The Terengganu Investment Authority (TIA) was duly established on February 27, 2009 with a projected fund size of RM11 billion. RM6 billion would be raised through bond issues in the capital markets collateralised by its annual royalties from Petronas, while the remaining RM5 billion would be raised with the backing of a guarantee from the federal government[27].

---

27 *The governance structure of TIA would have the Menteri Besar of Terengganu (MB Inc) holding 100 percent of ordinary shares (the Ministry of Finance Inc and the TIA Foundation would be issued one preference share each, entitling them to nominate one director each and to 10 percent of TIA's annual profits), the Sultan of Terengganu would chair a board of advisers, and a management team of professionals would be reporting to a board of directors (www.theedgemalaysia.com 18 & 19 May 2009). The Singapore Straits Times (July 15, 2009) reported that a key architect of TIA was Joe Low, a Penang-born businessman described as a member of Najib Abdul Razak's inner circle and also as an adviser to Sultan Mizan Zainal Abidin of Terengganu.*

The TIA however also had an unintended effect, i.e. setting a precedent whereby a state government could leverage on a guarantee provided by the federal government to raise investment capital from local and international financial markets for development projects over which the federal authorities may exercise only limited control.

In its inaugural RM5 billion capital-raising exercise in May 2009, TIA's thirty-year Islamic bonds were oversubscribed, attracting tenders from local and foreign investors whose bids exceeded RM8 billion within two days of its launch. As if to drive home the point, the Penang state government immediately requested a similar federal guarantee for a RM5 billion capital-raising exercise to finance priority development projects in the state[28].

In July 2009, Prime Minister Najib Abdul Razak, fresh from talks with leading officials of Abu Dhabi's sovereign wealth fund Mubadala Development, announced that the TIA would be federalised and re-named as 1Malaysia Development Berhad (1MDB)[29]. It would be wholly owned by the Ministry of Finance Inc (MoF Inc) and would report directly to the prime minister. Meanwhile, the management of Terengganu's oil and gas royalties would revert to the pre-TIA status quo, leaving unresolved for the moment the discretionary use of Terengganu's oil and gas royalties by an incumbent state government, an issue that had fomented much dissension and shifting alliances within its ranks.

This reversal by the federal authorities might have been a pre-emptive move to forestall further requests from other states for their own investment funds (which might weaken federal control over development financing):

> By becoming a [federal] sovereign wealth fund, 1MDB will have Malaysia as its priority instead of just one state, according to a source. It puts all states on equal footing at a time when there are a couple of states that are tinkering with the idea of establishing their own state-based investment funds. Establishing the 1MDB will also do away with the [pressure

28 "Now Penang wants its Sovereign Wealth Fund", <http://www.theedgemalaysia. com/commentary/14923-now-penang-wants-its-sovereign-wealth-fund.pdf> (accessed 26 May 2009).

29 "Terengganu Investment Authority to be federal body", The Star (22 July 2009).

on the] Government to provide further guarantees for other state-based funds.

The Star

July 22, 2009

Additionally, it could also reassure TIA's co-investors in Malaysian ventures (such as Mubadala's participation in a RM6.26 billion property development project in Pulau Bidong, Terengganu) that the investment vehicle for a joint venture would be insulated from local political uncertainties and discontinuities such as may erupt in states like Terengganu.

Meanwhile in Selangor, the state government was exploring its options vis-à-vis *zakat* (Muslim religious tithes) as a potential source of development finance for the state[30]. Since *zakat* contributions are currently deductible against federal income taxes, this could be yet another intriguing attempt at fiscal devolution which relies on the state's jurisdiction over Islamic affairs. The challenges are daunting though, given the parties involved and the potential stakes, not to mention Selangor's religious pluralism[31].

In East Malaysia, Sabah and Sarawak, accounting for 52 out of Barisan Nasional's 137 parliamentarians, have become crucial swing states in the federal power equation post-March 2008, providing leverage for increased development allocations as well as cabinet positions and political office, if not for reinstated autonomy.

If a durable two-coalition system emerges and over time approaches parity in electoral strength, there might eventually be less resistance to some degree of devolution, in anticipation of fluid scenarios in the (rotational) exercise of federal and state governmental power. This is unlikely to be a smooth process, and might well entail, as Dr Nungsari Ahmad Radhi envisages, an over-extended, centralised federalism forced to cede *de facto* jurisdiction at the periphery, when it overreaches in its ambitions relative to the resources that it can muster.

---

30 *"Selangor plans to bypass federal government with new tax system", The Malaysian Insider (13 July 2009).*

31 *"MB cadang orang bukan Islam bayar zakat perdagangan", HarakahDaily.Net (13 July 2009); "Zakat only for helping Muslims and nothing else", Bernama (19 August 2009).*

In 2008, Petronas' payments to the federal government (RM72.5 billion as dividends, taxes, and export duties) accounted for 45 percent of federal revenues in that year. Whether Petronas can continue to be a major source of federal largesse may increasingly depend on its foreign operations, which contributed 30 percent of its revenues in 2007, as domestic reserves of oil and gas are progressively depleted. Not surprisingly, this heavy reliance on Petronas' revenues has also prompted repeated calls for widening the tax base[32].

In 1999, the Indonesian parliament *(Dewan Perwakilan Rakyat)* enacted *Undang-Undang Pemerintahan Daerah No. 22 Tahun 1999* (Law No. 22, 1999 on Local Government) which devolved substantial responsibilities in public works, health, education and culture, agriculture, communications, industry and trade, capital investment, environment, land, cooperatives, and human resources to local governments while retaining security and defence, foreign policy, monetary and fiscal matters, justice, and religious affairs as central government prerogatives.

It is tempting to link this with Indonesia's declining oil production (since 1998) and its status as a net oil importer (since 2004). Notwithstanding oil and gas revenues contributing 33 percent of the central government's revenues from 1997-2000[33], the main impetus for Indonesia's decentralisation came from the 1997 financial crisis and the demise of Suharto's autocratic regime, which released pent-up demands for regional autonomy especially from its resource-rich provinces.

Depending on the adequacy of revenue sharing arrangements between central and local authorities in Indonesia, we might witness mounting pressures for the devolution (or sharing) of *revenue raising powers* (local taxation), to accompany the devolution of governmental responsibilities for meeting citizen needs and expectations.

---

32 *"Malaysia needs to implement new taxes, says IMF", www.theedgemalaysia.com (17 August 2009); "Govt. must reform tax; introduce GST or VAT says MIER", The Star (18 August 2009).*

33 *Etisham Ahmad & Eric Mottu, " Oil Revenue Assignments: Country Experiences and Issues", Fiscal Policy Formulation and Implementation in Oil Producing Countries, edited by Jeffrey M. Davis, Rolando Ossowski and Annalisa Fedelino (Washington, DC: International Monetary Fund, 2003), p.225.*

In Malaysia, the possible emergence of a national health (insurance) fund (in effect, a supplementary tax in the form of payroll deductions plus matching contributions from employers and the self-employed) may provide an opportunity to lobby for the decentralization of aspects of the financing (and provision) of healthcare. The Canadian model for national health insurance for instance comes to mind, where provincial and federal authorities have shared responsibilities along with the commensurate powers of taxation for the financing of healthcare.

There is little dispute that certain health functions and health facilities such as peak referral institutions, control of communicable diseases (immigration and trade-related health matters, quarantine), equalisation grants and cross-subsidies to poorer states, bulk procurement of pharmaceuticals, medical disposables and accessories, National Institutes of Health (research and the deployment of its outputs), international health engagements, etc., should remain as federal health prerogatives.

But there is no compelling reason why the Penang Hospital for instance should not be restructured to be a devolved institution reporting to the Penang state government, along with a devolved system for the allocation of requisite financial resources.

Indonesia required a financial crisis to catalyse the devolution of a highly centralised and militarised unitary state. What will it take for us in Malaysia to rebalance the existing jurisdiction between federal, state, and local governments?

[6]

Social Justice and the Penang Housing Question

Goh Ban Lee

Introduction

We have housing problems and will always have housing problems. What they are and how intense they are depend on whom one talks to. Indeed, an academic can build a good career just studying and writing about housing problems.

The focus of this paper, however, is on the role of the state government in improving housing conditions. Since Penang has had a new state government since the March 8, 2008 general elections, it is legitimate for the leaders to want a new agenda. There is also no doubt that Penangites are seeking changes, otherwise there would have been no reason for them changing the state government. At the same time, it is important to realise that March 8 was not a revolution. Furthermore, housing issues were probably not the compelling factors for the recent change of government.

The main objective of this paper is to identify the housing agenda for the next decade or so. To do that, it is useful to conduct a brief survey of existing housing situations. In the process, the paper will also touch on existing housing policy and strategies and the resources available to the state government to improve housing in Penang, including the mechanisms to regulate the housing industry.

Social Justice and Housing

Let us first briefly discuss the state's role in housing. Why should the government be involved in and even responsible for housing?

A compelling reason is because a society is responsible for the welfare of its members based on the principle that "all men (and women) are brothers (and sisters)". We are our brothers' keepers. As such, if there are those among us who do not have adequate shelter from the elements, it is our responsibility to ensure that this is corrected.

But even if one does not believe in the altruistic nature of human beings, there are also reasons why a society, through the government, must be responsible for the housing needs of its members based on the selfish principle of self-preservation. Since no one can do everything himself or herself in the production of goods and services, especially in a capitalist society, it is important to ensure that every member of society is healthy or at least not sick.

Housing is a basic ingredient to good health. At the very least, even the poorest require basic shelter to live and bring up families so that the production process is kept going.

Furthermore, even the richest person's housing needs depend extend beyond the confines of his or her house and garden. They also depend on a clean and safe neighbourhood and, as an extension to this, the entire city. It is not possible to have good housing if one's neighbours' houses are rat-infested or breed mosquitoes or are in seriously dilapidated condition. The rats and mosquitoes are not going to reside only in the houses of the poor. Security guards and high walls, even electrified ones, are no guarantee of safety.

The state government is, therefore, responsible for ensuring that everyone has adequate shelter.

State Power and Resources

But the state government is not all powerful in matters related to housing. Although Penang is usually seen as one of the richer states in the country, the reality is that the state government does not have huge financial reserves. Its annual budget is slightly more than RM440 million. It also does not own a lot of land, much of which was alienated during early colonial days.

The state government does have power over the use of land and collect certain "taxes" related to land. It decides on the amount of quit rent to be paid by every land owner and collects a conversion fee if a land owner applies to change the use of the land. There is also a subdivision charge.

Under the National Land Code, alienated land is usually classified as "Building" or "Industry" or "Agriculture". Since almost all new development projects are located at urban fringes, invariably the affected land has been under agriculture. As such, land owners have to seek the permission of the state government to change the use or subdivide the land. This gives the state government the power to impose conditions and collect taxes, usually a percentage of the difference between the value of agriculture land and building land.

However, in Penang, there is a unique land tenure called "First Grade" titles. Owners of such titles do not need to change land use, although they still have to seek permission for subdivision. As a general rule, the Penang state government has less power over land than other state governments.

There is a state executive councillor in charge of housing and he is supported by the State Housing Department (SHD). But the limited budget allocated to housing means that the roles of the councillor and the department are very limited, largely focusing on housing for the poor. As such, the state has to depend on assistance from the federal government even to build houses for the lower income groups. There have been occasions when the local councils were "persuaded" to use their land for joint venture projects.

Aside from the power over change of land use and land subdivisions, the state government does not have much direct role in land development by private developers. The main government bodies responsible for development control are the two local councils.

The state government, however, does have a big role in choosing the leadership of the councils. The Local Government Act also provides for the state government to pass general policies which the local councils must abide by. Furthermore, the chief minister is also the chairman of the State Planning Committee which can pass town planning policies that the local councils must also follow.

Existing Housing Policies and Strategies in Penang

The only housing policies in Penang that are legally binding are those in the Penang Structure Plan 2020 (PSP 2020) that was gazetted

in 2007 (see Appendix: Box 1). It consists of 15 policy statements (Box 1). Unfortunately, almost all are "pie-in-the-sky" feel-good statements that are applicable anywhere in the world. For example, the first policy statement, "Pembangunan Perumahan Yang Berkualiti Akan Terus Disediakan Bersesuian Dengan Permintaan Rakyat" (p. 4-63) is applicable in Kelantan, Selangor, or even Timbuktu.

The PSP contains some specific housing targets. It projects that Penang needs 185,000 new houses by the year 2020 with an average of 12,300 units of new houses per year (p. 4-65). It is left for the Local Plans to identify the amount of land required, and the location of the new houses.

The PSP also have strategies to achieve each of the policy statements (see Appendix: Box 2).

The PSP also addresses the issue of affordability. However, the policy statements are, again, too general. For example, it states that the state must: "Menetapkan harga yang mampu dimiliki dalam mancapai sasaran permilikan perumahan berdasarkan jenis, saiz dan lokasi dan dikawal selaras dengan Dasar Perumahan Negara dan Negeri" (p. 4-65). While the intent of the statement is good, there is no mechanism to control the price of houses built by private developers, except those in low-cost and low–medium-cost categories (Table 1).

The reality is that unless the government is in control of the housing market by being the biggest housing developer, it will have great difficulties controlling house prices. Since it does not have a huge land bank, its role in affordability is largely indirect, through planning and building standards and guidelines which have to be administered through the One Stop Centre in each of the two local councils.

Table 1: Type, Size and Price of Low-cost and Low-medium-cost Houses

Southwest District /Seberang Perai Utara/Seberang Perai Tengah/Seberang Perai Selatan–Low Cost House.

Type of low cost House	Area (Minimum)	Maximum Price for the Low Cost House		
		Zone 1	Zone 2	Zone 3
Landed (Terrace)	650 S.F	RM42,000	RM 40,000	RM 35,000
Landed (Cluster)		RM42,000	RM 38,000	RM 33,000
Flats (maximum 5 storey)		RM25,000	RM 25,000	RM 25,000

Northeast District–Low Medium Cost.

Type of House	Area (Minimum)	Zone 1 (RM)	Zone 2 (RM)	Zone 3 (RM)
5 Storey Flats	650 S.F	72,000	72,000	67,500
5 Storey Flats	570 S.F	63,000	63,000	58,500

Southwest District /Seberang Perai Utara/Seberang Perai Tengah/Seberang Perai Selatan–Low Medium Cost House.

Type of Low Medium Cost House	Area (Minimum)	Maximum Price for the Low Medium Cost House		
		Zone 1	Zone 2	Zone 3
Landed (Terrace)	650 S.F	RM 70,000	RM 65,000	RM 55,000
	700 S.F	RM 75,000	RM 70,000	RM 60,000
	753 S.F	RM 80,000	RM 75,000	RM 65,000
Landed (Cluster)	650 S.F	RM 65,000	RM 60,000	RM 45,000
	650 S.F	RM 70,000	RM 65,000	RM 50,000
	650 S.F	RM 75,000	RM 70,000	RM 55,000
Flats	650 S.F	RM 60,000	RM 50,000	RM 40,000
	650 S.F	RM 65,000	RM 55,000	RM 45,000
	650 S.F	RM 70,000	RM 60,000	RM 50,000

Source: PSP 2020, 4-68

The Realities

Despite so much emphasis on adequate housing for the people, there is no one agency where one can get a comprehensive picture of the housing situation in Penang.

There are several government agencies that have some information, including the Penang State Housing Department, local councils, Pusat Maklumat Harta Tanah Negara (NAPIC) and the Statistics Department. But they each provide only part of the picture. To complicate matters, much of the data is considered confidential by the keepers. Anyone interested in formulating housing policies and strategies not only needs the cooperation of these agencies, but must also undertake some costly studies.

The most recent published data on housing in Penang can be found in the Penang Structure Plan 2020 (PSP 2020, 2007) and its report of survey (RoS, 2003). (The Second Penang Strategic Development Plan – 2001 – 2010 and its technical report do not have much data on housing).

Housing Stock

One of the most significant findings in the Draft Report of Survey for the Penang Structure Plan Study 2002-2020, is that there was an oversupply of 70,467 housing units in 2000. More specifically, there were 355,436 housing units to cater to only 284,969 households (2003: 11-19). Furthermore, according to the PSP, as of 2005, the number of housing units in Penang was 470,331, an increase of 114,895 units within five years (2007:2-31).

However, according to NAPIC report, there were only 322,426 residential housing units in Penang in the third quarter of 2008 with another 51,612 units under various stages of construction (Property Stock Report Q3 2008). But NAPIC reports do not have household data. It is possible that the discrepancies are due to the methods of data collection.

Although there are some discrepancies between the two sources of data, it is fair to say that there is no shortage of housing units for the present population. Even to casual observers, many high-rise apartments, especially the high-end ones, are not occupied. In fact, some have as low as 30 per cent occupancy.

Housing for the Lower-income Groups

In a capitalist society, numbers alone do not mean adequate housing. There is the question of affordability. The poor still face the problem of access to adequate housing. In other words, there is still a shortage of low-cost houses and low–medium-cost houses.

More specifically, according to the PSP, out of the five districts in Penang, only the North-east District in Penang Island and Seberang Perai North on the mainland had a shortfall of low-cost housing units in 2007. If the situation still holds true today, there is adequate low-cost housing in the remaining three districts, namely the South-west District on Penang Island, the Seberang Perai Central District and Seberang Perai South Districts, both on the mainland (2007: 2-31). If this is the case, then it does not make sense to continue to require private developers to build more low-cost and low–medium-cost houses in these areas.

Yet the state executive councillor in charge of housing just announced that a RM35 million Public Housing Project would be undertaken on a 4.2ha land worth about RM10 million in Teluk Kumbar, which is in the South-west District on the island. It was also reported that 500 poor households would benefit from the project, with priorities given to those earning RM700 or less per month (The Star, 12.3.09).

There is a serious need for a good information system. Otherwise, it is possible that the needs of the poor may not be met or that resources are allocated for projects that are not really needed.

The issue of shortage of housing for the poor in Penang is puzzling. As early as in 1950s, even before the country achieved independence from Britain, there were efforts by the government to help lower income groups have adequate shelter. More specifically, George Town Municipal Council which eventually evolved into the Penang Island Municipal Council of today began building quarters for its lower-paid workers as early as 1946. Two years later, it also built low-cost houses for sale to the public at $2,775 each (Penang – Past and Present, 1966:86). It then went on to build many housing units to be rented to the poor, such as those in Trengganu Road and Cintra Street. After al-

most half a century, these are still among the most sought-after housing units for the lower income groups.

The Seberang Perai Municipal Council (MPSP) and its predecessor also built low-cost housing units to be sold to the poor. For instance, in 1959, the Butterworth Town Council built low-cost houses in Jalan Mohd Saad costing between $5,000 and $12,000 each.

The Penang State Government has also been building low-cost houses for the poor. They include those in Kampung Melayu, Nordin Street Ghaut, Riffle Range, Kedah Road and recently, in cooperation with the federal government and MPPP, the Lines Road area.

Besides building low-cost houses, the Penang Island Municipal Council (MPPP) has been promoting affordable housing. One of its successful strategies was facilitating private developers to build "low-cost housing units", defined as flats of not more than 700 sq. ft. each. There was no price control and the developers were free to sell to anyone they liked as the size of the flats was judged to be sufficient to restrict prices and discourage rich people from buying them. This policy was judged to be very successful (Goh Ban Lee, 1986).

Housing for the Young Middle-class

While Penang is still grappling with the issue of providing adequate housing for lower income groups, it is clear that the new middle-class, including those in professional and sub-managerial groups, is facing problems of affordability. Existing terrace houses in the popular middle-class residential areas such as Island Glades are selling for above RM600,000 each while those in the vicinity of Glugor and Sungei Dua are not much cheaper. New three-storey houses in George Town, including Jelutong and Glugor, are asking for above RM800,000. Indeed, similar houses in Relau are also asking for these prices!

The mid-management workers and young professionals who are the back-bone of the drive to turn Penang into a developed state have to settle for apartments in high-rise buildings if they want to live on the island. Even then, the asking prices in choice areas are above a million ringgit each and those in middle-class areas are selling at about half this amount. They must be prepared to live in the southern part of the island to find apartments that are below RM250,000 each.

Below is part of a letter from "Steven" that was posted on Lim Kit Siang's blog dated March 23, 2008. Despite the grammatical mistakes, the message is clear.

- I am a regular employee who works for an international company in Penang Bayan Lepas Free Trade Zone Industrial Area.
- I have been working here close to seven years.
- What I notice something seriously is the Penang landed housing property is going up tremendously...
- A quick check on the price is going to above RM600,000 and some could reach millions of dollars. As a result, only the upper income community or foreigners (who wants to utilize MMH2) can purchase these types of properties...
- Nowadays, it has been a trend for Penang housing developers to build luxury houses only, why they never build medium costs houses?

At present, there is no clear policy on this housing issue. There are also no strategies to foster the building of houses for this group of Penangites, although Chief Minister Lim Guan Eng did mention in his opening speech in the recent real estate conference organized jointly by InvestPenang and Seri that he was concerned about the difficulties faced by these people.

Poor Quality of Life in High-rise Apartments

It is clear that more and more Penangites will come to live in high-rise apartments, especially those who prefer to live on the island. In terms of housing issues, the poor quality of life in high-rise apartments is a badly neglected point. Among the problems identified are: lack of cleanliness, leaks, discoloured paintwork and damaged facilities including lifts, corridor lighting, "libraries" and gym rooms (Tiun, 2005). This is surprising as high-rise housing began to appear in the 1960s when the George Town City Council and the Penang State Government began to build low-cost housing for lower-income groups.

Even those who read nothing more than newspapers cannot miss these problems. Below is part of a report in The Star on March 12, 2009 under the heading, "Daily demos if lift problem not settled":

SOME 1,300 residents living in the Ampang Jajar flats in Permatang Pauh, Penang, have threatened to stage daily demonstrations at the state secretariat office in Komtar if the problem of lift breakdowns is not settled within the next 48 hours.

The flats association chairman Mat Fadzil Idris said they had been facing the problem for the past three months and only one of the six lifts in the three-block flats was working.

"We have complained to the state Housing Department for umpteen times but nothing has been done. ....

"Old folk, schoolchildren and pregnant women are the ones who suffer the most from the problem.

"If the problem is not settled within the next two days, we will hold demonstrations at Komtar until it is resolved," he said.

The problems were attended to the next day. Somehow, the state executive councillor in charge of housing was able to find RM230,000 to repair the lifts immediately (The Star, 13.3.09.)

Too little is known about the causes of poor quality housing in high-rise buildings. Incapable management or buildings designed with little understanding of occupant behaviour are possible causes for these problems. It could also be the result of inadequate funds for building management and maintenance.

Having said this, there is no doubt that many Malaysians have not yet learnt to live in high-rise buildings. There are numerous acts of non-compliance with basic house rules essential for living in congested areas. Rules on parking of vehicles are largely ignored. So are rules on use of swimming pools, BBQ appliances, garden benches, game rooms and even the use of lifts.

Deteriorating Housing Estate Conditions

The above statements do not mean that those staying in landed properties lead a first-world quality of life. The failure to upgrade existing residential areas as the country becomes richer is one of the many mysteries in Malaysia. Quality of life should reflect economic growth. Otherwise, it makes little sense to strive for growth.

Unfortunately, the realities on the ground are evidence of a deteriorating quality of life in existing housing estates. In some cases, this is caused by bad development control decisions by the relevant authorities, particularly the local councils. It makes little sense to approve multi-storey buildings, some higher than 20 stories in the vicinity of two-storey buildings without an adequate distance separating them. To make things worse, many of these high-rise apartments do not have adequate car-parks resulting in the residents parking their vehicles at the entrances of landed properties. The ugly Malaysian mentality certainly does not help matters.

It is useful to note that town planning was "invented" more than a century ago. Malaysia, or more specifically the Federated Malay States, adopted town planning as an instrument for developing liveable cities as early as 1920 (Goh Ban Lee, 1991). Today, millions have been spent on town planning and development control. There is no excuse for the deterioration of existing housing conditions as a result of incompatible development.

In some cases, the quality of residential properties has also deteriorated as a result of neighbouring properties undergoing massive renovations. It is common to see two-storey terrace houses being converted into three-storey ones. Some semi-detached houses have been extended so much that the immediate neighbours' houses look like badly constructed bungalow extensions. In most cases, the alterations are illegal. Yet there is seldom any enforcement action. In some cases, renovations and extensions might be legal, but this does not mean that they do not cause a deterioration in the living conditions of neighbours and even the whole neighbourhood.

Then there are cases of change of building use. These range from turning a residential property into a kindergarten to a car-repair workshop. In between are cases of changes into hair-dressing saloons, clinics, sundry shops and even houses of worship. The consequence is a deterioration of the housing quality of the area, with the immediate neighbours paying for it.

There are laws and mechanisms to prosecute these illegal renovations and change of building use. Unfortunately, the local councils have been unable or unwilling to enforce the law. This topic has been discussed in Non-compliance – A Neglected Agenda in Urban Gover-

nance (Goh Ban Lee, 2002). Suffice it to mention here that the situation has not improved in the last seven years or so.

Social Justice in the Distribution of Houses

In a multi-racial society, the distribution of wealth, including ownership of houses, is always an important issue. In Malaysia, where dominant political parties and non-government organisations are race-based, the distribution of ownership of houses among racial groups has been a major concern.

Penang, following the policy established by the federal government, has adopted the practice of requiring developers to reserve 30 per cent of their houses for Bumiputras, defined as Malays and other indigenous peoples. These are also given a five per cent discount on advertised prices.

It is fair to say that most developers have come to accept the conditions because they largely have no choice. Besides, when the policy was first introduced in the early 1970s under the New Economic Policy, developers were told that reserved units could be released to be sold on the open market after a six-month wait from the date of the launching of the schemes and after at least two advertisements had been placed in newspapers.

Over the years, the original conditions have been changed to the extent that they have become obstacles to an efficient housing market. Today, reserved units that are not taken up by Bumiputra buyers are not released until the developers obtain a clearance from a committee. Furthermore, they have to pay into a fund a sum equivalent to 30 per cent of the value of the five per cent discounts when units had been sold to non-Bumiputra buyers.

Since the March 8, 2008 general elections, the process of getting reserved units released has been less agonising. There is less uncertainty. For example, there is no longer a need to negotiate for discounts. But a more tolerable system does not mean a fair one, especially when one talks about social justice.

There is also the question of fairness when a Malaysian whose income is about one-third that of his/her colleagues has to pay full price while the higher income earner is eligible for a five per cent discount. It is not certain whether developers would lower the price of houses if there were to be no discounts for Bumiputras. But these feelings of "unfairness" are not doing society any good.

Housing Agenda from 2010 to 2020

It is clear that there is a need for a new housing agenda for Penang. The recent change of government provides good impetus for adjustments to the status quo. But more importantly, the situation as it is demands change. There is a need for clearer strategies by which to meet policies. The following are some of the more urgent for the next decade.

A Vehicle to Build Houses and Set Standards

The most effective way for the state government to solve housing problems, especially those related to affordability, is for it to have a vehicle, such as a housing board, for building houses. While it is always good to have a vehicle to do things directly, the idea of a board should be treated as an agenda, rather than as a project to be carried out without further deliberations.

The Penang Development Corporation (PDC) is ideally such a vehicle. In the early days of its incorporation in the early 1970s, it was the major mover in the development of housing in areas where the state government wanted to have development.

For instance, to push for the development and popularity of the Bayan Lepas Industrial Zone and the Bayan Lepas Free Trade Zone, the state government also incorporated the development of the Bayan Baru township. Apart from promoting industrialisation, PDC was also tasked with building houses. The first batch of houses built were single-storey terrace houses and single-storey semi-detached houses with prices ranging from about RM18,000 to RM40,000 each in the mid-1970s.

The PDC did not build low-cost housing in the first phase of the project. The terrace houses in Island Glades then were selling for between RM27,000 and RM50,000. Indeed, to attract buyers, the PDC even gave a stove, garbage bin and a choice of a fruit tree to each of the first batch of house buyers. Today, these houses are selling for RM400,000 to RM700,000 each!

The contributions of the PDC in building houses and the successful industrialisation of Penang deserve a book-length documentation. It is clear that the PDC's role has changed substantially. It is a sad reflection of how far things have gone awry when it is building houses costing more than a million ringgit each and selling large chunks of land to other property development companies. While the pros and cons of a board or company to build and manage houses are being considered, the state should not forget that the PDC was able to perform this role rather adequately. It is also useful to remember that the job that Invest-Penang is doing was also part of the portfolio of the PDC.

A Transparent System for Allocating Low-cost Houses

The allocation of low-cost and low–medium-cost houses has been and is done by the State Housing Department (SHD).The system of allocation should be made more efficient and transparent.

Although the workings of the SHD are still not clear, there is no doubt that they could be improved. Some of the ironic sights in Penang have been empty low-cost and low–medium-cost apartment blocks built by the government. Are such delays the result of inefficiency on the part of the housing department in the allocation of houses? Or were the allocations timed to make politicians look good by having pictures of them handing out keys just before the elections? It is also possible that the delays were the result of politicians not wanting to create controversies if the allocations were seen to be unfair. A study of the allocation process is long overdue.

The time is also ripe to review the criteria of eligibility for low-cost housing and low–medium-cost housing. Furthermore, the government should also have a policy on those who repeatedly turn down allocations.

It is important to note that low-cost and low–medium-cost houses built by private developers are also allocated by the SHD. As businessmen, housing developers need to sell their houses quickly. The process for getting a list of names and addresses of buyers can be improved.

Even after getting the list of buyers, there is no guarantee that there will be takers for all available housing units. The rates of rejection of offers are high. This may in part be due to addresses having been changed and not updated, and is not necessarily the fault of the department. The time taken for allocated buyers to respond to the A.R. registered offer letters and the need for a new list of applicants can be considerable. Any rejection or absence of replies also means developers have to go through the process once again.

The most logical solution is to allow the developers themselves to sell their housing units. Unfortunately, not all developers are socially responsible. There have been accusations of developers demanding inordinate amounts for "upgrading" works. It only takes one developer to behave badly for the state government to institute a system that causes problems for everyone. Indeed, almost all the laws and procedures have been instituted because of unethical acts by only a few bad apples. Making things worse, there seems to be a reluctance to punish the guilty parties. Instead, more laws and procedures have been put in place, thus punishing everyone.

There is a serious need to review the queuing system for low-cost and low–medium-cost houses. At the very least, the system should be made transparent. Anyone who applies for these housing units should know his or her position and the expected month of allocation.

The whole system of allocation, including the need for interviews, should be studied. It is tempting to suggest that no one should be allowed to interfere with the queue. But this would be too restrictive. It may be a good thing to allow the state executive councillor in charge of housing to grant certain applicants to jump queue. But such "interference" should be properly recorded and displayed in public notice boards and the department's website. If there are good reasons for queue jumping, there is nothing to hide.

Rental Housing

No matter how efficient the housing industry is, not everyone can afford to buy a house or wants to buy a house at a particular time. There is a need to make the rental housing market a robust one. This should cover all types of housing.

For Penang, if the state government is serious about its slogan of "a roof over every family", there must be provisions for rental housing for the poor. This means there must be housing units that are only for rentals, such as those belonging to the MPPP in Trengganu Road and in Cintra Street.

The very poor have no means by which to buy a flat. Even if it is RM25,000, they may not quality for a loan. For some households, there is no need to secure permanent houses yet. Additionally, there is such a need also for those who are waiting for the allocation of low-cost housing.

A paper on this issue was written long ago. Although the circumstances might have changed, the basic premises for the state government and the local councils maintaining a housing stock for rental purpose are still valid (Goh Ban Lee, 1985).

Improve Development Control

The development control process should be made more transparent and accountable. This could be a factor in the perceived indiscriminate development taking place in Penang. For instance, the deliberations of the OSC should be open to the public, like those of the Appeals Board, with the reasons for or against an application well explained.

It is also clear that the process of making development control plans, namely Structure Plans and Local Plans, needs to be investigated to find a better way to not only formulate them but also get them gazetted as legal documents. For example, there is no real need to gazette the Structure Plan as a legal document. It is too general in nature. It should only provide the basis for the making of Local Plans which should be gazetted as legal documents.

At present, it is clear that the whole process of making development control plans is very complicated and difficult. The fact is that after more than 30 years since the enactment of the Town and Country Planning Act in 1976, the state has only two Structure Plans and a few Local Plans in small areas in Penang. If development projects were held back waiting for these plans, Penangites would be in serious trouble today.

There is also an urgent need to study and review the development control standards and guidelines. Many of the standards and guidelines were formulated many years ago, and no longer apply to a drastically changed Penang. The standards and guidelines must also change, both to suit current realities and also to promote the implementation of new development ideologies, such as the promotion of sustainability.

For instance, there is a need for a review of the provision of car-parks. At present, the rules only require one car-park for each housing unit in high-rise buildings. The provisions for car parks for low-cost housing units are lower.

However, any casual observation will show that this is clearly inadequate. As a result, cars are parked along road sides, despite the no-parking signs and the yellow lines. Furthermore, in many cases, the cars are parked along roads in housing estates in such a way that a two-lane road has become one lane, thus causing problems to nearby residents and even to the apartment dwellers.

There is, of course, no necessity to make it mandatory for provisions for more car-parks. There are cities, such as Tokyo, that require those who want to own cars to show proof that they possess car-parks or have rented them. However, it should also be noted that in such cities, the public transportation system is excellent.

There have also been calls for a review of density control and the mechanics of calculations. On the one hand, housing developers are pushing for higher density. On the other, critics of recent development projects are calling for higher standards and stricter development control. A total review of density control and height control are urgently needed.

More specifically, the current rules that govern units per hectare yet fail to be strict in their specifications on building heights, appear to be inadequate. It has led to the development of very tall buildings with large housing units, some as big as 600 sq. m. each. It has also led to very haphazard urban design with high-rise buildings everywhere.

There is also a need to ensure that the local councils enforce compliance with land use and intensify the use of guidelines and rules. Too many buildings are allowed to be extended or undergo change of use without action being taken against the owners. As a result, the quality of many existing housing areas has deteriorated. The whole question of non-compliance with municipal rules and regulations should be studied to find policies and strategies to ensure compliance and improve the quality of housing in existing housing areas.

(The call for a review of development control standards and the making of development control plans, however, is predicated on a much improved town planning. So far, there have been serious ques-

tions about the quality of the development control plans, such as the PSP and the Kuala Lumpur City Plan 2020. See Goh Ban Lee, The Sun, Aug. 26, 2008; Sept. 23, 2008).

From Quantity to Quality

The housing policy should shift from promoting quantity to quality, especially for houses catering to lower income groups. Indeed, the recent challenge issued by Chief Minister Lim Guan Eng to housing developers to improve the quality of houses for the lower income groups has set the tone (The Star, 26.5.09). But housing developers do not operate in a vacuum. They are guided by planning standards and by-laws. While there have been some modifications, the definition of low-cost housing is about 30 years old and that of low–medium-cost about 15. It is time to review the criteria and definition of these types of housing.

There is also a need to improve the quality of housing in high rise apartments. The parliament finally passed the Building and Common Property (Management and Maintenance) Act in 2007 to institute a systematic procedure in the management and maintenance of properties with strata land titles. It also provides for the creation of a Commissioner of Buildings (CoB) to ensure that the Joint Management Body (JMB) or Management Coroporation (JB) that manages a high-rise building performs according to the law. The CoB is also charged with the power to ensure that the JMB or JB maintains proper accounts and property owners fulfil their obligations.

Making the presidents of the two municipal councils CoBs was a wrong move and the state government should hold talks with the Minister of Housing and Local Government to reconsider this decision (The Sun, Aug. 12, 2008).

Penang can play a role by spending some time on making the CoB more effective. For instance, the task of a CoB could be more than waiting for complaints from the residents. There is a need for pro-action. This means that the CoB should draw up programmes and activities to teach those living in high-rise buildings on the roles and responsibilities of living such places.

Fair Distribution of Houses

The state government has to address the question of fairness in the current housing policies and strategies.

While there is no doubt that the poor and the lower income groups have benefited from many programmes to build low cost and low–medium-cost houses, there is the question of consistency and commitment. For instance, it makes little sense that the repainting of blocks of flats in Taman Tun Sardon has been left half done since the March 8, 2008 general elections. Many blocks are left with two walls having fresh yellow and orange colour paint while the other two have been left unpainted. There appears to be too much politics and too little social justice in helping the lower income groups attain better housing conditions.

It is also time to review the effectiveness of the policy and the strategies to improve property ownership of Bumiputra. The effects of this policy on the housing industry should also be of concern. Rehda has made some concrete proposals. For instance, it proposed that discounts should only be given for properties below RM250,000 each. Apparently, some federal government leaders have also broached the idea of scrapping the discounts for properties costing RM500,000 and above (Chua Tee Yong, 2009).

There is also a need to ensure that the mechanism for getting clearance to sell the unsold Bumiputra units is clear and the decision making process transparent and accountable. The payments for the release of reserved units should also be reviewed. At the very least, there should be a mechanism to let the public know how much has been collected from the developers and how the monies have been spent to help Bumiputras improve their housing conditions.

Gated Communities

Gated communities are getting popular in Malaysia. In Penang, a few schemes have been built and some existing housing enclaves have been turned into "guarded communities", meaning building illegal guard houses with boom–gates have been erected.

The main reason for the growing popularity of gated communities is security, although the preference for well-maintained facilities also plays a part.

However, some social scientists have raised the fear that gated communities are symbols of elitism and social exclusion. Furthermore, they are also antithetical to liveable cities where access, especially for pedestrians, is paramount. By building walls and gates, gated communities create obstacles. Since some gated communities can be relatively large, this can cause problems of access. Indeed, gated communities of 20 acres can cause problems for pedestrians who have to circumnavigate the walls to get from one place to another.

Even if the state government does not want to ban gated communities, there is a need to draw up guidelines to regulate them. For example, they must not be bigger than 15 acres each. Furthermore, existing housing estates must be prevented from building illegal guard houses on road reserves and having boom-gates across public roads.

Having stated the above, the state government and the local councils should be aware of the need for safer cities. There should be a more serious effort to implement the steps recommended by the National Council for Local Government to foster safer cities.

Conclusion

Periodically, state and local government leaders, property developers, professionals involved in housing development and maintenance and non-governmental organisations must take stock of the effects and efficacy of existing housing policies, strategies, standards and guidelines. Are they getting the results expected? Do they need changes or modifications? Can they be improved to make them more effective in making housing situations better? Do they need to be amended to suit the changing development ideology? Has the social justice ideal been neglected?

Hopefully, this paper points to certain areas that should be on the agenda when the questions above are answered.

Acknowledgement

The writer wishes to thank En. Mohd Firdaus for his insightful contributions to this paper.

Appendixes

Box 1 Housing policy statements from Penang Structure Plan 2020.

DS28	Pembangunan Perumahan Yang Berkualiti Akan Teru Disediakan. Bersesuaian. Dengan Permintaan Penduduk.
DS29	Agensi Awam dan swasta Akan Digalakkan Terlibat Dalam Penyediaan Perumahan Mampu Milik.
DS30	Pembangunan Perumahan Hanya Akan Dibenarkan DiKawasan-Kawasan Yang Telah Dikenalpasti.
DS31	Pemajuan Perumahan Akan Dilaksanakan Dengan Segera Setelah Kelulusan Kebenaran Merancang Diperolehi.
DS32	Pembangunan Perumahan Kos Rendah Dan Kos Sedarhana Rendah Akan Dilaksanakan Menepati Garis Panduan Yang Telah Ditetapkan.
DS33	Perkampungan Tradisional Dan Perkampungan Dalam Bandar Akan Dikekalkan dan Prasarana Dinaiktaraf.
DS34	Merancang dan Membangunakan Semula Kawasan Setinggan Seiring Dengan Matlamat Setinggan Sifar Di Atas Tanah Kerajaan Menjelang Tahun 2010.
DS35	Penyediaan Kemudahan Masyarakat Yang Berkualiti Akan Dipertingkatkan Bagi Memenuhi Keperluan Penduduk
DS36	Penyediaan Kemudahan Pendidikan Dari Peringkat Asas Sehingga ke Peringkat Tertiari Akan Diperting-

katkan Selaras Dengan Falsafah Pendidikan Sepanjang Ayat.

DS37   Penyediaan Kemudahan Kesihatan Yang Mencukupi dan Berkualiti Akan Disediakan Berdasarkan Piawaian dan Keperluan Penduduk.

DS38   Penyediaan Kemudahan Kebajikan Akan Disediakan Mengikut Keperluan Kumpulan Sasar Seperti Orang - Orang Tua, Anak – Anak Yatim, Kanak – Kanak

dan Orang Kurang Upaya.

DS39   Penyediaan Perkhidmatan Keselamatan Seperti Polis, dan Balai Bomba Akan Disediakan Mengikut Keper- luan dan Unjuran Yang Ditetapkan.

DS40   Penyediaan Perkhidmatan Pos Akan Disediakan Bagi Memenuhi Keperluan Penduduk.

DS41   Kawasan Lapang Yang Berpotensi Akan Diwartakan Sebagai Kawasan Rekreasi Awam.

DS42   Penyediaan Kemudahan Keagamaan Yang Terancang dan Mencukupi Akan Disediakan Selaras Dengan Pen- ingkatan Penduduk dan Keperluan Piawaian Perancan- gan.

Source: PSP 2020 (p xviii)

Box 2   Example of strategies for housing policy DS28

Menyediakan keperluan tambahan unit perumahan sebanyak 185,000 unit sehingga tahun 2020 dengan purata penyediaan sebanyak 12,300 unit setahun.

Menetapkan harga yang mampu dimiliki dalam mencapai sasaran pemilikan perumahan berdasarkan jenis, saiz dan lokasi dan dikawal selaras dengan Dasar Perumahan Negara dan Negeri.

Menyediakan unit – unit perumahan yang mempunyai saiz yang bersesuaian serta menepati keperluan golongan kurang upaya.

Penentuan had ketumpatan dan nisbah plot pembangunan akan diperincikan di dalam Rancangan Tempatan dan Rancangan Kawasan Khas atau oleh pihak berkuasa perancang tempatan berkaitan.

Memperkukuh dan memperluaskan sistem pangkalan data maklumat perumahan yang disediakan oleh NAPIC (National Property Information Centre) bagi mengintegrasikan semua maklumat atau data – data mengenai hartanah perumahan di Negeri Pulau Pinang termasuk maklumat setinggan dan pemilikanhartanah.

Menggalakkan pemilik hartanah menyertai program pemuliharaan dan pembaharuan bandar melalui Agensi Pemuliharaan dan Pembaharuan bandar, melaksanakan program bantuan untuk penduduk miskin yang terlibat.

Menyediakan pembangunan perumahan mengikut kumpulan sasaran dengan mensyaratkan peruntukan sekurang – kurangnya 30% daripada rumah – rumah yang dibina dalam skim – skim perumahan baru dijual dan diberi keutamaan kepada kaum Bumiputera khususnya di kalangan kumpulan berpendapatan rendah.

Membina rumah kos rendah dan sederhana rendah juga perlu

mengambilkira citarasa masyarakat setempat yang lebih ber-
minat kepada rumah jenis landed.

Menetapkan had pendapatan yang melayakkan pemohon untuk memiliki perumahan kos rendah dan kos sederhana rendah
dinaikkan masing – masing kepada RM 2,500 dan RM 3,500
dan had umur pemohon yang layak memohon perumahan juga
digalakkan supaya diturunkan dari 21 tahun (semasa) kepada
18tahun.

Menyediakan pembangunan perumahan mengikut kumpulan sasaran dengan memberi keutamaan mengikut kumpulan
sasaran melalui penyediaan bekalan rumah kos rendah dan
sederhana rendah yang mencukupi.

Meningkatkan bekalan perumahan kos rendah dan sederhana
rendah melalui penawaran insentif yang lebih baik kepada
pemaju.

Membenarkan fleksibiliti bagi rekabentuk rumah kos rendah
dan rumah kos sederhana rendah untuk disesuaikan dengan
komposisi masyarakat yang terdiri daripada warga emas, ibu
tunggal, golongan orang kurang upaya (OKU) dan lain –lain.

Source: PSP 2020 (pp.4-63)

References

Agrawal, Pramod. "Two decades of low-cost public housing in
    Penang: a critical appraisal". Universiti Sains Malaysia,
    1978.

Atkinson, Rowland and Flint, John. "Fortress UK? Gated Com-
    munities, the spatial revolt of the elites and time-space
    trajectories of segregation". Keynote paper presented at
    the conference entitled Gated Communities: Building So-
    cial Division or Safer Communities. Glasgow, 18-19 Sept.
    2003.

Blendy, Sarah and Lister, Diane. "Gated communities: (ne)gating community development?" Paper presented at the conference on Gated Communities: Building Social Division or Safer Communities, 18-19 Sept. 2003, Glasgow.

Cheah, S. C. "Gated community getting popular". *The Star*, 13 September 2004.

Chua Tee Yong. "How about property liberalization?" *Malaysian Insider*, 4 May 2009.

Ernawati Mustafa Kamal. "Dissertation, Corak pemajuan perumahan oleh pemaju swasta di Pulau Pinang". Universiti Sains Malaysia, 2004.

Goh Ban Lee. "Housing Delivery System: An Academician's Perspective". In *Housing the Nation: A Definitive Study. Cagamas*, 1997.

Goh Ban Lee. "Rental Housing - The Forgotten Shelter". Paper presented at the Seminar on Shelter Housing in Penang, organised by Parti Gerakan Rakyat Malaysia. KOMTAR, 11 Aug. 1985.

Goh Ban Lee. "Penang structure plan report of housing study", Pulau Pinang: Pusat Penyelidikan Dasar, Universiti Sains Malaysia, 1986.

Goh Ban Lee. "Housing in Penang State: Towards Sufficiency in Human Settlement". Paper presented at the Seminar-cum-Workshop on Housing in Penang State, organised by the Housing Bureau of Parti Gerakan Rakyat Malaysia. Penang, 21 August 1988.

Goh Ban Lee. "The Effects of Recent Urban Planning Policies on the Real Estate Market". Paper presented at the Third Real Estate Convention on the Malaysian Real Estate market - Emerging Trends, organised by the Institute of Surveyors. Subang, 1-2 November 1988.

Goh Ban Lee. "Access to Land and Housing in Asia/Pacific: Towards Some Solutions - The Case of Penang, Malaysia". Paper presented at the XVII Pacific Science Congress: Towards the Pacific Century - The Challenge of Change. Honolulu, 27 May - 2 June 1991.

Goh Ban Lee. "A Critical Review of Government Policies on Affordable Housing in Malaysia". Paper presented at the Conference on Affordable Housing - New Concepts, Ap-

proaches and Challenges Towards the Year 2000, organised by the Housing Developers Association. Kuala Lumpur, 7-8 October 1991.

Goh Ban Lee. "Privatisation of Housing Industry - issues and Challenges". Paper presented in ISIS-HIID Seminar on Implications of Privatization on the Housing Industry, organised by the Institute of Strategic and International Studies. Kuala Lumpur, 20 February 1993.

Goh Ban Lee. "Housing In Malaysia - Inadequacy in the Midst of Plenty". Paper presented at the National Housing Conference, organised by the Institute of International and Strategic Studies (ISIS). Kuala Lumpur, May 1997.

Goh Ban Lee. "Non-compliance – A Neglected Agenda in Urban Governance". Skudai:Institute Sultan Iskandar of Urban Habitat and Highrise. 2002.

Goh Ban Lee. "Seeking security in gated enclaves". *The Sun*, 5 July 2005.

Gurjit Singh. "Up close and personal with gated and guarded communities". In *Property Times, New Straits Times*, 30 July 2005.

Lee Lik Meng. "Study of financial contributions imposed on housing development in Penang State: final report December 1986". Persatuan Pemaju Perumahan Malaysia, Penang. 1986.

Marina Emmanuel. "Affordable housing for all in Penang", *New Straits Times*, 26 May 2003.

Marina Emmanuel. "Call to scale down Penang high-rise projects". *Business Times*, 2009.

Mahazir Ismail. "Pengagihan dan Pembekalan Perumahan di Pulau Pinang" Dissertation. Universiti Sains Malaysia. 1998.

Mak, K. W. "Debate continues on gated community". *The Star*, 28 August 2004.

Noor Liza Hasan. "Measuring housing customers satisfaction: a case study of Penang Development Corporation (PDC)". Dissertation. Universiti Sains Malaysia. 2003.

Nurwati Badarulzaman. "The prospect of Housing Market in Seberang Perai, Penang". 1998 <http://www.hbp.usm.my/

methods/Research/methodhousing.html> (accessed 5 May 2009.

Repass, James. "Gated Communities are enemies of democracy". Providence Journal, 21 July 2006.

Salleh Buang. "Walls that exclude". *Property Times, New Straits Times*, 6 March 2004.

Salleh Buang. "The lure of 'Privatopia'". *Property Times, New Straits Times*, 15 October 2005.

Steven. "Penang housing development". In Lim Kit Siang's blog, <http://blog.limkitsiang.com/2008/03/23/penang-housing-development-comment/> 2009.

Tan, Bernard. "Gated communities – the concept and vision". Paper presented at the Seminar on Gated Community Schemes, organised by The Dept. of Lands and Mines. Kuala Lumpur, 15-16 Sept. 2003.

Timmer, Vanessa and Seymoar, Nola-Kate. "The Livable City". Published paper. International Centre for Sustainable Cities. Vancouver, 2005.

Yong, Chai Seng. "Proses pembangunan perumahan dipihak swasta : kajian kes di Pulau Pinang". Universiti Sains Malaysia, 1984.

Yeoh, Mooi Mooi. "Residents' satisfaction on low cost housing in Penang". Universiti Sains Malaysia. 2004.

New Straits Times. "Shock find of car workshop in midst of food outlets". 4 April 2002.

The Star (Metro). "Quiet neighbourhood not without its problems". 11 May 2004.

The Sunday Star. "Incidence of poverty a hard problem to tackle". 25 April 2004.

The Malay Mail. "Temple by day and nightclub by night". 31 August 1999.

The Sun. "CoB appointments on council should be full time". 12 August 2008.

The Sun. "Housing quota questioned". 29 October 2007.

The Star. "Housing evolution". 26 May 2009.

[7]

Some Thoughts on Private Higher Education in Penang

Sin I-Lin

Introduction

Attracting tertiary-level students has long been the objective of Penang and this is no exception for the relatively newly-minted state government. Similar to state governments of the past, the present one has the broad aim of positioning Penang as a centre for educational excellence in the region, country and within the larger global education marketplace. What remains unclear, though, is the specific policy stance, goals and intended outcomes of the Penang state administration in its move to build a higher education hub. The purpose of this working paper is to propose questions and strategic directions that the state government should pay attention to when seeking improvements to the private higher education landscape in Penang. This paper is only a start to what is hoped will contribute to a drafting of a comprehensive framework against which various relevant parties can refer to in formulating and evaluating policy directions, measures and standards related to the promotion of private higher education in Penang.

Context

Penang is a relatively small spatial unit of 1030 square kilometres with a population (including foreign nationals) of about 1.56 million (SERI 2009). Its key challenge arises from its high population density but limited land area and natural resources. As such, Penang's strength lies in its large educated, English-speaking population, although human capital has to be constantly nurtured and developed in order to meet the needs and demands of a changing economy and society.

The state houses a number of leading and well-established primary and secondary schools in the country, as well as reputable international schools and a public university which is accorded the Accelerated Program for Excellence (APEX) status, that is, identified by a national selection committee to have the best potential to be of world-class standard. Previous and present Penang state governments alike see the importance in improving and extending quality education beyond these traditional sites of study, most notably, to the burgeoning private higher education sector.

Private higher education is a rapidly growing industry in Malaysia, the marketing of which can and has contributed to significant amounts of revenue for the country. The commoditisation and expansion of private higher education is enabled by liberalizing policies aimed at addressing three primary issues of concern: one, the local unmet demand for a wide range of higher education choices; two, the lack of government resources to efficiently provide more educational seats, infrastructure, services and facilities; and three, the shortage of higher level human capital to fuel an emergent knowledge-based economy (Lee 2004). Malaysia has some 452 registered private higher learning institutions (including branch campuses of foreign universities), out of which a mere 6% (or 30 institutions) or so are located in Penang (MoHE 2009). This is in contrast to 24% in Kuala Lumpur (KL) and 25% in Selangor (MoHE 2009). There are a couple of branch campuses of prominent out-of-state private higher learning institutions (PHEIs) in Penang and a host of smaller institutions which operate solely within the state. Penang has no foreign university branch campuses.

Private higher education at the state level largely comes under the purview of the Federal Government which closely regulates the sector in areas such as institutional licensing, standard and quality assurance, course provision and accreditation, the medium of instruction and compulsory subjects (Lee 2004). The setting up of branch campuses by foreign universities is upon invitation by the central government. State development plans for education are restricted by budget limitations and heavy dependence on federal allocations for development expenditure. Given the strong intervention of the Federal Government in the private higher education market at state and national levels, a question arises as to how much room is left for states in the development of their respective academic markets. A related question is, with numerous resource and regulatory constraints, what are the key areas of concern and practical strategies for states interested in building those markets?

Previous Directions and Concerns

In policy discourse, the benefits of constructing a centre of excellence for private higher education has often been tied to the potential income revenue it will generate and the trickle-down effects it will have on the state's economy. Accordingly, the performance of the PHEIs is viewed largely in terms of economic competitiveness in various levels of markets seeking educational consumers (Tan 2006; SERI 2005a). Apart from retaining students from the state, Penang is known to aspire to become a preferred study destination for inter-state and international students. Hence, the outward migration of tertiary-age Penang students, particularly to Selangor, KL and overseas is deemed worrying (Tan 2006; SERI 2005a). What has also been of concern is that despite increased provision of educational choices, Penang has not been able to attract substantial numbers of students from other states, apart from the Northern region (SERI 2005a). Its private tertiary student population lacks the diverse demographic profile characteristic of education markets which incorporate a global, cosmopolitan identity.

Previously, efforts to expand and internationalize the private higher education sector have seen the state government, especially through the Penang Education Consultative Council (PECC) and with the Socio-economic and Environmental Research Institute (SERI) as its secretariat, organize and participate in education exhibitions in other states of Malaysia and in potential student markets such as China, Indonesia and South Korea. The success or failure of such initiatives is not known, although the slow growth, if any, of student enrolments at the PHEIs in recent years is suggestive that Penang has not made its mark as an attractive study destination.

State governments in Penang traditionally assume a complementary role in higher education, facilitating peripheral training and educational activities while leaving high-cost and longer term educational projects and programmes to the central government (Lee 2004). Despite limited jurisdiction, there are key areas in which the state government can and should intervene to ensure better provision and evaluation of

quality private higher education in the state. The following sections of this paper deal with these areas.

Catch Phrases and Buzz Words

There are many positive catchwords and phrases used in policy discourse to describe what Penang envisions to be: a "model of excellence in education", a "success in the education service", a regional, national and international "knowledge hub", a "centre of educational excellence" where "quality", "world class education" is attainable, to name a few (Penang State Education Department 2009; SERI 2005a; Penang State Executive Committee for Education, Economic Planning and Information 1996). When marketing Penang private higher education, bold statements asserting that Penang is indeed a "hub for excellent international education" have been used (SERI undated). However, these glossy descriptions are vague and lack in specifics on how private higher education in Penang is or heading to become all that has been proclaimed.

Reference to a "hub" or "centre" carries different meanings. At the regional level, it could mean positioning Penang to be the core of educational development and activities in the Northern region of Malaysia. Extended further, it could mean making Penang a prominent study destination in the South East Asian or Asian region. At the more modest national level, it points to a plan to enhance Penang's potential to become the leading private higher education provider in the country, matching or surpassing Kuala Lumpur and Selangor as the dominant academic centre. The most ambitious level would be to strategically engineer the state to be an international academic powerhouse within the global education marketplace. While marketing at the international level is ideally the education development plan for Penang, and for that matter, Malaysia, it is perhaps important not to be fecklessly optimistic about what can be done within a short time to transform the private higher education landscape.

Recommendations

What should be of immediate focus is to operationalize concepts and set out a collection of reliable indicators against which high quality education and excellence can be measured. The priority should be not as much to achieve final outcomes as to continue improving the quality and standards of private higher education. Definitions of a high quality centre of excellence in education should include the following criteria:

- have credible PHEIs which collectively, have the capability and capacity to offer a diverse and flexible range of programmes at different levels and modes and at a relatively affordable cost
- have highly skilled human capital with appropriate academic and professional qualifications and experience in teaching, administration and research
- have efficient and effective infrastructure, facilities and support services to create a conducive learning and working environment
- produce employable, creative and flexible graduates who have competent technical knowledge and soft skills

This is, of course, not an exhaustive list but should cover the fundamental areas for Penang to work on.

A common recommendation to expand the base of skilled human resources in Penang comes in two basic forms (SERI 2005a; 2005b; 2004; DCT Consulting Services 1997): 1) encourage PHEIs to increase the types and modes of industry-relevant courses, so as to attract and retain more talents; 2) promote the growth of more institutions to cater to the varying interests, preferences and financial capabilities of educational consumers. While widening access and increasing the number of students as potential knowledge workers is a laudable economic and social justice goal, there is a need to remember that Penang is a small state and there is only so much that it can do to play host to inter-state and overseas students. Limited affordable middle-class housing and commensurate jobs to apply upgraded skills particularly in the declining manufacturing sector are issues faced by present students and young graduates in the state. It would be a misguided policy to expand the private higher education market without first thinking deeply of its implications on the already stiff competition for livelihood in Penang.

For the limited space it has, it might be said that Penang has quite an impressive number of PHEIs, but perhaps too many offering duplicate courses (SERI 2005b). Institutions are mostly small in size and in student numbers. A study of the facility profile of PHEIs in Penang in

2004 (SERI 2004) revealed that the majority operated in rented premises and buildings (60%) and had no more than 250 students (64%). Many did not have the capacity to provide hostel accommodation, transportation and extended services to students.

The state government should play facilitator and provider to:

• encourage and stress the importance of institutions delivering all round, relevant and up-to-date courses, focusing on areas of strength

In discourses on the knowledge-based economy, higher education is regarded as an important tool in packaging workers with specific high-end knowledge, skills and creativity to meet the demands of a rising new economy (Brown and Hesketh 2004). A knowledge-intensive labour market requires individuals to be not just recipients of knowledge, but also to be self-motivated agents managing their own learning and applying what they know to produce efficient and innovative results. The knowledge worker is one who is competent in both hard and soft skills. PHEIs play an important role in developing graduates for suitable employment and it has to be stressed on them the need to at all times offer and deliver balanced, comprehensive and up-to-date education to respond to the shifting needs of the economy. It is essential for PHEIs to link up with various industries and sectors to enable practical training for students.

The appointment, probation and appraisal of academic staff should be based on their abilities to demonstrate up-to-date expertise and experience in teaching and researching their subject areas, in addition to professionalism and commitment to achieve and maintain high standards of learning for students. Professional developmental support has to be given to enable staff to fully contribute to the desired objectives. The recent decision by the Tertiary Education Committee of the PECC (2009) to organize workshops and seminars to enhance academic staff learning is an example of how the state government can facilitate knowledge sharing among the academic community in Penang. Initial workshops and seminars to be conducted by staff of PHEIs with appropriate specialization will touch on academic writing, and assessment and evaluation in education. This will be followed by other relevant topics when the need arises.

It has been brought up many times before in various reports and sites of discussion that instead of competing against each other, PHEIs ought to work together to market the Penang education brand (SERI 2004; DCT Consulting Services 1997; Penang State Executive Committee for Education, Economic Planning and Information 1996). The institutions have to reduce the duplication of courses and specialize in different areas of strength. This will allow them to utilize their resources more efficiently and to quickly build up their reputation in those select areas. Partnerships between local institutions and the merging of smaller entities into bigger units will enable PHEIs in Penang to draw from a larger pool of educational resources such as a wider reference collection to better provide for their students and staff.

The reality of competitiveness of PHEIs in Malaysia is such that institutions gain more credibility among students, parents and employers when they have strong partnerships and affiliations with leading learning and training institutions of advanced Western countries. As such, a short to medium-term strategy for PHEIs is to establish and strengthen collaborations and links with reputable overseas Western institutions to provide reputable quality programmes of international standards. This is not to ignore the need to localise content and delivery appropriately to ensure local relevance and to meet the interests of students seeking a unique Penang study experience. Dependence on overseas institutions for franchise, twinning, advanced standing and joint venture programmes, however, raises the question of whether PHEIs in the long run will be able to move from peripheral positions to the core of the global knowledge production system. In the long term, it is necessary to develop at least one private academic and research-intensive institution which has good potential to contribute to the global production of knowledge in its areas of specialization.

Private higher education has to be more inclusive, particularly with respects to the distribution of learning opportunities for less academically inclined individuals. To this end, further development of a dual sector private higher education system in Penang is required to equally provide academic-based education focused on teaching and research, and a skills-based one emphasizing vocational education and training. The state government represents an important medium to communicate these ideas.

- Promote the formation of niche areas in the Penang education brand

The respective strengths that the institutions build up on could develop into distinct niches that will help carve out the Penang education brand. Penang faces stiff competition from KL, Selangor and other emerging or traditional education markets all claiming in some way or another to offer value for money world-class education, a vibrant entertainment and social scene and a unique, international experience. Positioning Penang as an attractive study destination does not mean playing catch up to the bigger markets by increasing the number of higher learning institutions and by duplicating the range of courses available, nor does it mean reconstructing the physical and cultural landscape to be bigger, better and brighter than the rest. Moreover, the issue of concern should not be about how Penang can retain its students and at the same time, steal the market share of inter-state and international students who would normally choose to study in KL and Selangor. Penang is not and should not aim to be a second KL or Selangor. For obvious reasons such as a bigger population and being the most developed region of the country, KL and Selangor will always have higher tertiary-level student enrolments and a more diverse student population. On the other hand, Penang will continue to attract a large proportion of inter-state students from the northern states, naturally due to its geographical proximity. This should not be seen as worrisome as it actually represents Penang's comparative advantage in the Northern market.

The real issue on the agenda is to identify and solidify areas in which Penang can specialize and, at the same time, contribute to a network of higher education hubs that will collectively boost knowledge creation in the South East Asian region and beyond. Penang should continue to maximize on its strengths in for example, manufacturing, tourism, information communications technology and logistics and tap into new niche areas such as professional development, the trades, and arts and culture. When reputational capital is built and the necessary infrastructure, facilities and services are in place, students from various locales will come. However, despite the best efforts to make Penang more attractive, the search for adventure and independent living away from parents, for example, will likely motivate some young adult Penangites to move out of the state, at least temporarily. The outflow of these students can be counterbalanced by the in-migration of out-of-state and overseas students.

- actively create appropriate jobs for the expanding pool of knowledgeable workers

A strong incentive to entice locals to return to Penang upon completing their studies elsewhere is to have suitable job opportunities available. This applies to out-of-state students in Penang who can be encouraged to remain and participate in the state economy. While ideally, every worker with an advanced level of education and training will be able to utilize their specialized knowledge in a tertiary-level job, realistically, not everyone will be able to engage in actual knowledge work. Massification of higher education has brought about an oversupply of highly qualified job candidates in a congested market not ready to absorb a high proportion into managerial and professional positions. The state government has to actively work to enhance the employability of the workforce, particularly by reducing the mismatch between supply and demand of skilled knowledge workers. When declaring intentions to develop a certain niche area, it is crucial to follow through with the plan within an acceptable timeframe, so as not to mislead students and parents into choosing courses with bleak employment prospects.

- ensure there are sufficient and appropriate accommodation for students, particularly for those from abroad and other states

Private and rental housing, particularly on the island, is relatively scarce and not cheap. It would be demanding and unrealistic to place expectations on the PHEIs, especially the smaller scale ones, to obtain accommodation premises to house students. Yet, nearby and affordable living arrangements are greatly required by students, more so if they are from overseas and out of state. One possible way to improve the availability of student housing is for the state government to assist in acquiring several flat or apartment units at strategic locations. Rent should be kept at an affordable rate. The government has to work closely with the PHEIs, private agencies, developers and neighbourhood housing associations to identify and allocate areas suitable for student living. This may well call for the setting up of a free central-

ized online database system to facilitate students in their search for suitable accommodation. Home owners and housing agents who are willing to offer their service without commission will be allowed to add rental postings. The state government will have to enforce certain guidelines to ensure that the premises meet minimal health and safety standards and that they cater for a variety of living arrangement needs while not compromising the needs of the local neighbourhoods. In the event that demand for government or institution-provided housing exceeds supply, a guarantee of accommodation is to be given to only new first-year full-time students who are not usually resident in Penang. An accommodation guarantee is common in most universities in the United Kingdom whereby new full-time undergraduates and postgraduates from outside the European Union are given top priority in places at university halls and residences.

Ultimately, though, private developers should be convinced of the viability of a market in accommodation for students and young working adults. Certain waivers can be given by the state government, but the financing, building, allocation and maintenance of the units will essentially be left to the developers. Partnerships between PHEIs and the developers should be encouraged where developers provide affordable rental housing while the PHEIs offer rental guarantee.

• Improve public transportation system

It cannot be assumed that every student has easy access to private transportation by which to   commute around Penang. This is especially so for out-of-state and overseas students. Even if such access is available, it is likely to pose a significant cost to the student budget. As such, Penang has to be a student-friendly city with a safe, reliable and highly accessible public transportation system in place. Buses which form the main form of transport in the state should service areas in which students would regularly go to, such as the place of study and the main sites for leisure and entertainment. Services ought to have extended journey times during the morning and evening peaks. Apart from that, all bus stops should include a proper waiting area with benches, lighting and roof shelters. More importantly, they should have a display of the name of the stop, a map of the bus stop location and the surrounding area, operator names, bus numbers and enquiry telephone numbers, fare and zone structures, detailed and up-to-date information on routes, first and last bus timings and bus intervals, and, emergency help numbers. Furthermore, user-friendly websites have to be designed to provide convenient and accurate information on bus services. In addition, concessions should be considered for registered students at PHEIs. With good and affordable public transportation, students and the larger Penang population will be more mobile and less reliant on private vehicles.

- Encourage the setting up of a one-stop education centre, along the lines of organizations such as IDP Education Australia and the British Council

Attracting students to come has to be accompanied by a genuine commitment to provide accurate information and support services to them. While PHEIs are likely to have their own student support section, having a one-stop education centre where present and prospective students could obtain free general information, career counselling and professional advice on anything to do with studying in Penang is worth considering. For an example, the centre could offer impartial information on the various programmes and courses offered by the PHEIs and link up interested students, parents and sponsors with the respective institutions. Information could also be disseminated on an easy-to-find centralized website. The centre could also administer the free centralized online accommodation database system proposed earlier.

Private tertiary-level students, whether home or international, contribute more than just income revenue to the state. They add vibrant character and diversity to the social and cultural fabric of Penang. Providing them with a central platform to interact and exchange views and experiences through classes, outings and community engagement activities will encourage their personal development and further sociocultural contributions to the state. The one-stop centre could function as a basic get together place where interested students and graduates of various PHEIs could meet in occasional continuing education or hobby classes such as creative writing, cooking and dance. Joint food, sports and volunteering outings with students and alumni members of public higher learning institutions are further examples of activities that can be organized. Fees have to be kept at a minimum. PHEIs with more fa-

cilities and resources may already have a wide range of extra-curricular activities running, but for institutions that do not, their students and alumni members will greatly benefit from these social bridging and bonding activities. The activities may help break down stereotypes attached to students and graduates of different institutions and foster better social interaction and understanding among individuals of various cultures and socio-demographic profiles. This, together with housing and transportation, may seem like secondary issues to work on, but it is the very small, fundamental issues that if properly addressed, will significantly raise the quality of life of students and workers in Penang. The state will then emerge as a more attractive destination to live, study, work and play in.

Towards a Comprehensive Private Higher Education Strategy

There is a pressing need for the state government to go into details and spell out, among other things, its specific policy purpose with regard to building a private higher-education hub, the scope of the policy, terms of reference, possible action plans, their likely implications, methodology for research and consultation, the cost and timeline for implementation and the indicators by which progress can be monitored and the impact assessed. Monitoring and reviewing the state and quality of private higher education in Penang has to be conducted on an ongoing basis involving systematic research and consultation incorporating the views and input from various participants in the education scene. This has been done to a certain extent, although perhaps lacking in follow through and rigour. At present, institutional profile questionnaires are administered by PECC to the management of PHEIs only when funding is available. As the PHEIs are not bound by statutory obligation to complete the questionnaires, non-response from several institutions pose limitations to the completeness of data collected. The benefits of achieving full response rates have to be understood by the PHEIs. Essentially, the state government has to ensure that adequate funding is allocated to build a comprehensive and reliable ongoing database covering all aspects of private higher education in Penang. Only when clear policy direction and good quality data are available can policy makers, stakeholders and other players effectively evaluate and contribute to the improvement of private higher education in the state.

Conclusion

This paper has proposed some of the key areas of concern and offered suggestions in relation to enhancing the state government's complementary but active role in nurturing a high quality knowledge hub in Penang. Many issues and recommendations brought up here are not new, yet they have never really been followed up on, mainly because of a lack of co-ordination and urgency. However, they remain pertinent and it should be of utmost priority for the new state government to commit to further assessment, planning and implementation within an efficient timeframe.

Acknowledgments

This paper was written during my one-month visit at the Socioeconomic and Environmental Research Institute (SERI). My thanks to YB Liew Chin Tong and Ms. Fatimah Hassan for their valuable comments.

References

Brown, Phillip and Anthony, Hesketh. *The Mismanagement of Talent: Employability and Jobs in the Knowledge Economy.* Oxford and New York: Oxford University Press, 2004.

DCT Consultancy Services. *The Future of Education in Penang Report.* Unpublished, 1997.

Lee, Molly. *Restructuring Higher Education in Malaysia.* Penang: USM, 2004.

MoHE (Ministry of Higher Education, Malaysia). "Senarai IPTS [List of PHEIs]", June 2009. <http://jpt.mohe.gov.my/menudirektori.php> (accessed 10 August 2009).

PECC (Penang Educational Consultative Council). *Mid-Term Report.* Unpublished, 2009.

Penang State Education Department. *"Department Profile",* 2009. <http://jpnpp.edu.my/index.php?option=com_content&view=category&id=42&Itemid=75&lang=en> (accessed 12 August 2009).

Penang State Executive Committee for Education, Economic Planning and Information. *Establishing Penang as a Cen-*

tre of Excellence for Education, Proceedings of the Second Penang Economic Seminar, edited by Tan Pek Leng. Penang: Penang State Executive Committee for Education, Economic Planning and Information,1996.

SERI. Penang Statistics, Quarter 2, 2009. <http://www2.seri. com.my/Penang%20Statistics/2009/Q2%20April-June%20 2009.pdf> (accessed 12 August 2009).

SERI. *Final Report for Study on the Competitiveness of Private Institutions of Higher Learning in Penang*. Unpublished, 2005a.

SERI. *First Phase Report: A Study on Penang's Private Institutions of Higher Learning*. Unpublished, 2005b.

SERI. *Report on the Study on the facility profile of private institutions of higher learning in Penang*. Unpublished, 2004.

SERI. *Education @ Penang - Your Gateway to Excellent International Education*. Undated brochure.

Tan, Toh Wah. "Can the Education Industry Meet the Expectations of New Economic Growth? - The Role of Institutions of Higher Learning and Universities", December 2006. <http://www.seri.com.my/ap/seminar-on-new-sources-of-growth-for-penang-8-dec-2006.html> (accessed 18 August 2009).

[8]

Re-examining
State Finances and Governance:
The Challenge for Penang

Suresh Narayanan, Lim Mah Hui and Ong Wooi Leng1

Introduction

Malaysia embraces a federal system of government with a strong centre—so strong that some have dismissed it as a "flawed federation" (Holzhausen, 1974). Nowhere is this more obvious than in the conduct of financial relations. The Centre has retained for itself all the major revenue sources, rights of undertaking expenditures and powers of borrowing. The states, on the other hand, have such limited revenue sources and borrowing powers that the system fosters a permanent dependency of the states on the Centre for development funds.

This has never been a major issue in the past because the Centre and the majority of the states have been under the control of a single political party. At any one time in the post-independence period no more than two states have been under opposition rule. And on such occasions, the Centre has not failed to use the opportunity to strike home the fact that states that vote opposition parties into power are likely to pay the price in terms of reduced and often delayed Federal fund disbursements.[2] The affected states have invariably been powerless to renegotiate the terms of disbursement because innumerable obstacles stand in their way.

---

1   *Prof Suresh, Senior Fellow at Universiti Sains Malaysia; Dr Michael Lim, SERI Senior Research Fellow; Ong, SERI Research Analyst.*

2   *See Loh (2008), for some recent examples.*

In the 12th general election of 8 March 2008, the Barisan Nasional (BN) lost its two-thirds majority in parliament and control of five of the 13 states. This led to initial optimism that the old tactics of bullying a state by cutting down or delaying development allocations would no longer work. After all, the most developed states of Penang, Perak and Selangor were in opposition hands and any action that reduced economic growth in these key states would adversely affect the growth and economic performance of the national economy as a whole. Yet the early actions of the Central government do not demonstrate an appreciation of this fact; a series of measures were announced that appear to be designed to 'punish' opposition-held states rather than foster joint development. For instance, the Entrepreneurial and Cooperative Development Ministry replayed a familiar tune from the past by ordering Mara, rather than the State Economic Development Corporations (SEDCs), to disburse funds for Federal projects under the Ministry (The Star, 27 April 2008). This deprived the states of revenue equivalent to 5% of the value of Federal projects implemented in the states.

Clearly, in Malaysia where a single party has controlled both federal and most state governments since independence, federal-state relations have been akin to intra-party relations. Some time will no doubt elapse before the former is recognized and treated as distinct from the latter. Until that time arrives, however, it is prudent for states such as Penang to optimize the internal resources available to it.

Levels of Government

The prevailing system of government in Malaysia is divided into three tiers: federal, state and local. In this paper, we will concern ourselves with the federal and state levels. The Federal constitution specifies the division of responsibilities with respect to expenditure, revenue-sharing and borrowing between the federal and state governments. The federal government controls a wide array of exclusive powers while shared powers are few, with federal law always taking precedence over state laws in case of inconsistencies.

While the Federation pays for federal responsibilities, the states must pay for their own responsibilities and, in the case of shared responsibilities, the Federation pays only if expenditures are related to federal commitments or state commitments undertaken in accord with federal policy and with federal approval.

Under the constitution, the federal government enjoys exclusive powers to levy and collect all taxes and other forms of revenue except from a few minor sources assigned to the states. In fact, state revenues are limited to collections from import and excise duties on petroleum products (Terengganu, Sabah and Sarawak), export duties on timber and other forest products (for Sabah and Sarawak) and excise duties on toddy in all states. State revenues can be raised from forests, lands (quit rents, fees for TOL, grazing permits and conversion) and mines and entertainment taxes. Non-tax revenue includes licenses and permits, royalties, service fees, profits from commercial undertakings (such as in water, gas, ports and harbours), land sales, rents on state properties; and non-revenue receipts include proceeds, dividends and interests, grants and reimbursements from the Federal government.

The state is only allowed to borrow from the Federal government or from a bank or other financial sources approved for that purpose by the Federal government for a period not exceeding 5 years. Furthermore, the Federal government prescribes the terms and conditions which will apply to all loans raised by the state or guaranteed by it. However, the state governments are constrained in their ability to guarantee loans. They can offer no such guarantees except with the approval of the Federal government and subject to conditions set by the latter (Ummikalsum, 1991).

Revenue, Expenditures and Deficits: An Overview

State revenue is divided into Operating and Development revenue. The former comprises largely of revenue raised within the State while the latter consists primarily of loans and grants from the Federal government to finance major development projects.[3] In a similar fashion, expenditures are classified as Operating and Development spending. Operating expenditures maintain existing infrastructure, services and facilities while development spending creates new infrastructure, services and facilities. In general, development expenditures are seen as contributing to increasing the productive capacity of the economy.

---

3   It is odd that loans should be considered 'revenue'.

Table 1 shows these categories of revenue and expenditure for the 9 year period from 2000 to 2008, though the data for 2008 are only estimates. Table 2 shows the annual rates of growth of these categories between 2000 and 2004 and from 2005 to 2008.[4]

Table 1: Total Revenue, Total Expenditures and the Budget Deficit, 2000-2008 (RM million)

	2000	2001	2002	2003	2004	2005	2006	2007	2008*
Operating Revenue	230.96	215.52	231.31	246.67	257.44	274.89	280.50	295.86	282.9
Development Revenue	161.01	132.34	100.13	102.54	105.8	163.22	75.43	152.28	162.53
Total Revenue	391.97	347.86	331.44	349.21	363.24	438.11	355.93	448.14	445.43
Operating Exp.	248.15	263.52	248.66	233.05	228.90	191.70	269.63	252.25	278.56
Development Exp.	179.58	112.55	93.84	79.99	98.42	106.04	110.67	129.39	162.53
Total Expenditure	427.73	376.07	342.50	313.04	327.32	297.74	380.30	381.64	441.09
Surplus/ Shortfall in Operating Budget	-17.19	-48.0	-17.35	13.62	28.54	83.19	10.87	43.61	4.34
Surplus/ Shortfall in Development Budget	-18.57	19.79	6.29	22.55	7.38	57.18	-35.24	22.89	-
Surplus/ Deficit in Overall Budget	-35.76	-28.21	-11.06	36.17	35.92	140.37	-24.37	66.50	4.34

Sources: Report of the Auditor-General on the Accounts of the State of Penang, 1980 and 1990; Penang Financial Statement, 2001 and Penang State Budget, 2008.
*Notes: * Estimated*

4   *All rates of growth are continuously compounded rates.*

Operating revenue grew slowly between 2000 and 2004, with an annual rate of growth of only 2.8%. This declined drastically to about 1% growth in the 2005-2008 period. The annual rate of growth of operating expenditure, on the other hand, picked up from a negative 2% between 2000-2004 to a robust 13.3% growth in the 2005-2008 period.[5] Despite the fact that operating revenue growth edged ahead of operating expenditure in the first period, deficits were evident in the operating budget in 2000, 2001 and 2002. In the later period, when operating expenditure growth outpaced operating revenue growth, net surpluses were recorded. However, if operating expenditure maintains its rapid growth vis-à-vis operating revenue, the future may well see persistent deficits emerging in the operating budget.

Table 2: Annual Growth Rates of Revenue and Expenditure (%), 2000-2008

	2000-2004	2005-2008
Operating Revenue	2.8	0.96
Development Revenue	-10.0	-0.14
Total Revenue	-1.9	0.55
Operating Expenditure	-2.0	13.3
Development Expenditure	-14.0	15.3
Total Expenditure	-6.5	14.0

Source: Computed based on Table 1

A rule-of-thumb suggests that operating revenue must at least cover operating expenditures. In the case of Penang, after three years of operating deficits (2000-2002), operating revenue has exceeded operating expenditures from 2003 onwards. Although the surplus has averaged RM30 million per year, it has varied considerably in size and it is unclear whether it is on a downward trend.

---

5   Note that the Operating expenditure figures shown here will not coincide with the figures published in the Financial Reports. This is because we have subtracted from the published figures the amounts that are transferred to Development revenue each year. If these transfers are not subtracted we will be unable to derive the overall budget deficit/ surplus figures shown in the table above.

Re-examining State Finances and Governance

Turning to the Development budget, development revenue fell in both periods, though the rate of decline in the second period was considerably slower. In a similar fashion, development expenditure that had been falling at an even more dramatic rate than development revenue in the first period saw a hefty 15% rate of annual growth in the second period, well ahead of development revenue growth in this period.

The development budget maintained a surplus in all years except 2000 and 2006 and is expected to be balanced in 2008. In the early period, the surpluses were generated because development expenditure growth was declining at a faster pace that the decline of development revenue growth. In the later periods, surpluses were maintained despite the fact that development expenditures were growing at a more rapid rate in the face of declining growth in development revenue. If this trend persists, the development budget of the future will accumulate deficits again.

Looking at total revenue and expenditures, both components registered negative growth rates between 2000 and 2004, with expenditures falling at a more rapid rate than revenue. This helped reign in the size of the overall budget deficit in 2001 and 2002 and contributed to the surpluses in 2003 and 2004. In the subsequent period, both registered positive rates of growth, with expenditures growing more rapidly than revenue. Despite this, the overall budget showed surpluses in all years except 2006, although surpluses seem to be shrinking since then.

It is interesting to note that between 2000 and 2003, the share of development expenditure in the total was shrinking from about 50% in 2000 to 26% in 2003. Since then it has shown an overall rising trend, reaching about 37% in 2008. This suggests that the State budget surpluses of later years have been achieved largely by trimming operating expenditure rather than development expenditure—a positive development.

However, the generally favourable picture of Penang's budgetary health diminishes considerably when we appreciate how vulnerable it is to fluctuations in Federal funding. To illustrate, in 2000, Federal loans amounted to RM62.8 million. Had these not been forthcoming, the overall budgetary deficit of the State would have more than doubled from RM35.8 million to RM98.6 million. Similarly, estimated Federal loans for 2008 amounted to RM97 million. If not for this, the estimated surplus of RM4.34 million would have turned into a hefty deficit of RM92.7 million. This vulnerability underscores the need for the State to be more dependent on its own sources of revenue given the reality of the prevailing political situation which suggests that Federal loans may not always be so freely forthcoming.

Sources of Revenue

State revenue, as previously discussed, is divided into operating and development revenue. Operating revenue is derived primarily from State sources, while development revenue comprises curiously of federal loans, federal grants and a portion transferred from the operating budget which is classified as 'contribution to development funds'.[6]

Operating Revenue

State operating revenue can be broken down into three major categories: tax revenue, non-tax receipts, and non-revenue receipts (Table 3). Of the three, non-tax receipts accounted for the biggest share in 2008, followed by tax revenue and non-revenue receipts. Each of these will be discussed in turn.

Non-tax Receipts

Non-tax receipts consists of revenue from land sale, land applications and land ownership transfers (services payments), licenses and permits, dividends and income from investments, rentals and penalties. Together they accounted for 40% of all revenue in 2008.They recorded a high 9.1% growth rate in the 1980-1990 period but slowed down to 3.2% in the second ten-year period before recovering to 5.4% per annum growth between 2000 and 2008.

Within non-tax receipts, services payments, dividends from investments and receipts from the sale of goods (land) were the most important components in 2008. They accounted for 30%, 29.4% and 25.8% of non-tax revenues, respectively (see Appendix Table 1).

---

6   Some portion of the operating expenditure is transferred to development revenue. This has the effect of lowering operating expenditure to amounts that are lower than the published figures. The published figures for development revenue, on the other hand, already incorporate these transferred amounts.

The growth of revenue from services payments appears to have remained stable over the period under consideration. Most of the incomes from services payments are derived from charges to register shifts in land ownership, land application fees, pawn registration fees and miscellaneous other sources (see Appendix Table 2). Of these, the fastest growing component has been revenue from registration of land ownership changes. Sadly, the revenue from the Penang Hill railway was not only small but has also stagnated between 2000 and 2008.

Table 3: Sources of Operating Revenue, 1980-2008 (RM Million)

	1980	1990	2000	2008*	Growth 1980-90	Growth 1990-00	Growth 1980-00	Growth 2000-08
Tax Revenue	11.49	35.05	87.97	107.42	11.8	9.6	10.7	2.5
Direct taxes	11.49	-	83.26	101.92			10.4	2.6
Indirect taxes	-	-	4.71	5.5			-	2.0
Non-Tax Receipts	22.78	54.47	74.32	113.6	9.1	3.2	6.1	5.4
Licences & permits	1.84	-	8.67	9.01			8.1	0.5
Services payments	2.1	-	14.9	34.05			10.3	10.9
Receipts from goods sold	9.27	-	25.88	29.31			5.3	1.6
Rentals	2.12	-	2.5	3.23			0.8	3.3
Dividends & Investments	6.98	-	19.38	33.41			5.2	7.0
Penalties& punishment	0.46	-	2.98	4.58			9.8	5.5
Non-revenue Receipts	22.87	45.84	68.67	61.88	7.2	4.1	5.7	-1.3
Returned expenditure	2.62	-	0.42	0.07			-8.7	-20.1
Receipts from Fed. Govt. agencies	20.25	-	68.25	61.82			6.3	-1.2
Total revenue	57.14			282.9	9.0	5.5	7.2	2.6

Sources: Appendix Table 1
Notes: * Estimated

The growth of returns from investments and dividends has risen from 5.2% over the 20 year period (1980-2000) to 7.0% between 2000 and 2008. Dividends accrue largely from interest from fixed deposits and investments including dividend income from shares held in Telekom, Malaysian Airports Berhad and the Water Authority (PBA). (See Appendix Table 3.)

In sharp contrast to returns from investments, the growth of receipts from goods sold has dipped sharply from 5.3% between 1980 and 2000 to just 1.6% between 2000 and 2008, as has its share in total revenue from 16% to 10% (see Appendix Table 3). Income in this category consists largely of land premiums for ownership distribution and shifts in stipulation of land use. It is disconcerting that revenue from land sales, the only significant state resource, is dwindling both in terms of growth and its contribution to operating revenue. This suggests an urgent need to re-look at how this resource is being managed.

Tax Revenue

Tax revenue consists of two main items—quit rent and entertainment duties (indirect taxes)—that accounted for about 38% of all revenue in 2008. Tax revenue sources open to the State are few; as noted previously the Federal government has reserved for itself most of the lucrative sources of taxation. The only sources of tax revenue for the State are quit rents charged on land and entertainment levies.

The per annum growth of tax revenue appears to be slowing down rapidly—from 11.8% between 1980-90 to 9.6% between 1990-2000 and a mere 2.5% between 2000-2008. Consequently, although the share of tax receipts in total revenue recorded increases for 1980, 1990 and 2000, it has remained constant (at around 38%) for 2008 (Appendix Table 1). Even this was made possible only through the collection of arrears in the payment of quit rents.

Penang's tax base is narrower than those of resource-rich states like Sabah, Sarawak and Selangor where taxes on natural resources generate substantial state revenues. Given that land is limited in Penang and that the publicly held land bank is only around 12% of total land, the State is likely to face a serious shortfall in tax receipts in future years if grave attention is not paid to how land is managed.

Entertainment taxes contribute little to operating revenue and came largely via the cinemas in the State (Appendix Table 1)

Non-revenue Receipts

Non-revenue receipts consist largely of grants from the Federal government. These grants fall into three basic categories: tax sharing grants, general purpose grants and specific purpose grants. The first category refers to taxes imposed and collected by the Federal government with the receipts being returned back to the States in a specified proportion based on the origin of collection. These grants were important when export duties were imposed on tin, iron and other mineral ores. The structure, rate and proportion of sharing are determined by the Federal government though the States are free to spend their allocations without restrictions. Such grants are not relevant to Penang.

General purpose grants are given to states based on provisions in the Federal Constitution or by a formula determined by the Federal government. These include the capitation grant based on the state population, the revenue growth grant, state reserve fund grants and special grants (to Sabah, Sarawak, Selangor and Kedah only).

Finally, specific purpose grants are tied to a specific purpose such as the road grants, economic development grants, cost reimbursement grants, service charge grants and grants for religious schools and institutions.

In Penang, non-revenue receipts—more specifically, grants and other receipts from the Federal government—that accounted for the biggest chunk of the state's operating revenue in the past appears to be on the decline. For example, in 1980 it accounted for 40% of total revenue but by 2008 its share had declined to a mere 22% (Appendix Table 1).

Between 1980-90, non-revenue receipts grew strongly at 7.2% per year but slowed down to 4.1% over the succeeding 10 years before registering a negative 1.3% rate of growth between 2000-08. The main grants and receipts from the Federal government are detailed in Appendix Table 4. While per capita grants and grants for operating expenses have increased by about 1.7 and 1.6 times, respectively, between 2000 and 2008, no road grants are anticipated.

Penang has not been receiving big grants from the Federal government even while under Barisan control. This is evident from the fact that well before 2008 (when the State fell into opposition hands), federal funds as a proportion of operating revenue had been on the decline—from 35.4% in 1980 to 29.6% in 2000. Of course, it fell further to a mere 21.9% with the Opposition takeover of Penang in 2008 (Appendix Table 1).

The contribution of Federal funds to the State's revenues is likely to fall further in the immediate future. First, while Federal government payments to MPPP and MPSP were channelled through the State in 2000, the amounts allocated for both were not only reduced but were paid by by-passing the State in 2008. This explains the drastic reduction in funds in the 'Others" category from RM18.1 million in 2000 to just RM2.0 million in 2008 (see Appendix Table 4).

Another component of receipts from Federal agencies is the 'service charge for Federal projects'. This refers to the 5% charge levied on Federal projects implemented in Penang using State personnel. Although receipts from this source was projected to increase from RM7.31 million to RM10 million between 2000 and 2008, it is likely to fall in the future—a familiar mechanism used by the Federal government to deny opposition-held states of vital funds is to channel the implementation and monitoring of Federal projects in the state through Federal agencies. This tactic deprives the states of the receipts from the 5% service levy chargeable on Federal projects. This was evident in the case of Sabah and Kelantan—when the former fell to the opposition PBS party and the latter was controlled by PAS. While grants to these states, guaranteed under the Federal constitution, were given directly to the state governments, development funds allocated under the Sixth Malaysia Plan (1991-95) were redirected through the Federal government-controlled Federal Development Offices that were set up in these states to administer the funds (Loh, 2009).

Development Revenue

The share of Development revenue in total revenue fell from 41.4% in 2000 to 38.5% in 2008. The main sources of development revenue are evident from Table 4.

The main source of development revenue was Federal loans; it is therefore a gross misnomer to call it 'revenue'! The loans went to the Water Authority and to financing the Jelutong Expressway. It accounted for 60% of all development 'revenue' in 2008, up from the 39% share in 2000. Federal grants for development, on the other hand, accounted for only 8% of development funds, although this was a larger share relative to the 2000 figure.

Table 4: Sources of Development Revenue

Sources of Estimated Income	2000 (RM million)	%	2008* (RM million)	%	Growth 2000-08 (%)
Federal loans to Penang Water Authority and for building of expressway	62.70	38.9	97.00	59.7	5.6
Returned loans	7.42	4.6			
Monthly installment from the selling of low-price houses	7.89	4.9	5.10	3.1	-5.3
Lease receipts (rental paid by PBA)	-	-	7.60	4.7	-
Contribution from consolidated state funds	72.50	45.0	-	-	-
Contribution to development funds (transferred from operating expenditure)	-	-	40.00	24.6	-
Sale of low-cost houses	1.78	1.1	-	-	
Federal grants based on economic development, infrastructure and security of life stage (capitation grants from federal government)	8.72	5.4	12.83	7.9	4.9
Total of Estimated Income	161.01		162.53		-0.12

Sources: Penang State Financial Statement, 2001 and Penang State Budget, 2008.
Note: *Estimate

State revenue sources accounted for only RM52.7 million (or 32%) of development funds in 2008. Of this, one quarter (or RM40 million) was in effect transferred from the operating budget. Thus, Federal loans (rather than grants) and funds reassigned from the operating budget financed most of the State development in 2008.

The Nature of Expenditures

As indicated previously, expenditures can be divided into operating and development expenditures. While the former supports existing goods and services, the latter creates new goods and services.

Operating Expenditure

Three components took up the bulk operating expenditures in 2008: fixed contributions, charges and payments, emoluments and supplies and services. Each of these will be discussed in turn.

Fixed Contributions, Charges and Payments

This component accounted for nearly 40% of operating expenditures in 2008 despite the fact that it recorded a negative rate of growth between 2000 and 2008 (Table 5). It had used up 65% of operating expenditure in 2000.

A detailed examination reveals that the 81% of expenditure was undertaken by the State Treasury department and disbursed as state grants (see Appendix Table 6). Of the RM86.2 million set aside under state grants, RM40 million represents the transfer made to development revenue. The rest was made up of assessment payments to MPPP and MPSP for state buildings, medical expenses for existing and retired state officers and so forth.

Another 17% was disbursed as state grants by the Chief Minister's office and this includes payments made to the state museum, Penang library, Majlis Sukan Negeri and similar entities.

Table 5: Operating Expenditure (RM million)

	1990	2000	2008*	Growth 1990-2000 (%)	Growth 2000-2008 (%)	Share of Total in 2008 (%)
Emoluments (corresponding to higher salary for civil servants)	31.87	50.47	115.88	4.7	10.9	36.4
Supplies and services (management, rentals, transportation and trips, office rentals, utility cost, post and raw materials)	19.35	32.87	68.65	5.4	9.6	21.6
Asset acquisitions (equipments and appliances for government departments)	1.17	2.60	2.02	8.3	-3.1	0.6
Fixed contributions and charges/payments (state debt, gifts, annual contributions to local authorities, other contributions and assistance)	54.06	161.52	126.92	11.6	-3.0	39.8
Other expenditures (refunding)	0.91	0.68	5.09	-2.9	28.6	1.6
Total	107.36	248.14	318.56	8.7	3.2	100.0

Sources: Appendix Table 5
*Note: *Estimate*

Emoluments

Emoluments took up about 36% of the Operating expenditure in 2008 relative to the 20% in 2000. The annual rate of growth of emoluments increased from nearly 5% between 1990 and 2000 to about 11%

in the 2000-2008 period. The nation-wide reorganization of departments and the creation of additional posts in 2008 and salary revisions account for this rapid expansion. The offices involved in the expansion are the Chief Minister's Office and Secretariat, the five district and land offices and the State's religious department (see Appendix Table 7). The salary bill more than doubled for the Chief Minister's Office and Secretariat, each of the five district and land offices and the State's religious department. The bill in the State Mufti's office saw a greater than four-fold increase.

However, the biggest chunk of emoluments in 2008 (62.4%) was paid out by four departments: the Chief Minister's Office and Secretariat, the Public Works Department, the State Treasury and the State Agriculture Department. The comparable share in 2000 was 59%.

Supplies and Services

Expenditures on supplies and services took up 22% of operating spending in 2008, substantially higher than the 13% share in 2000. It also recorded an almost 10% growth rate per annum between 2000 and 2008. Details on these expenditures are shown in Appendix Table 8.

The Chief Minister' Office and Secretariat incurred 48% of all spending in this category in 2008 and payments for 'professional services' constituted the bulk of the spending. A large part of these payments are allocations for programmes started by various committees established under each executive council member. The size of this item ballooned more than two-and-a-half times relative to the 2000 figure.

The Irrigation and Drainage Department accounted for another 16% of the payments with much of it going towards maintenance works. The payment for 'professional services" in the State Treasury also saw a spectacular seven-fold increase between 2000 and 2008 and represents largely expenditures on training and upgrading courses for staff. In contrast, the maintenance bill for Public Works actually declined by some RM0.76 million between the two periods.

Development Expenditure

Table 6 gives the details of development spending by the various Departments in the State.

Table 6   Development Expenditure by Departments

Department/Office	2000		2008*	
	RM million	%	RM million	%
State Agriculture Department	1.64	0.9	4.00	2.5
State Forestry Department	0.80	0.4	3.00	1.8
State Department of Veterinary Services	1.10	0.6	2.00	1.2
Penang State Chief Minister's Office and Secretariat	111.46	62.1	117.90	72.5
Penang Botanical Gardens	0.70	0.4	1.00	0.6
Public Works Department of Penang	35.08	19.5	10.00	6.2
State Religious Department	5.01	2.8	5.00	3.1
State Department of Irrigation and Drainage	10.00	5.6	10.00	6.2
State Treasury Department	13.80	7.7	9.63	5.9
Total Development Expenditure	179.59	100.0	162.53	100.0

Sources: Penang State Budget, 2000 and 2008.
Note: *Estimate

The biggest expenditure appears under the State Chief Minister's Office and Secretariat; about 73% of development spending occurred via this Office in 2008. This is explained by the fact that development expenditure is financed either by using State revenue directly or through Federal loans. For instance, out of RM 117.90 million spending estimated in 2008, the RM97 million, financed through Federal loans, were credited to the State Chief Minister's Office and Secretariat for disbursement to the relevant projects departments. Thus, all State agencies have to borrow through the State Chief Minister's Office and Secretariat. Furthermore, spending on land acquisitions to build committee halls, roads and the like, financed through State revenues, also appears under the Chief Minister's Office and Secretariat.

To illustrate, in 2008, RM90 million was allocated to the Water Authority, RM14 million went towards land acquisition to build the Jelutong Expressway and other projects and RM3.74 million was spent on low cost housing.

Apart from the above, most development spending took the form of public works and financing Drainage and Irrigation.

It is sad to note that the development allocation for the Botanical Gardens—an important attraction in eco-tourism—was small (RM0.7 million) in 2000 and increased by only RM0.3 million in 2008

Summary and Policy Recommendations

State finance is constrained by the asymmetry of power between state and federal governments in Malaysia, with the latter controlling most revenue sources. Despite the fact that the state has managed to maintain small surpluses in most years since 1980, the fact remains that Federal government funding, either by way of grants or loans, has been an important source of funding. While in the past this over-dependence on the Centre might not have been an issue, a Penang ruled by an opposition party can no longer feel as secure as it had been before. The Federal government has a history of using the availability of Federal funds as an instrument for pressuring opposition-held states; it is therefore prudent for the State to become as self-reliant as possible by maximizing States sources of receipts and decreasing unnecessary expenditures or leakages. In the longer-run, in concert with other opposition-held states, it should also seek a review of the Federal-state financial arrangements that reduces the present dependency on the Centre.

On the revenue side, of the three major sources—tax revenue, non-tax revenue and non-receipts revenue (mainly federal loans and grants)—tax revenue, as a percentage of total revenue, has almost doubled from 20% in 1980 to 38% in 2000, and thereafter stayed constant at 38% in 2008. Non tax-revenue has hovered at about 40% between 1980 and 2008. Most significantly, non-revenue receipts has almost halved from 40% to 22% in the same period. This percentage is likely to further decrease with the State falling to an opposition party and the reduction of the 5% service fee received by State from the Federal

Re-examining State Finances and Governance

government as the latter starts to use more Federal (rather than State) agencies to implement development projects in Penang.

Quit rent forms the largest component of tax revenue; there has been no major revision of the rates over the past decade and the substantial increase in revenue from this source noted for 2008 was the result of better collection of arrears. As quit rents are a major revenue source, the rates should be regularly reviewed to keep pace with inflation or rise in property prices. It is noteworthy that the rate of growth of receipts from quit rents was 2.6% per annum, between 2000 and 2008, considerably lower than the 4.3% growth of the Penang House Price Index (PHPI) during the comparable period.[7] There is therefore considerable scope and justification for judicious increases in the quit rent rates. Given the mounting arrears, the efficiency of the collection of quit rents should also be reviewed.

The second largest source of revenue is non-tax revenue, the major component being service payments, followed by receipts from land sales and income from dividends and investments. Income from service payments is made up primarily of payment for land ownership transfer.

One potential source of revenue is for the State to consider appropriating a substantial, if not the entire proportion, of the increase in land value upon its conversion from one use to another. To illustrate, assume that an owner of a piece of land that is gazetted for agricultural use applies for the land to be converted to housing or commercial use. Upon the conversion being approved, the value per square foot of the land will increase substantially without any additional effort on the part of the owner. Presently, this increase is entirely appropriated the owner. It is suggested that the State appropriates this increase in value (or a substantial part of it). A similar principle should apply for reclaimed land as well.

The State should also consider introducing a property transfer charge on a sliding scale such that properties that are held for shorter periods are taxed at higher rates; this would be a source of revenue and also discourage excessive speculation in property investments that regularly result in property asset bubbles.

---

7   *PHPI data were obtained from SERI.*

The second important source of non-tax revenue is receipts from land sale. The Penang State government owns only about 12% of total land in the state. Past practices of conversion of leasehold land into freehold land have been less than desirable and have deprived the State of an important source of revenue. This administration must give serious thought to how to manage this revenue source more effectively. In particular, it should review the policy of conversion of leasehold to freehold land. (Please see Appendix A)

The third crucial source of non-tax revenue is income from dividends and investments. Much of this is derived from interest on fixed deposits and investment income from PBA and other privatized entities. The State treasury should review its investment portfolio to consider partial investments in government bonds and securities based on its cash flow needs to enhance yields. Performance of State corporations like the PBA and others should be monitored regularly with a view towards improving their returns.

Finally, as noted previously, receipts from Federal government agencies have been declining. In the longer term, the State, in co-operation with other opposition-held states, must seek to change the existing Federal-State arrangements that allow them access to so very few sources of self-funding. Some renegotiation of the revenue-sharing arrangements becomes imperative. While this may have been unimaginable previously, with four[8] opposition states working in concert towards a common objective, now may be the most opportune moment to attempt this.

Renegotiating tax sharing arrangements is an area that has been suggested before but has remained fruitless because of the poor bargaining power of just one or two opposition-held states (Umikalsum1991). With five states (and Sabah possibly throwing its indirect support to any change that will grant it more control over state resources), it is worth revisiting this suggestion. The idea is to extend the current revenue-sharing mechanism with respect to mineral resource taxes (which benefits only mineral rich states) to taxes on income and sales. Such an arrangement will ensure all states get a share of the taxes raised in their respective jurisdictions and, more importantly, the revenue obtained

---

8 *At the time of writing the position of Perak is unclear.*

will have a direct relationship with the level of economic activity in the respective states.

Another area that can be revisited is the basis on which grants are given. For example, the size of the capitation grant is determined by population size while the revenue growth grants are based on population and the GDP. A more meaningful method of giving grants should take into account the tax base of the state; states with limited revenue bases should receive higher transfers from the Centre (Abdul Rahim, 2000; Wilson and Sulaiman, 1997).

Turning to expenditures, these have been rising at a faster rate than revenue especially between 2005 and 2008. The largest percentage rise is in supply of services expenditure which went from 18% of total operating expenditure in 1990 to 22% in 2008. It was growing at about 7.3% per annum, much faster than the inflation rate. In particular, attention should be focused on why professional services in the Chief Minister's office (22%) and State Treasury office (8%) are high, and the category of minor maintenance in the Department of Irrigation and Drainage (12%) and the Chief Minister's office (9%) are also high. The State should begin to set yearly operational targets to control or reduce this category of expenditure and appoint appropriate state organizations, possibly with the participation of independent public individuals or organizations, to monitor this process. The introduction of competitive and open bidding by the present administration is a step in the right direction.

Fixed contributions and charges at 50% of total operating expenditure in 1990 formed the largest category; though this declined percentage wise from 65% in 2000 to about 40% in 2008.

Emoluments form the second largest category of operating expenditure; this has fluctuated from between 30% of total operating expenditure in 1990 down to 20.3% in 2000 and rising again to 36% in 2008. Emoluments have risen on average at a rate of 11% between 2000 and 2008. The departments with the highest emolument expenses are the Chief Minister and Secretariat Office (22%), Public Works Department (21%) and State Department of Irrigation and Drainage (11%).

Development expenditure should be regarded as investments for generating future income. In 2008, $97 million or 60% of development revenue were federal loans for PBA and highway expenses, $53 million (33%) were from state sources and the remaining $13 million were federal grants. Seventy-three per cent of development expenditure was absorbed by the Chief Minister's office. The other three departments with substantial development expenditures are the Drainage and Irrigation Department, the Public Works Department and the State Treasury, with each absorbing 6% of total development expenditure.

The office with the lowest development expenditure is the Penang Botanical Garden with a paltry $1 million, equalling 0.6% of total development expenditure. The Botanical Garden and Penang Hill are among the jewels of eco-tourism spots in the state. Since eco-tourism is crucial to Penang's economy, serious considerations and planning must be given to develop and upgrade these two sites to become star attractions for both tourists and local residents. Substantial improvements and sustained maintenance of these facilities can be followed by modest charges so that they not only become self-sustaining but actually generate a small surplus for the State coffers. (Please see Appendix B.)

This paper is an initial attempt to examine state finance with the objective of enhancing state financial capacity. It is recommended that the Penang State government make publicly and easily available, through print and websites, audited financial data in order to make its finances transparent and also to encourage more research and suggestions from the public.

To conclude, the message is very clear: the State needs to trim wasteful expenditure, maximize collections from existing revenue sources, look for new sources of revenue, and plug leakages in spending.

Acknowledgments

We are grateful to Chet Singh, Toh Kin Woon, Leong Yueh Kwong and Maheswari for useful discussions. The helpful explanations of state finances provided by Puan Hashimah Mohd. Hashim, the Deputy Financial Officer and Encik Roslan A. Rahman, the State Treasurer, are also acknowledged. However, all views and interpretations are our own.

Appendix

Appendix Table 1: Sources of State Revenue, 1980-2008

Revenue	1980		1990		2000		2008*	
	RM million	%	RM million	%	RM million	%	RM million	%
Tax Revenue	11.49	20.11	35.05	25.89	87.97	38.10	107.42	37.97
Direct Taxes (quit rent)	11.49	20.11	-	-	83.26	36.00	101.92	36.03
Indirect Taxes (entertainment duties)	-	-	-	-	4.71	2.00	5.5	1.94
Non-Tax Receipts	22.78	39.87	54.47	40.24	74.32	32.20	113.6	40.16
Licenses and Permits (alcohol manufacturers, pawn shops, import and export of fauna, production of stone materials, Water Enactment, public entertainment)	1.84	3.22	-	-	8.67	3.80	9.01	3.18
Services Payment (Land application, land ownership transfer)	2.1	3.68	-	-	14.9	6.50	34.05	12.04
Receipts from Goods Sold (land premium for ownership distribution, shifting in stipulation)	9.27	16.22	-	-	25.88	11.20	29.31	10.36

Revenue	1980		1990		2000		2008*	
		%		%		%		%
Rentals (government furniture, houses and buildings)	2.12	3.71	-	-	2.5	1.10	3.23	1.14
Dividends and Investments (interest from fixed deposit)	6.98	12.22	-	-	19.38	8.40	33.41	11.81
Penalties and Punishment (notice and penalty for late land taxes, breaking of contracts)	0.46	0.81	-	-	2.98	1.30	4.58	1.62
Non-Revenue Receipts	22.87	40.02	45.84	33.87	68.67	29.70	61.88	21.87
Returned Expenditure (refund from previous year surplus expenses)	2.62	4.59	-	-	0.42	0.20	0.07	0.02
Receipts from Government Agencies (receipts from federal government, road grants & population grants)	20.25	35.44	-	-	68.25	29.60	61.82	21.85
Total Revenue	57.14	100.0	135.36	100.0	230.96	100.0	282.9	100.0

Sources: *Report of the Auditor-General on the Accounts of the State of Penang, 1980 and 1990; Penang Financial Statement, 2001 and Penang State Budget, 2008.*
Note: *2008 data are estimates*

Appendix Table 2: Components of Services Payments

	2000		2008*	
	RM million	%	RM million	%
Land application	2.54	17.0	5.00	14.7
Preparation & registration of land grants	1.31	8.8	2.25	6.6
Registration of shifting the land ownership	3.99	26.8	13.00	38.2
Pawn registration	1.60	10.7	3.97	11.7
Caveat registration	-	-	2.70	7.9
Penang Hill railway fare	2.11	14.2	2.00	5.9
Others	3.35	22.5	5.13	15.1
Total Services Payment	14.90	100.0	34.05	100.0

Sources: Penang Financial Statement, 2001 and Penang State Budget, 2008.
Note: *2008 data are estimates

Appendix Table 3: Components of Dividends and Receipts from Investments

	2000		2008*	
	RM million	%	RM million	%
Dividends from shares in listed companies	-	-	10.50	31.4
Interest from money balance in the bank-Current account	0.34	1.8	0.50	1.5
Interest from fixed deposit	12.76	65.8	22.00	65.8
Interest and receipts from loans	5.41	27.9	-	-
Others	0.87	4.5	0.41	1.2
Total Dividend and Receipts from Investment	19.38	100.0	33.41	100.0

Sources: Penang Financial Statement, 2001 and Penang State Budget, 2008.
Note: *2008 data are estimates

Appendix Table 4: Components of Receipts from Government Agencies

	2000		2008*	
	RM million	%	RM million	%
Grants based on population	13.63	20.0	22.60	36.6
Grants for State roads	18.62	27.3	-	-
Service charge for Federal projects	7.31	10.7	10.00	16.2
Additional revenues	3.72	5.5	16.18	26.2
Grants for Operating expenses	6.83	10.0	11.00	17.8
Others	18.14	26.6	2.04	3.3
Total Receipts from Government Agencies	68.25	100.0	61.82	100.0

Sources: Penang Financial Statement, 2001 and Penang State Budget, 2008.
Note: *2008 data are estimates

Appendix Table 5: Components of Operating Expenditure, 1990-2008

	1990		2000		2008*	
	RM million	%	RM million	%	RM million	%
Emoluments (corresponding to higher salary for civil servants)	31.87	29.7	50.47	20.3	115.88	36.4
Supply and services (management, rentals, transportation and trips, office rentals, utility cost, post and raw materials)	19.35	18.0	32.87	13.2	68.65	21.6
Asset acquisition (equipments and appliances for government departments)	1.17	1.1	2.60	1.0	2.02	0.6
Fixed contributions and charges/payments (state debt, gifts, surrenders to state government, annual contribution to local authorities, other contribution and assistances)	54.06	50.4	161.52	65.1	126.92	39.8
Other expenditures (refunds)	0.91	0.8	0.68	0.3	5.09	1.6
Total Operating Expenditure	107.36		248.14		318.56	

Sources: Report of the Auditor-General on the Accounts of the State of Penang, 1990; Penang Financial Statement, 2001 and Penang State Budget, 2008.
Note: * 2008 data are estimates

Appendix Table 6: Components of Fixed Contribution and Charges/Payments

	2000		2008*	
	RM million	%	RM million	%
Penang State Chief Minister and Secretariat Office (general administrative: in-state contribution)	23.81	14.7	21.63	17.0
Scholarship, donation and study loan	0.86	0.5	0.90	0.7
State grants	22.95	14.2	20.65	16.3
Rewards	-	-	0.09	0.1
State Treasury Department (management: in-state contribution)	135.93	84.2	102.48	80.8
State grants,	111.79	69.2	86.15	67.9
Insurance claim and compensation	0.004	0.002	3.00	2.4
Dividends, interest and other State debts (Low cost houses, PBA projects)	19.30	11.9	5.25	4.1
Pension to Governor and DUN members	3.01	1.9	4.64	3.7
Rewards	1.83	1.1	3.44	2.7
State Welfare Department (outside services: in-state contribution)	1.78	1.1	2.78	2.2
State grants	1.78	1.1	2.78	2.2
Total Expenditure	161.52	100	126.89	100

Sources: Penang Financial Statement, 2001 and Penang State Budget, 2008.
*Note: *2008 data are estimates*

Appendix Table 7: Components of Emoluments Expenditure by Departments

Department/Office	2000		2008*	
	RM million	%	RM million	%
Penang State Chief Minister and Secretariat Office	11.99	23.8	24.89	21.5
Public Works Department of Penang	11.01	21.8	24.48	21.1
State Department of Irrigation and Drainage	4.89	9.7	12.46	10.8
State Treasury Department	2.06	4.1	10.41	9.0
State Agriculture Department	2.69	5.3	5.31	4.6
State Religious Department	1.91	3.8	4.31	3.7
District and Land Office of North Seberang Perai	1.55	3.1	3.58	3.1
District and Land Office of Central Seberang Perai	1.64	3.3	3.46	3.0
District and Land Office of South West	1.31	2.6	3.07	2.7
District and Land Office of South Seberang Perai	1.26	2.5	2.74	2.4
District and Land Office of North East	1.26	2.5	2.67	2.3
Office of Land and Mines	2.09	4.1	3.28	2.8
State Syariah Court	0.91	1.8	3.06	2.6
State Department of Veterinary Services	1.30	2.6	2.80	2.4
State Department of Town and Country Planning	0.86	1.7	2.33	2.0
Penang Botanical Gardens	1.07	2.1	2.22	1.9
State Forestry Department	0.89	1.8	1.62	1.4
State Welfare Department	0.62	1.2	1.19	1.0
State Mufti Office	0.22	0.4	0.94	0.8
His Excellency The Head of State Penang Office	0.39	0.8	0.74	0.6
Toddy Department	0.28	0.6	-	-
Water Supply Department	0.24	0.5	0.28	0.2
Total Emoluments Expenditure	50.44	100.0	115.84	100.0

Sources: Report of the Auditor-General on the Accounts of the State of Penang, 1990; Penang Financial Statement, 2001 and Penang State Budget, 2008.
*Note: * 2008 data are estimates*

Appendix Table 8: Components of Supplies and Services

Department/Office	2000 RM million	2000 %	2008* RM million	2008* %
Penang State Chief Minister and Secretariat Office (general administrative: in-state contribution)	15.43	46.9%	32.69	47.6
Professional services and others	5.65	17.2	14.75	21.5
Travelling and lodging	1.39	4.2	2.47	3.6
Communication and utility	1.74	5.3	3.25	4.7
Rentals	1.05	3.2	3.96	5.8
Minor maintenance	4.41	13.4	6.45	9.4
Others	1.19	3.6	1.81	2.6
State Department of Irrigation and Drainage	6.16	18.7	11.00	16.0
Professional services and others	0.06	0.2	0.34	0.5
Travelling and lodging	0.13	0.4	0.27	0.4
Communication and utility	0.75	2.3	1.41	2.1
Rentals	0.16	0.5	0.48	0.7
Minor maintenance	4.66	14.2	8.04	11.7
Others	0.40	1.2	0.46	0.7
Public Works Department of Penang	3.96	12.0	4.05	5.9
Professional services and others	0.31	0.9	0.50	0.7
Travelling and lodging	0.23	0.7	0.34	0.5
Communication and utility	0.36	1.1	0.60	0.9
Rentals	0.002	0.0	0.08	0.1
Minor maintenance	2.71	8.2	1.95	2.8
Others	0.35	1.1	0.58	0.8
State Treasury Department	1.15	3.5	6.20	9.0
Professional services and others	0.77	2.3	5.62	8.2
Travelling and lodging	0.06	0.2	0.16	0.2
Communication and utility	0.03	0.1	0.08	0.1
Rentals	-	-	0.02	0.0
Minor maintenance	0.20	0.6	0.11	0.2
Others	0.09	0.3	0.21	0.3
Other Departments	6.17	18.8	14.71	21.4%
Total Expenditure	32.87	100%	68.65	100

Sources: Penang Financial Statement, 2001 and Penang State Budget, 2008.
Note: * 2008 data are estimates

Re-examining State Finances and Governance

Appendix A

Ideas on Enhancing Revenue from Proper Management of State Land

As the analysis shows, revenue from land sale forms about 10% of State revenue, with another 12% from land application and land ownership transfers. Hence a judicious management of land matters can enhance this important source of revenue.

The State should enact and implement new and transparent policies for land management.

We suggest the following ideas for discussion and consideration.

1) When agricultural or recreational land is converted to development land, the value of the land immediately rises with the benefit going to the land-owner, without any contribution on his/her part. The State can enact a policy whereby the rise in land value from conversion reverts to the State as is practiced in some countries. This will form a huge source of revenue for the State. As a rough illustration, one acre of agricultural land in the Tanjong Bunga area converted to development land could yield $8.7 million (assuming $200 psf x 43,560 sq ft). One hundred acres of such conversion would yield $870 million - equivalent to 3 years present State budget. Private individuals and developers should base the viability of their projects on such market rates rather than from windfall gains.

2) All land reclamation should be carried out by the State and the benefits accrue to the State. In the past, the Penang State has lost billions of dollars of revenue by allowing private companies or individuals to benefit from land reclamation and conversion of reclaimed land to freehold land. This practice should be terminated. There are legal opinions to support that reclaimed land cannot be converted into freehold land

3) Presently there are numerous bungalows and buildings in Penang Hill that are not properly maintained and therefore

have violated the conditions of the leases. The State should take action to repossess these buildings and re-develop them into recreational bungalows in line with a proper master plan to develop Penang Hill into an eco-friendly and sustainable site that can generate revenue for the State and for the enjoyment of its citizens and tourists.

4) The State should seriously reconsider its policies of converting leasehold land into free hold land when the lease expires. By keeping its leasehold status, the State can benefit from revenue and also keep the cost of land from escalating.

Appendix B

Proposal to Improve Penang Botanical Garden

The Penang Botanical Garden and the Penang Hill, pristine, luxuriant tropical jungles in the island are the jewels in the Pearl of the Orient (if this term can still be justifiably used). However, their state of neglect is obvious to any casual observer. This is also reflected in the development budget allocated to the Botanical Garden – a paltry $1 million for 2008.

We propose the following measures to develop the Botanical Garden to one that is worthy of its status.

1) Set up an advisory committee consisting of highly qualified professionals with experience to provide vision, direction, guidance, and assistance to the staff of the Botanical Garden to re-develop the Garden. (The Singapore Botanical Garden can be an example to consider.) This committee can also include some representative users to provide feedback and input on policies.

2) The State to increase the budget for the Garden and to upgrade staff skills.

3) Upgrade the Garden incrementally. Begin by selecting one or two sites to develop and beautify, e.g., an orchid garden, or a cacti greenhouse, or a Japanese garden. Invest maximum effort to develop it. Once the first site is successfully completed, move on to the next.

4) Raise public funds by appealing to the citizens of Penang for donations – big and small. For example, propose to philanthropists to sponsor individual sites in the Garden that can be named after that philanthropist. E.g. XX Lee Rose Garden, YY Yap Japanese Garden etc.

5) For smaller donations, any one giving more than say $5,000 (as an example), can have his/her name in a plaque in the Garden. The State can consider match- funding smaller donations.

6) Once people see visible progress, the State can consider charging modest entrance fees for local users (this can be fine tuned with discount for regular users, children and elders) and higher fees for foreign tourists. We believe people are willing to pay for quality services and facilities. This serves as a source of revenue for the State.

References

Abdul Rahim Anuar, Fiscal Decentralization in Malaysia, in *Hitotsubashi Journal of Economics*, vol.41, (2000): 85-89.

Holzhausen, W. *Federal Finance in Malaysia*. Kuala Lumpur: University of Malaya Press, 1974.

Loh, F. "Restructuring Federal-State Relations". In *Aliran,* 2008. <http://www.aliran.com/index.php?option=com_content&view=article&id=640:restructuring-federal-state-relations&catid=69:vol-28-2008-issue-no-3&Itemid=10> (accessed 20 June 2008).

Umikalsum, M.N. "Fiscal Federalism in Malaysia, 1971-1987". Ph.D. thesis, Faculty of Economics and Administration, University of Malaya, 1991.

Wilson, S., and Sulaiman, M. "Decentralization and Fiscal Federalism in Malaysia". In *Malaysia's Public Sector in the 21st Century: Planning for 2020 and Beyond*, edited by S. Wilson and M. Sulaiman. Kuala Lumpur: Malaysian Institute of Economic Research (MIER), 1997.

[9]

Tweaking the State Delivery
Mechanism: The Case of the MPPP

Ooi Kee Beng & Goh Ban Lee

The Historical and Political Contexts

The methodology used in producing this paper is experimental in that, aside from the customary reliance on secondary sources, the study derived most of the ideas about reforming the local government offered herein from in-depth interviews with the President of the Majlis Perbandaran Pulau Pinang (MPPP, the Municipal Council of Penang Island), Tan Cheng Chui, and other sources linked to the state government and the council.

Although both the DAP and PKR, the component parties of the Penang Pakatan Rakyat State Government, did promise to bring back local government elections in the 2009 general elections campaigns, it is clear that this cannot be done under the present laws. The adoption of the Local Government Act 171 in 1976 ended all constitutional provisions for local elections despite recommendations by the 1968 Royal Commission of Enquiry to Investigate into the Workings of Local Authorities in West Malaysia that local councils throughout the country, except the federal capital, Kuala Lumpur, should be elected (Athi Nahappan 1968: 105-6).

At present, any support from Putrajaya for the reinstatement of local elections cannot be expected until and unless there is a change of government at the federal level. While awaiting the return of local government elections, measures to democratize and improve local government being considered by the Penang state government include the setting up of an independent panel to act as the advisory body in the ap-

pointment of councillors. Fair representation without election in such a body is to be sought by ensuring sufficient distribution among members of the panel where gender, geographical abode, ethnic background and education level are concerned. At present, the MPPP consists of 24 councillors, as does its distant cousin, the Majlis Perbandaran Seberang Perai (MPSP), across the Penang Straits.

This panel is also to consider holding "informal" elections at chosen residential areas where the local resident association is pro-active and stable.

Given the overly centralised nature of governance in Malaysia at the moment, however, the most pressing question for improving governance in Penang is not so much broadening democracy in local politics as improving the quality of public services and making the main apparatuses for the providing of those services – the MPPP and the MPSP – efficient, economically and otherwise.

Where the state economy is concerned, its future was already looking increasingly bleak before the present global crisis, and before the change in state government in 2008. Figures from 2005 show that 43% of the state GDP was from manufacturing, but most of the employment in this sector – as much as two-thirds – was in low-value assembly industries. Comparisons of Mean Monthly Household Income by State between 1999 and 2004 reveal that Penang families had the lowest annual growth of *all* the states. No doubt Penang in 1999 was at a level lower only than the Federal Territory and Selangor, but it is telling that while Penang household incomes grew at an annual average of 2.5% during the first five years of this decennium, the same period saw Selangor families, in comparison, increasing their income by 6.9% per year – 2.7 times faster than was the case in Penang. The national yearly average for that period was 6.6% (Rimmer & Dick 2009: 101; Halipah 2006). However, it is also useful to note that the Mean Household Income in Penang, at RM3,531 per month in 2005 was still higher than that of the national figure at RM3,249 (Ninth Malaysia Plan 2006: 378).

The deteriorating macro-economic situation Penang, along with the less than lukewarm relations between the state and the federal governments and, lastly but most importantly, the centrally initiated and sustained processes of centralisation and privatisation, act as the harsh context within which we are to perceive the seriousness of the problems faced by the MPPP, the state, and the people of Penang not to mention the country, as well as the possible solutions that can be realised despite the many constraints.

According to the 9th Malaysia Plan, the state government is to provide suitable land sites for development and shorten the approval process at the Land Office, encourage inter-state cooperation for regional development and get its local authorities to improve the investment environment. While this directive remains, the political changes of March 8, 2008 mean that the focus of the new state government is more on state development than on compliance to federal planning objectives.

State development in such a situation is tantamount to state governance development aimed at encouraging locally driven economic growth, supplemented by efforts to attract foreign investments. Improving governance means improving the delivery apparatus – mainly the local councils in this case – towards (some would say back to) becoming a responsive and flexible machine that is systematically regulated and manned by motivated personnel proud of being a part of the local councils.

The present structure of local government in Penang came into being with the amalgamation of the city council and four district councils into two local councils on 15 December 1976 (Report 1971: 4). This restructuring had the aim of placing weaker local councils under richer ones in the hope that the former would draw advantages from the latter.

Major Issues

1. The state government and its local councils

This paper is written in light of the new possibilities presented by the end of long-term Barisan Nasional rule in Penang. That should perhaps be made apparent from the beginning. Understandably, the reforms suggested express a rationale of going "back to basics".

Central to the discussion about reforming the MPPP is the relationship between the elected state government on one hand, and the councillors and MPPP leadership it appoints on the other. As has often been pointed out, if the local government is popularly elected and holds

significant powers in providing public goods, then the role of the state government would be minimised to the extent of becoming irrelevant. However, at the same time, a local government badly subsumed under the state government is also badly sheltered from political battles, which would directly affect its ability to manage its finances and provide public goods.

The importance of this relationship is plainly reflected in their budgets. For 2009, the state of Penang has a budget of RM477million. This is not much more than the combined budgets of the two local governments, which is about RM390 million (The MPPP's budget is RM222 million, and the MPSP's is RM 165 million).

The new state government, pressured by its own inexperience in the exercise of power, its need to show quick results, the tentativeness among civil servants and foot-dragging by the federal government in implementing measures to improve the workings of the local authorities, cannot therefore ignore the possibility of turning the MPPP into the model of good and effective governance that its as yet winning slogans about transparency, accountability and competence wish to bring into being.

The local authority is at the frontline of the delivery process. How it performs is tantamount to how the state government performs, at least in the eyes of most voters, and on good grounds.

The first rule to get right thus concerns drawing a distinct boundary between the competencies of the two. With the state deciding ideological direction and developmental strategies, the local government can act confidently in carrying out its responsibilities of planning, implementation and enforcement. This enables the MPPP to participate meaningfully in the development of Penang, and to provide badly needed feedback on policy efficacy.

This requires that the state government provides a clear set of developmental goals and policies. Ad-hoc piece-meal proposals should be avoided, even if there is pressure to demonstrate that the state government knows what it is doing. But there is no need to hold back the implementation of elements of good governance as part of the state government's declared policy of adherence to CAT principles – competency, accountability and transparency.

Transparency becomes necessary and can be experienced as an unavoidable factor in good governance. Indeed, one could easily argue that bad governance depends on vague boundaries between politicians and civil servants, and on the lack of grounded and definite instructions.

Accountability requires definite ideas about what is demanded by superiors and what is required – and what is fair to require – of the lower ranks. Of course, competence cannot be judged unless the service required is clearly proposed. Indeed, training and recruitment policies are dependent on this basic condition.

Keeping goals secret and vague may be necessary in many political contexts, but not where steering a local council is concerned. Building morale among salaried civil servants calls for a strong profiling of areas of responsibilities, not only within the state executive council, but within the bureaucracy as such.

With the keen centralization of public services that has been going on in Malaysia over the last three decades, the overlapping of power among various authorities at the local level has become a major problem in the delivery of basic public goods. This is worsened by the fact that some authorities are controlled by the state, like the MPPP, some are federally controlled, and some are hybrid structures.

Together with the federal eagerness for so-called privatization of state bureaucracies, and the politicization of Malaysian life in general that as yet un-reviewed affirmative action policies has brought about, the centralization of local government activities constitutes a trinity of external processes that have weakened the power and ability of local governments, and caused much of the complicated problems they face today.

At the point where the delivery of public goods takes place, the state government therefore has the unenviable role of playing the spider in a sinister web of overlapping authorities. Paradoxically, this overlap of jurisdiction has not meant excessive governance. On the contrary, it has led to poor governance, and encouraged a shirking of responsibilities. What have emerged today are pockets of no-man's-land where irresponsibility and illegality are rewarded, both among government officials and common citizens.

For example, the state government was slow in ensuring that all reclaimed lands would come within the boundaries of the MPPP. As a result, large tracts of land were developed without going through the normal development control process that all private land owners are otherwise subjected to. Development control process was under the State Town and Country Planning Department. Whether or not Penangites are proud of the resultant built environment is another question.

The strengthening of the state apparatus and the state government in particular, depends therefore on the drawing of clear hierarchic relations within the state executive council, and on filling up the pockets of no-man's-land where incompetence, unaccountability and non-transparency rule.

The spider has a lot of web-repairing to do.

As long as lines of authority and the pecking order are not clear, and the shirking of responsibilities all the way down the line is starkly rewarded, politicians and top administrators become "fire-fighters" concerned with solving immediate problems, and moving where they can and de-prioritizing important issues that will subsequently have a hard time regaining priority in the future.

It is thus in the interest of state governments to revive the efficacy of the local government apparatus in delivering public goods and to keep the solving of local problems at as local a level as possible. That way, accountability can be better realised.

2. Human resources and MPPP legal power

And so, it is back to basics. Much needs doing: the competence and the authority of the political masters, where the nitty-gritty of local governance is concerned, has to improve successively, perhaps through clearly delineated areas of responsibility and accountability where exco members are concerned, and; perhaps as the way to kick off the whole process, pressure could be brought to bear from below through a "No Wrong Door" principle where complaints lodged with one authority, even if it is not clearly the right one, has to be facilitated within the MPPP bureaucracy acting as a single entity.

The human capital that the MPPP possesses – about 2,500 personnel – should be better utilized and developed. There is space for further recruitment of new professionals. At present, MPPP staff consists of

72% Malays, 20% Indians and 5% Chinese, making a need for better ethnic representation a pressing problem.

Keeping morale high remains a major concern. Does the staff know what is demanded of them? Are recruitment, appointment and promotion procedures seen as fair? Are they being properly trained? Are they given the right roles? Are the right people being recruited for the right jobs? What mechanisms are available to remedy wrong decisions?

The last is perhaps most important given how "fire-fighting" as policy has become the norm. A reliable system for collecting and assessing feedback from the implementation level is required. It must not be assumed that a systematic monitoring of the quality of the delivery of services actually takes place. That must be ascertained instead. Otherwise, a bad spiral downwards comes into being, and the end product will deviate from the original plan.

An area that has been neglected is the upgrading of posts in the two councils, especially in view of the exercise for comparable positions in the state and federal governments. For example, the Municipal Secretary of MPPP stands at a position that is lower than that of heads of many state departments. For all intents and purposes, it should be higher than theirs, or at least be placed at the same level.

It is indeed important that a structure plan is adopted along with high development control standards. But without a serious system for feedback upwards and for serious handling of this feedback, the opportunity costs for deviations will be unnecessarily high, economically, functionally and politically.

Feedback is necessary knowledge, without which vagueness and fire-fighting measures will continue to be regarded as virtues.

Much concern has been expressed since the general elections that the new governments in the states of Kedah, Perak, Selangor and Penang would face silent opposition and foot-dragging from civil servants used to the old apparent symbiosis between the political elite and the bureaucratic elite.

But what may be more significant factors where political loyalty is concerned are inter-personnel loyalties built up over a long period of employment and political stability (or inertia, depending on one's politics). Such ties, built up over time, dissipate dedication to the functions of the council. Favours were done, favours still need to be repaid, and

favourites had been picked over time. A network of mutual protection is strongly in place.

The sudden change in government has therefore threatened this network, and so, immediate loyalty to the new administration cannot be expected. Suspected conspiracies at the civil servant level may therefore not be of an ideological nature, but of a personal and therefore more changeable, nature.

What is more advisable as a general principle is for the state to encourage a sense of professionalism in the system, especially where a relatively healthy body like the MPPP is concerned.

At the moment, where work at the implementation level is concerned, there are two types of task force. The first is the operational staff that handles the common day-to-day routines. This is supported by the so-called extraordinary task force, meant to be deployed under extraordinary circumstances, when matters get out of hand. This is used in response to serious complaints, which could lead to inputs like drain cleaning, rubbish collection or getting rid of illegal parking attendants.

For example, illegal parking attendants are a nuisance in Penang. Complaints about them are plentiful but though eye-catching offenders, they come very low on the priority list of the police, due to a lack of manpower and other reasons.

> The MPPP cannot make arrests. What it does now is to deploy a task force that makes citizen arrests. These offenders are taken to the police where a report is made. When the police can't help us, we can turn things around and help the police instead (Tan Cheng Chui, interview 8 Feb 2009).

Unlike in Singapore, for example, where the lines of authority are clear, and one authority has the full right to serve notice on other authorities should they break regulations or the law, the MPPP's hands are often tied even when misdemeanours committed by other authorities are evident and the solution easy and obvious. The Land Transport Agency in Singapore, for instance, can fine the National Environmental Agency if the latter's personnel is caught blocking traffic.

The George Town City Council used to be in charge of most things that had to do with local government. For example, it used to provide piped water and electricity; it managed sewerage and ran a bus service. The process continues. At the moment, solid waste management is on the verge of being taken over by the federal government. The centralisation that has been dictated by the federal government has resulted in (1) leaving patches of no-man's-land in the delivery of public goods; (2) allowing local knowledge, skills and expertise to be ignored and overshadowed by distance planners who are more detached from the places their planning affects so intimately (as in the case of solid waste management); (3) taking away the clarity of purpose and action that only a strong local government can have; (4) diminishing the power and ability of the local government to act forcefully on issues that need tending to, and (5) making it difficult to hold any person, department or authority fully responsible for negligence and incompetence.

With well-defined powers, the MPPP will be able to minimize many of the ill-effects stemming from the serious overlapping of authority. The right to serve notice – without fear or favour – on other authorities appears vital if the downward spiral in the delivery of public goods is to be reversed.

> The public does not care how things get done. They only care about things getting done. They are not interested in internal squabbles and fighting, or how internal rules hamper public service. All they care about is that things get done and that it is the council's job to get them done (Tan, interview).

One important benefit that would come from the serving of notices between authorities is that they provide further knowledge about how each of these authorities is functioning. The political fallout from government departments breaking rules openly and going unpunished is easily underrated. In the eyes of the public, the "arrogance" of such behaviour undermines the authority and integrity of the government in general.

Furthermore, this can only worsen the present lack of civil responsibility found among Penangites and for that matter Malaysians in general. Non-compliance with municipal rules and regulations is one of the important reasons why Penang is not clean and pleasant despite its many by-laws and planning and building standards (Goh Ban Lee, 2002).

How he or she "got away with it" and "beat the system" becomes viable social games that the common man or woman feels pride in relating to friends and relatives. Rules lose integrity, and non-compliance becomes rational behaviour for the individual. Confidence in the government's sincerity and ability to implement its own rules is seriously damaged.

The strength of the British principle of local governance which Penang inherited – and was proud to inherit – once upon a time, and which Singapore polished further, was the simple message to the public: "Don't think you can get away with it". Some element of fear of the government was instilled in the public, but of the kind stemming from the fact that law would be implemented, not that the law would be misused or ignored.

> My enforcement people are told that when we serve a "compound", it must be clear that the offender will be punished within a week if nothing is done. This is especially important when there is a lack of resources. That is when you have to prioritize your actions according to efficacy. Make your actions count, and instil fear in the public that chances of them getting away with an offence are not good. For example, in the area around Upper Penang Road, where you are bound to have a large number of various offences being committed, such as illegal parking, etc, or illegal structures being put up, you have to strike unhesitatingly. Don't let offenders think that you are not serious, and that there will be no follow-up to council actions. Once we allow that, then our job becomes that much harder. The public will think the authorities are only going through the motions. So you see, the need for extraordinary task forces is quite evident at the moment (Tan, interview).

The present structure puts great pressure on state assemblymen, who are the ones that the public blames for the slow or lack of response to local complaints. Since the MPPP is the local body on the island, and is in the end the authority with the strongest moral obligation to see to it that public services do not descend to an untenable level, the exasperated politicians tend to rely on the willingness of the MPPP to be accommodative and to go the extra mile.

Should the Public Works Department (Jabatan Kerja Raya, JKR) fail to respond to a serious complaint about roads, for example, assemblymen have to bear the brunt of public anger, and to solve the problem quickly, the MPPP is called in to do some "fire-fighting". This recurring condition alone suggests that restructuring is needed to make areas of competence agree more closely with the reality of local government. A centralisation at the local level is needed to counteract the ills of federal centralisation.

Lack of good governance also leads to a dispersal of responsibility, professionalism, technical knowledge and basic documentation, allowing for blind spots in public administration to appear. The resultant lack of transparency and competence lays the ground for a culture of unaccountability. For example, on Penang Hill, where an overall mapping of the drainage system is missing, and the drains have consequently not been maintained, there are presently 50 official landslides spots where disaster is waiting to happen (Liew Chin Tong, interview 10 May 2009).

The management of rivers is another example. The responsibility of different aspects of river control and maintenance rests with different authorities. While drains are managed by the council, big drains and rivers are under the control of the Department of Irrigation and Drainage.

In order to counteract the serious everyday deficiencies of the locally decentralised system, the MPPP has been resorting to its task force resources. For example, in the face of the controversial centralisation and privatisation of solid waste, one section has been retained by the council for the purpose of preserving expertise, for maintaining a benchmark for other areas in the state to follow, and for backup purposes in case of emergencies (Tan, interview 13 May 2008).

The Penang Solid Waste Management Project was launched at the beginning of 2006 and was ready for implementation by early 2008, just before the general elections (UNDP 2008: iii). An immediate source of tension issues from how the Solid Waste Management Department at the Ministry of Local Government executes this outsourcing of this basic public service. It picks concessionaires who are given the right

to demand that the sum used by the local authorities for solid waste management be handed over to them. Not only is the wisdom of such a procedure dubious, the required sum of money is not one that is already in the bank, and that can be handed over on request. It is one that has to be collected through hard work by the local councils.

> The latest rumour is that the department will piggyback on the assessment bill system of the local government, getting everything for nothing in the process (Tan, interview).

Issues raised long before the implementation of the Bill, and which have become highly pertinent now, are: Where should residents lodge complaints, to the local authorities or to the Ministry of Housing and Local Government?; How will local councils be able to control concessionaires which they have had no hand in appointing?; and, will statistics about costs and volume, and other relevant information, be available to the public? (Goh 2009).

In accordance with the Federal Constitution, the National Council of Local Governments is the forum where the chief ministers and *mentri besar* meet under the chairmanship of the deputy prime minister.

> Before March 8, compliance to central decisions was the norm. Hopefully, with several PR representatives in that council now, things will get more exciting. If, as suspected, the quality of solid waste management deteriorates, the state government, whether responsible or not for agreeing to the project, will be blamed. The solid waste project remains highly controversial and contentious, and any reversal of it requires a change in government at the federal level. (Tan, interview).

3. Managing available sources of information

Basic to efficient modern public administration is a good and up-to-date ICT system. Indeed, MPPP was one of the first authorities in the country to become computer literate. However, not much has happened in recent years, and the synergy that an integrated computer system would have provided has not been obtainable. This is partially blame-able on the decentralisation at the local level wrought by the eager-ness of federal politicians and bureaucrats to centralise public services, but the lack of easily accessible and assessable information has helped foster a culture of non-transparency, unaccountability, and consequentially, incompetence.

Departments have become unable and unwilling to piggyback on others and to be piggybacked upon.

The lack of development in the computerisation of local government is due in no small measure to the lack of vision and to the computer illiteracy of the top management. Incompetence at the top is always a serious flaw.

An effective measure to be taken at this point to remedy the deteriorating situation is to upgrade the MPPP's computer section into a department. Once it is a department, it can start planning for the whole council. So whatever computer upgrading, whatever new software is needed, will be controlled from that one department. It is only then that we can achieve an integrated computer system that works for the whole local government. This department can become advisors for the rest, and will be able to maximize computer usage, whether software or hardware. Such centralization is worth investing in. In the long run, a lot of resources will be saved. Once you automate as much as possible, the system will be able to maintain a high level of integrity. There will be less wastage of manpower and travel miles if all new information is fed back into the system so that all involved can check things out at will (Tan, interview).

Since transparency and accountability are best ensured if information is freely available and accessible, developing ICT and upgrading the computer unit into a department are necessary steps to take, both for ideological reasons and for reasons of efficiency.

Efficiency should not only involve the collection of duties and assessments. Far from that, enforcement time, which has always been a major concern, can be shortened, and an integration of the complaints system can be achieved through Information and Communication Technology (ICT) centralisation at the MPPP.

With a central database that is successively expanded, the MPPP and the state will be equipped with useful information that can be used in various areas, such as planning, implementation and enforcement, as well as control and monitoring.

Even if there was a good master plan, the state and its councils must have access to updated and reliable statistics about common people and their living conditions if it is to plan, and implement plans, successfully. It is important that planners and implementers know what is out there, and know what bigger picture they are functioning within.

With details about age groups, geographical concentration, income patterns, etc., structural and local plans will have greater integrity and usefulness. Politicians will be able to resort to them, and have a better idea of the issues they decide upon and talk about, and what the social needs of the moment actually are.

Easy access to information contained in the databases of other authorities will also help MPPP function more efficiently. For example, the ability to check up on car number plates on JPJ (Jabatan Pengangkutan Jalan) computers immediately would make the enforcing of traffic and parking regulations more effortless.

Once a central system for collecting and computing data were available, information on traffic conditions, for example, could be shared out to road users without delay. Not only would this help drivers to plan their trip instantaneously, it would also strengthen public confidence that the state was on top of things, and that it was not asleep.

> Getting the infrastructure in place is the first thing you need to do. Within MPPP, we do have an integrated system. But between authorities, we have the problem of "Little Napoleons". But more than being a mere protecting of individual turf, or keeping information secret in order to enhance one's own relevance, such behaviour within the civil service also hides the fact that information kept in our databases are not up to standard or up to date (Tan, interview).

The possibility of putting the blame for a lack of information makes it easy to hide incompetence and negligence. With a reliable central database available, the chances of reversing the downward spiral of non-transparency, incompetence and unaccountability would be significantly raised.

> It should be seen as a basic public service for authorities to make information easily accessible on the Internet. The Internet can be garnered to better governance

at all levels. Authorities are paid to collect and compute information, so why is that information then kept from the public? Transparency is indeed very important at this level. Whatever figures we have, whatever information we have, should be available to the public and to other authorities. That way, competence is kept high, and the correctness and updatedness of information are ensured (Tan, interview).

Indeed, it is hard to argue that the public would not appreciate reliable information about housing development projects, and about the developers and every party involved in them. Given such a tool, the common man would have better chances of making informed decisions, or learning to make informed decisions. More importantly, they learn to turn to the government for reliable information.

4. Funding matters

Undoubtedly, a local authority on an island would be ineffectual and even irresponsible if it did not maintain a land bank, and manage that well at the same time.

Ensuring that MPPP assets are properly managed over the long term is therefore an important state matter as well as council matter. No conflict of interest need exist between the optimal use of assets over time and the fulfilling of planning goals. Unfortunately, in the past, choice pieces of municipal land have been sold to private developers.

> Careless unlocking of land resources will quickly get MPPP into trouble. Given the political culture in the country, care is needed to safeguard these assets (Tan, interview).

Cost-effectiveness must also be a vital consideration, and economic sense should steer the functioning of the council. Continuous purchasing of land, for example, is advisable. Once any MPPP land is exploited, the principle should be that new acres should be acquired to replenish the bank. The basic idea is that in the long run, not only does the council make money out of land use; it is kept economically healthy while continuing to provide services.

A principle of economic self-sustenance at council level, especially given the distrust and conflict of interests that mark the relationship

between the state and federal governments, should be seriously considered. Independence from federal funding is needed if local competence is to be strengthened and distant dictates avoided.

> Relying on federal government funds does not only mean that your hands are tied, and that the central authority will dictate terms to you, it also means that it will bring in its own contractors and developers, and what this means in the end is that the federal government can claim that it gave projects to the state; but in reality, the state and its councils are left with subsequent problems, and are left paying for the maintenance.

> We should generate our own funds instead. Of course, politicians do wish that taxes taken by the federal government should be ploughed back into the state, but the projects that come from the centre tend to be for the well-being of people connected to the centre, and tend not to be sincerely meant for nation-building or for serving the public. That is my general experience. How things will change from now on is an open question.

> Federal funding comes with a wish to clip the wings of the local authorities. There is an insidious centralism behind federal planning which assumes that the success of local authorities subtracts from the authority of the federal government and its many arms.

> Instead of taking functioning local authorities as the benchmark for good governance, you get many cases of the federal government undermining such authorities instead (Tan, interview).

The reality of such disappointing experiences with federal authorities and government departments suggests that local councils should try to generate more funds by themselves. More importantly, representatives of state governments in the National Council for Local Government should push for automatic federal annual allocations to the local authorities since the existing tax regime greatly favours the federal government. If experiences since March 8, 2009, are any indicator, things may get worse in the foreseeable future. Circulars, guidelines and academic surveys from the Ministry of Local Government have increased steadily over the last few months.

After the shift in power in Penang state in 2008, the ranking exercise that had been taking place before is now strongly suspected of having become a political game.

> We had to open up our books for the central authorities to humiliate us. The ranking should be done by the people instead, the people we serve, not by central bureaucrats with dubious aims (Tan, interview).

5. Review of standard operational procedures

Given the great changes wrought on local governance by federal ambitions to privatize the delivery of public goods in the wake of rapid urbanisation, changing technology and economic development, it is not surprising that bylaws and regulations quickly become outmoded. These rules need reviewing if local governance is to be improved.

Such reviews should be geared towards Key Performance Indexes such as the rationalizing of processing periods, and should reflect a style of governance that is more proactive than what has been experienced in recent decades.

These KPIs should include the complaint turnabout as well. By showing serious concern to complaints, local governance goes back to the people. With a new sense of engagement, comes a need for greater transparency.

A restructuring of the system requires an ambition to turn MPPP personnel into specialists. Without specialisation, it is difficult to demand accountability and transparency of the staff. Black-and-white appraisal of staff entails clear lines of responsibility, which means that the KPI's must be clearly formulated as well.

Summation

Federal disregard for – and inability to understand – local government concerns remains a problem. Without appreciation for the importance of feedback at the point of implementation, a lack of follow-through becomes inevitable, culminating in a lack of cooperation

within the structure of local governance, and in non-transparency even in routine procedures.

It is vital that the state realises how important a well-informed reform of the structure of local government is to its own ability to perform and to deliver on the promises it made in the general elections. Major challenges involve stemming problems issuing from the sustained federal drive towards centralisation, privatization and outsourcing, and the excessive politicization of public goods delivery.

Much is gained if politicians provide the ideological rationale and the clear directives that local government needs to reform itself and deliver necessary public services, and maintain separation of functions.

A patent relationship between the state government and the MPPP in that the latter receives clear directives from the state executive council, on which it can immediately act, is necessary.

While a thorough reform of the system within its larger national context is needed in the long run, the points of entry for immediate reforms include the following:

1. Value-add where human resources are concerned. This includes training, better placement of skills, promotion based on meritocracy as the norm, clear directives and KPIs being announced, as well as the recruitment of new professionals. In the end, "I work for the council" should once again become a statement of pride. Promotion based on meritocracy has been sidelined too long.

2. Managing and maintaining MPPP assets aside from human resources. Cost effectiveness should inform all planning and all policy making. Maintenance and operational costs should be given equal consideration. In order to be cost-effective, feedback is required and should be prioritized. Without feedback, no learning and adapting to new situations are possible. The concept of opportunity costs should be widely proselytized, and within this should be considered the economic value of good civics. Keeping the state and city clean and functioning is easier if public civic-mindedness is inculcated broadly, either through education or a system of fines. Managing funds is a major issue, as is the maintenance of land ownership over the long term.

3. Upgrading the computer section into a department. This can be the first step in computerizing public administration, and holds the potential to reverse the work culture presently sliding into incompetence and defensiveness.

4. Review of standard operational procedures, involving the implementation of clear KPIs, without which demands for accountability are not always fair.

5. Promotion of community relations and participation in the policy-making process. Public consultation, feedbacks, involvement, publicity & promotion and media cooperation are some pertinent considerations for better governance and best practices.

As Tan Cheng Chui often and fervently states, "with the right political will, the MPPP can be improved greatly". In the final analysis, the onus is on the state government to develop a culture of excellence within itself, in the public administration, and consequently, in the people of Penang.

Bibliography

Annual Report 2007. Municipal Council of Penang Island.

Anwar Fazal. "The struggle for local democracy in Malaysia – Challenges and Opportunities". Paper presented at the National Convention of Citizens and Residents Association on Planning and Local Government Acts, in Kuala Lumpur. 19 Dec 1999.

Athi Nahappan. Report of the Royal Commission of Enquiry to Investigate into the Workings of Local Authorities in West Malaysia. Government Printers. 1968.

Goh Ban Lee: Non-compliance – A Neglected Agenda in Urban Governance. Johor Baru: Institut Sultan Iskandar of Urban Habitat and Highrise. 2002.

Goh Ban Lee. "The demise of local government elections and urban politics". In Mavis Puthucheary and Norani Othman (eds): *Elections and Democracy in Malaysia*. Bangi: Penerbit Universiti Kebangsaan Malaysia. 2005

Goh Ban Lee. *Counselling Local Councils*, Fomca: Kuala Lumpur. 2008.

Halipah Binti Isa. "The Ninth Malaysia Plan and its Implications on the Penang Economy. Paper presented at the Seminar on the 9th Malaysia Plan organized by the Socio-economic & Environment Institute, Penang. 29 April 2006.

Khoo Boo Teik. *Ethnic Structure, Inequality and Governance in the Public Sector. Malaysian Experiences*. Democracy, Governance and Human Rights Programme Paper Number 20. United Nations Research Institute for Social Development. December 2005.

Lim Hong Hai. "Malaysia: Distilling the Lessons of Forty Years". In Ho Khai Leong: *Rethinking Administrative Reforms in Southeast Asia*. Singapore: Marshall Cavendish 2006.

Norris, Maurice. *Local Government in Peninsular Malaysia*. University of Birmingham. 1980.

Report of the Committee to Study the Implications of the Report of the Royal Commission of Enquiry to Investigate into the Workings of Local Authorities in West Malaysia, Part 1. Government Printers. 1971.

Report by the Local Government Elections Working Group, Penang. 20 April 2009.

Report of the Local Government Working Group for the Penang Local Government Consultative Forum 2008, Penang. September 2008.

Rimmer, Peter J. & Howard Dick. *The City in Southeast Asia. Patterns, Processes and Policy*. Singapore: NUS Press.

Rüland, Jürgen. *Urban Development in Southeast Asia: Regional Cities and Local Government*. Boulder, San Francisco and Oxford: Westview Press. 1992.

Tennant, Paul. "The Abolition of Elective Local Government in Penang", in *Journal of Southeast Asian Studies*, Vol. 4, No. 1. 1973.

UNDP. *Malaysia Developing a Solid Waste Management Model for Penang*. Kuala Lumpur: United Nations Development Programme. 2008.

Pilot Studies for a New Penang

Interviews

Tan Cheng Chui, acting president of Majlis Perbandaran Pulau Pinang, on 8 February 2009 and 13 May 2009 at the Penang Sports Club, Penang.

Liew Chin Tong, Member of Parliament for Bukit Bendera, Penang and member of the Local Government Elections Working Group, on 10 May 2009 at Putra Marine Resort, Penang,

[10]

Positioning Penang for Sustainable Growth

Nungsari Ahmad Radhi & Hamdan Abd Majeed

Penang has always been a story of change. It has evolved dramatically over the centuries, starting out as a forest-covered land with an economy based primarily on agriculture and regional trading back in the 18th century, to a manufacturing hub in the 1970s, a transformation that put Penang on the world map.

And so it had turned from a resourced-based economy into an economy steeped in trading, alongside the emergence of a cosmopolitan and culturally-diverse city, with its own distinct identity that set it apart from the rest of Malaysia. But as other nation states rose, coupled with the removal of its free port status, its days as a trading hub were coming to an end. Penang needed to change, and it had to change quickly.

This gave birth to the Penang we are all familiar with today. The past three decades saw the rise of a new economic phenomenon: the Free Trade Zone and the concept of off-shoring. We saw rapid industrial development with a focus on the electric & electronic industry (E&E). We had a period where the GDP grew by 11 percent, or 40 percent per capita higher than the national average. Few other places in the world experienced the kind of growth Penang did.

Today Penang is a technology hub, producing 50 percent of the world's microprocessors. Once an agriculture-driven industry, it is now a Free Trade Zone economy, driven by multinational corporations and

supported by a host of small-medium enterprises. These firms have since expanded their operations in great numbers, sophistication and diversity, and are currently moving up to engage in higher value-added activities. There is little doubt that the base is widening.

But is Penang prepared for the next phase of change? According to a survey done by Khazanah about a year ago, firms' activities are dramatically changing, and they are no longer just manufacturing-based. But in order for change to happen, a whole host of enabling environment changes need to happen first, including an upgrading in knowledge intensity. This simply is not happening as quickly as it should.

The World is Changing. Penang is Not.

In fact, Penang's growth, once the marvel of the world, has actually decelerated over the years. Its primary engines of growth, manufacturing and tourism, have slowed after peaking in the 1990s. Meanwhile, competition has intensified with the emergence of new growth cities like Hanoi, Chennai, Guang Zhou and Shenzen, among others. Our immediate competitors, Hong Kong, Singapore and Taiwan, have made the quantum leap, even though Penang had started out at par or ahead of them.

Penang is at a crossroads. What are our options? How do we take advantage of what we have already built, and get Penang back on track once more in today's economy?

One way is to leverage on Penang's existing ecosystem of firms. The George Town Conurbation currently has some 2,500 companies engaged in a variety of industries, with a heavy concentration on the E&E industry. We should embrace what we already have and enhance it. Leverage on the past to enhance the present, and shape the future. Keep in mind, however, that shaping the future requires a close partnership with private companies, the Federal Government and various institutions.

Penang should also avoid what is called "blind diversification". Do not diversify for the sake of it; by trying to be good at everything, you'll invariably turn up being excellent at nothing. If Penang is to distinguish itself from its competitors, it must deepen its specialisation in order to see some benefit on scale effect. Select a few sectors according to three criteria: scale economies, their link to supply chains or their regional advantages, and existing strengths and capabilities you could build on. And among Penang's strengths include the fact that it is already part of a global supply chain network, as well as its already established logistics capabilities and skilled workers. It is imperative that the state maintain and build on these.

Penang has existing growth areas that are struggling right now — focus on strengthening and optimising them. With the manufacturing sector, there should be a focus on the high technology segment of the value chain. With the tourism sector, specialised medical tourism and boutique MICE are big growth areas; in fact, Penang is presently the largest market when it comes to medical tourism.

Other than helping existing growth areas, the state could also promote growth in new areas, areas such as agribusiness (modern farming, supply chain management, halal hub), life sciences (biotechnology, medical devices and diagnostics) and business process outsourcing and information technology outsourcing , which involves leveraging Penang's MSC status along with the presence of large multinational corporations.

Thirdly, we need to rebrand this new Penang. Penang needs to be looked at as a secondary regional city, a "sticky space" for retaining local talent while attracting new talent from around the world. No longer "just" a manufacturing hub, Penang needs to be seen as a destination for high-value individuals to visit and conduct their businesses. It needs to be seen as an attractive enough place where high-value workers would actually want to live and work.

For this to happen, a paradigm shift is required. Charles Landry once said, "Penang happens to stand at the cusp of a rare opportunity to put itself at the centre but it cannot be grasped by a business as usual approach. It needs clarity of purpose and vision and talented people to make it happen." Penang must be ready to embrace a new way of thinking, and embrace its potential as a secondary regional city. The fact is that Penang is not competing with other nations — it is competing with other cities, like Bangkok and Singapore and so on. This competition is intense, but can be a good thing for Penang, even an advantage. The future is through networks and partnerships, and Penang has already established itself as part of the technology nodes of Asia.

Penang is not going to be another big city like Bangkok, and it should not try to be. It should be distinguished by something uniquely Penang. Penang has a lot of social capital to work with, and it needs to develop and take advantage of this existing technology network. The challenge lies in how Penang positions itself in the Network Economy. To be a valued member of this network, Penang needs to possess knowledge content and branding, improved infrastructure, quality of governance, economies of scale and critical mass, quality of information, and the ability to stay ahead of the competition. It may be a tall order, but it is achievable. Penang's biggest asset has always been its people, and it simply is not doing enough to leverage on them.

The rewards could be enormous. Penang could be the business and services hub of the Bay of Bengal. Why not? It is already well-placed to become a hub for the Northern Corridor, the Indonesia-Malaysia-Thailand growth triangle (IMT-GT) and the Bay of Bengal. The Corridor is well situated as the dominant economic mass in the IMT-GT, and Penang has the highest economic density and lowest distance to market for a large local area in the triangle. The economics of geography suggest that high density localities (such as Penang) are best placed to attract new firms and exploit economies of scale. Penang needs to be ready to take advantage of that, as it is strategically located to benefit from regional growth, while supported by good infrastructure and connectivity through road, sea, air and rail. It also has access to a large hinterland of resources, human capital and technology.

The opportunity that lies ahead of us is in taking advantage of our past, position and people. In the first half of the 21st century, the fastest growing poles will be the Middle East, China and India. In light of that, which country is culturally, geographically and resource-wise best placed to take advantage of these countries' growth? Malaysia, with its melting pot of Muslims and Chinese and Indian citizens! And Penang is already a strong brand. Its food, beaches and colonial heritage are large tourism draws. The core of George Town is now a UNESCO World Heritage Site, and Penang is well-known as the culinary capital of Malaysia, thanks to its renowned street food. And thanks to its manufacturing sector, it is also known as the Silicon Valley of the East.

Let's contextualise Penang's next evolution by looking at its history. From 1786 to 1969 it was a trading hub. It was agriculture and resource-based and became a cosmopolitan and culturally-diverse city. It featured a dynamic secondary city with its own distinct identity and economy. It then evolved into a manufacturing hub, and it experienced unprecedented growth. It became a technology hub, with half of the world's microprocessors produced in the state.

But there is a risk that this route may lead to a middle income trap, where wages stagnate even as inflation rise. The fact is that you do not want Penang to compete on a low-cost basis — this is simply not a viable option if Penang truly wants to develop and evolve. The competition instead lies between cities, for talent. We live in a world that is defined by competition for talent. Penang's diaspora and cosmopolitanism can be an asset for the knowledge economy.

Obviously, this does not come without its fair share of challenges, and the challenges Penang will face are tremendous. Not only does it have to deal with increasing competition between cities for talent, it is also facing the challenges that face a middle income country. It is losing out in competitiveness to its rivals, no thanks to an attrition of talent that prefer to work elsewhere, along with weak clusters. Penang faces significant structural issues and distribution challenges as well. The George Town Conurbation is the key to unlocking Penang's potential to be the heart of the region, by leveraging on its past, place and people: it has an rich endowment of industry, heritage and history; its geographical location as an urban centre; and its cosmopolitan living heritage. The Northern Corridor Economic Region is especially critical to the national equation, contributing 20 percent of the GDP.

To define its next evolution, Penang will need a city-centric strategy. It is necessary to nurture and attract global talent, since creative and capable people are the primary source of long-term economic growth. Along with its economic strategy, there must also be a spatial strategy that will enable Penang to become a sustainable and liveable city, supported by an ecosystem that is seamless and interconnected with the right level of spatial density. It also needs to take advantage of the potential of virtual agglomeration with an institutional arrangement for the 21st century.

Penang is facing a myriad of issues and problems at the moment. But we cannot wait until the housekeeping issues are over and done with before moving on with Penang's evolution. This evolution, in

whatever form it may take, must happen now. And sometimes we need to wing it along the way and see what happens.

[11]

The Wage-Productivity Question and Women in the Workforce: A Labour Statistics Approach for the Penang State Government[1]

Hwa Yue-Yi

Introduction

Since the conclusion of the 1970s glory days, Penang's manufacturing sector has been hemmed in by price competition from peer economies on one side and stunted technological growth vis-à-vis developed nations on the other. Newer local industries, such as tourism, are also stranded in the limbo between aggressively low labour costs and progressively sophisticated infrastructures. Furthermore, the state lacks the instruments to assess the full symptoms of its ailing competitiveness. Such powerful statistical instruments are available on a national level but sorely underutilised by policymakers.

With today's advanced data management technology, it would be an indefensible waste to bypass labour market data analysis in the pursuit of effective employment policy. This need for informed labour policy development is accentuated by the nature of the state government's mandate: although it has limited influence over economic demand, whether from federal government initiatives or private investment, it could play a significant role in harnessing the local workforce for sustainable growth in the economy. Furthermore, the relatively small

---

1   The research for this paper was conducted during an internship at the Socio-economic and Environmental Research Institute (SERI), Penang, under the supervision of Senior Research Fellow Dr. Chan Huan Chiang during the summer of 2009.

workforce in Penang makes policy formulation all the more delicate. Hence, understanding the particulars of the labour market becomes crucial.

This paper makes a case for the establishment of a body of Penang-specific labour market indicators that are routinely updated and shared with local stakeholders. The first section gives an overview of workforce statistics in Malaysia. It examines issues in data dissemination, as typified by the Department of Statistics' Labour Force Survey, and in statistical rigour, as exemplified by the Ministry of Human Resources' Electronic Labour Exchange.

The second and third sections consider avenues through which data-driven policy development could optimise potential GDP[2], which is the product of productivity and workforce strength. These sections examine two facets of potential GDP: (a) the relationship between wages and productivity and how this interacts with Penang's high-investment industries, and (b) raising female labour force participation for economic vitality and family welfare gains. The fourth section extends this discussion by proposing a number of actions for the state government, and the final section concludes.

Labour Statistics for Penang: Potential and Problems

Official labour statistics in Malaysia run the gamut from the quarterly Business Tendency Survey, which observes general economic climate sentiments from 465 industry leaders, to the decennial Population and Housing Census, which incorporates comprehensive employment information from all living quarters in the country. Falling in between are a range of Department of Statistics (DOS) sector-specific surveys of varying detail[3], as well as records of retrenchments, worker protections and the like, which employers are legally required to report.

In stark contrast to this wealth of labour market information, there is a paucity of both rigorous employment data analysis and statistical indicators in labour policy, whether at federal or state levels. That said, it would be equally unproductive to swing to the other end of the spectrum, scrutinising spreadsheet after spreadsheet of human resource

---

2   *Or Gross Regional Product, in the case of Penang.*

3   *See "Surveys and Censuses" at <www.statistics.gov.my>.*

numbers as an end in itself. The prudent middle ground is to select certain labour market measures that can sketch a reasonably accurate picture of the landscape and thus shape policy decisions. This representative selection of statistics can then serve to track the impact of policy actions.

There is no need to quantify the employment situation with perfect precision, in part because policies aim at a moving target—which renders the highly accurate decennial census data obsolete by the time it is released—and in part because statistics is a discipline that understands uncertainty. However, it is essential to have an idea of how imperfect the data are.

To illustrate the role of statistical measures in labour policy, consider the unemployment rate. Theories on the trade-off between unemployment and inflation, as well as technocrats who argue that a robust investment climate can coexist with high unemployment, may claim that such statistics are irrelevant. For Penang, an additional argument against the centrality of the unemployment rate is the fact that Penang's labour supply includes individuals currently residing elsewhere in the federation, whether professionals who cut their teeth in the Klang Valley or factory employees from Kedah and Perak—to say nothing workers from other countries.

If, however, the state government contemplates social justice, or the quality of life in Penang, or the inefficiency of providing public services to economically inactive residents, then the employment rate becomes a matter of vital interest—even if different datasets yield conflicting signals. For example, if retrenchment figures reported by firms show higher unemployment than corresponding data from surveys of private households, this contradiction may suggest robust growth in the informal sector, as distinct from taxable employment in registered companies.

Although there is tremendous room for study and application in any of the data frames currently available, this paper will focus on two major statistical instruments: the DOS Labour Force Survey (LFS), a monthly household survey, and the Ministry of Human Resource's (MOHR) Electronic Labour Exchange (ELX).

The Labour Force Survey and Issues in Output

The LFS is a rich and rigorous dataset, but the potency of its statistics is hampered by their very limited dissemination. Like the decennial census, the LFS complies with international statistical standards, uses household interviews and is administered by the DOS. Unlike the Census, data is collected every month, rather than every ten years; from a sample of living quarters, rather than every listed residence; and with a focus on employment, rather than a broad spectrum of social, economic and housing characteristics. In addition, the Wages and Salaries Survey and the Migration Survey are appended to the LFS annually.

In addition to demographic particulars, the LFS collects detailed information on the labour market activity of all working-aged members in a surveyed household (see Chart 1). Respondents are asked not only about work patterns during the reference week, but also the reasons behind their choices. For example, individuals who are neither employed nor actively seeking work can give any of 13 different reasons for their lack of activity, including "believe no suitable work available", "going for further studies" and "bad weather" (DOS 2009a). Such specificity allows for analysis of workforce motivations, and thus for the creation of policy that engages these motivations.

All this employment information comes from a total of 68,000 households annually. These households are drawn from the decennial census sampling frame to characterize rural and urban areas of each state and the federal territories of Malaysia (DOS 2009b). Once tabulated, LFS responses are weighted against both the composition of the sample and national population estimates to yield numbers for the entire country. These benchmarked data are the source for the national employment rate and other key metrics. According to a Department of Statistics statement, the LFS has the highest response rate among all its household surveys (DOS 2003).

Strict standards govern this important survey. The LFS complies with the International Labour Organization's statistical methods, facilitating direct comparison with data from other countries. Furthermore, job sectors and descriptions in the LFS are classified using the Malaysia Standard Industrial Classification (MSIC) and the Malaysia Standard Classification of Occupations (MASCO), as are corresponding data from other government agencies, e.g. Ministry of Finance records of the GDP disaggregated by sector. The LFS also benefits from ongoing DOS refinements of staff skills, technology and statistical processes.

While the collection and preparation of data is given scrupulous attention, very little seems to be allotted to its publication. To wit: the LFS is comparable to the United States Current Population Survey (CPS) in terms of scope and analytic capacity. From the perspective of data dissemination, however, the LFS is the poor cousin of its U.S. counterpart, particularly in the areas of publication frequency, data availability and level of detail (see Table 1).

Granted, the comparison is an unfair one due to the countries' relative sizes: the United States channels far more financial and intellectual resources to employment accounting than Malaysia can. One could also argue that there is little need for labour market statistics in Malaysia: according to the DOS, demand for statistics is highest for national accounts, external trade, manufacturing, services and population (DOS 2003).

Although on some levels it may be justifiable for the DOS to levy a fee for detailed data releases, this is simply not an efficient use of resources. With current information systems, the main cost of a dataset is collecting and tabulating data. Additional dissemination incurs comparatively insignificant cost—and generates substantial gains for policymakers, academicians, entrepreneurs, not-for-profit organizations and students. These gains are then multiplied to communities through well-grounded decisions and advocacy. As much as the public release of, say, wage statistics by ethnic group may initially rankle, the government needs to furnish its people with a wide range of information if it is serious about building the evaluative and data navigation skills that are hallmarks of a knowledge-based economy[4].

The problem of inadequate dissemination is not exclusive to the DOS or the LFS. With the exception of Bank Negara, which makes comprehensive statistics available free-of-charge on its website, it is difficult to name a governmental agency that regularly puts detailed data in the public domain. The Ministry of Human Resources has made some headway with its annual compilation *Labour and Human Resources Statistics*, which can be downloaded for free at <www.mohr.gov.my>. However, most of the data in *Labour and Human Resources*

---

4   See, for example, <http://www.epu.gov.my/knowledgebasedeconomy>.

Statistics appear in very broad categories. As such, they can serve as general year-on-year indicators, but do not permit high-level analysis that can suggest cause-and-effect and so help to guide policies.

The Electronic Labour Exchange and Issues in Accuracy

All the employment information in the volume *Labour and Human Resources Statistics* is retrieved from a self-reporting system called the Electronic Labour Exchange (ELX), which hosts the job-matching platform JobsMalaysia (launched in 2002 as the Job Clearing System). This system is administered by the MOHR, which also uses ELX data for the monthly Labour Market Report available on its website. Different MOHR agencies also utilise ELX numbers for various purposes. The Penang Labour Department, for one, relies on employment data from the ELX, as well as retrenchment, closure and Voluntary Separation Scheme (VSS) records which employers are required by law to report[5].

Unlike the weighted samples of the LFS, the ELX presents cumulative counts. The primary flaw of these counts is that the ELX is an online system and depends on voluntary reporting, thus introducing chronic selection bias. Certain categories of people—for example, tech-savvy urbanites—are the most likely to use the system and therefore will be overrepresented. Furthermore, there is no incentive for registrants who obtain jobs through other channels to update their particulars. This vulnerability is demonstrated by the fact that active registrants rose from 190,237 in June 2008 to 315,442 active registrants one year later (MOHR 2009a), a 65.8 percent increase that probably reflects increased penetration of the interface more than anything else.

Nevertheless, the strengths of this database are arguably as compelling as its weaknesses. Despite the cumbersome separations into "active registrants" and "new registrants", the data are reported with a useful range of classifications: not just age, gender, industry and occupation, but also state, work experience, graduate/non-graduate status

---

5   As noted by Hoe Lean Fatt, director for the Penang branch of the Labour Department, during a meeting with the Socio-economic and Environmental Research Institute on August 21, 2009.

and type of skill certificate[6]. Moreover, the ELX is one of the rare systems that interacts simultaneously with individuals and establishments, generating data on job movements, i.e. vacancies and placements, as well as individual employment statuses. A further benefit is that ELX does not entail tedious data entry.

The dual function of the ELX, as a recruitment tool and a data collection mechanism, renders it an even worthier object of study and investment. As such, efforts to improve the statistical accuracy of the ELX will also reap returns for its job-matching capabilities, and vice versa. On the obvious level, regular publicity campaigns—which become even more important when economy is stricken and the job market tight, as at the time of writing—will improve the coverage of the system. Drawing more workers and employers into the system will strengthen the incentive for others to register: the larger the pool, the higher the probability of a good match. Also, although it might not be possible to offer registrants incentives to update their employment statuses, system administrators could easily send out periodic reminders to that end, whether through e-mail, SMS or the post.

Regardless of how extensive ELX coverage may one day become, there is a pressing need to introduce statistical treatments of the data that go beyond generating tables, to allow controlling for its biases. It is convenient to merely extract and publish the numbers directly. However, this sort of complacency is detrimental to the accuracy, and hence the policy relevance, of this data frame. Before the ELX can become a consequential labour market indicator, a whole body of technical documentation needs to be developed. On the most basic level, there are no available definitions of terminology: it is unclear what is meant even by "active registrants"—whether this group comprises everyone who has registered at some point, those who have accessed the system in the last month, those who state that they are unemployed, or some other description.

To further refine ELX statistics, it is important to introduce some sort of weighting for its inherent selection bias. LFS metrics, for example, are weighted against annual population estimates from the census (DOS 2009). In a similar vein, it would be possible to benchmark

---

6   *Although most of these details are also included in the LFS, they are reported in far more general terms.*

the proportion of urban workers, or graduates, or 18 to 25 year-olds, in the ELX against the corresponding percentage from the LFS or census estimates. Alternative weighting methods could also be attempted, such as matching ELX registrants and internet usage statistics for each zip code.

It must be noted that the contention here is not cumulative counts from a sample versus weighted estimates for the whole country; there is nothing wrong, per se, with using month-by-month changes rather than absolute numbers. Rather, it is a matter of formulating some concept of who the ELX registrants are, relative to the composition of Malaysia's workforce. As it is, all that an increase in active registrants conclusively says is that more individuals with Malaysian identity cards have filled in an electronic form.

As with limited dissemination, accuracy issues also plague numerous labour statistics instruments in Malaysia. The bottom line is that one cannot diagnose the economy using a broken stethoscope and blurry X-ray prints and expect to nurse it effectively.

Productivity and Wages

One question that can be answered with appropriate statistical instruments is whether productivity gains translate into wage increases, and vice versa. This wage-productivity relationship is pivotal for Penang due to the nature of her industries. Unlike the rest of Malaysia, which maintains a comparative advantage in resource-based exports, Penang holds a comparative advantage in technology-intensive industries, which imply higher skills and wages (Yusuf and Nabeshima 2009).

Although many studies examine the wage-productivity dynamic on the level of employees within individual firms[7], Millea (2002) evaluated both the conventional theory (i.e., increased productivity leads to higher wages) and the efficiency wage theory (i.e., higher wages lead to increased productivity) using wage and productivity statistics from manufacturing sectors in six OECD countries. Similar analysis could be carried out for Penang using wage data across manufacturing subsectors in the LFS and productivity metrics from the Malaysia Productivity Corporation. Comparison would be aided by the fact that both of these data sources use the Malaysia Standard Industrial Classification.

Other wage-productivity interactions in Penang that warrant statistical study are considered below.

Foreign labour

Despite perennial discussion about whether lower-tier foreign workers should be phased out of the local economy in order to accelerate the shift to highly skilled local labour (UKM 2002), little has changed. Within Penang, many factories rely on cheap low-skilled foreign labour, which keeps short-run expenses down. However, this may come at the cost of future gains, because the longer the workforce is held to low skill levels, the further Penang's competitiveness is eroded.

LFS data on wages, nationality, industry and occupation would be helpful for gauging the contributions of low-wage foreign workers in Penang. Should analysis reveal that it is expedient to depend more on the native labour force, the impetus for change must come from the government (perhaps through stricter quotas), as individual employers are caught in the dilemma of losing greatly if they retrench while competitors do not.

The minimum wage option

Fold and Wangel (1997) recommend that Penang institute a minimum wage to increase efficiency, motivate local labour reserves to enter the market, reduce dependence on foreign labour and stabilise workforce turnover rates. If statistical investigation reveals that productivity in Penang does increases as wages increase, a minimum wage could force employers to pursue drastically more efficient production processes, whether through investments in technology, R&D or human capital development. Although such a move may initially spark mass layoffs, it may be fundamental to Penang's economic sustainability.

Malaysia lags far behind other countries—including Indonesia, Thailand, the Philippines and Vietnam—in instituting a minimum wage. Currently, Malaysia merely has a wage floor of RM500-600 for plantation workers, although in July the MOHR announced an upcoming minimum wage for workers in textile, hospitality, safety and electronics (Bernama 2009a). It is becoming increasingly clear that Ma-

laysia cannot afford to ignore minimum wage issues, not least in the ignominious wake of domestic worker salary disputes with the governments of Indonesia and the Philippines (Shyamala 2009; Kaur and Jamaluddin 2009).

Possible approaches to the minimum wage question include comparing wage growth over time with changes in the Consumer Price Index, as well as benchmarking the wage distribution against a selected poverty line. If these analyses reveal that market forces do not adequately provide for basic needs, it is only apt that a wage floor be introduced. From a societal perspective, a criminologist recently urged for more wage regulation on the basis that many employed persons in Malaysia turn to crime as they do not earn enough to support their families (Loh 2009).

Skills training

In addition to advocating a minimum wage, Fold and Wangel (1997) argue that Penang's economy requires solid training structures in order to transcend its competitiveness slump. Whether state planners opt to focus on high-end manufacturing, services or both, the workforce must be suitably equipped. Skills training is rightly touted as the path to a high-capital economy, but whether existing training programmes reap returns is an open question with respect to productivity for investors and wages for workers. The two areas requiring statistical analysis are training needs and training programmes.

One method of assessing training needs would be extracting LFS information on unemployment by industry and occupation, and then developing programmes that aim to raise the minimum qualification level within each industry to that of a desirable occupation class. Alternatively, it may be more useful to gather ELX vacancy data and then to prepare workers for fields that show high vacancy rates. A study of training deficiencies ought also to take into account future demand. If, for example, the state intends to intensify the production of biomedical devices and pharmaceuticals, appropriate skills infrastructures must be established early since investments in education generally yield high profits only after a time lag.

Another area of analysis that should not be neglected is the efficiency of training institutions, which also has consequence in Penang's progress as a hub for education. The state must find ways to replicate the longstanding contributions of the market-oriented Penang Skills Development Centre (PSDC). Given that a high value-added manufacturing economy insists on not just skilled workers but also industry-relevant degree holders and research linkages, Universiti Sains Malaysia (USM) could and should be a linchpin in the economy (Yusuf and Nabeshima 2009).

Anecdotal evidence, however, suggests that local universities do not currently produce employable, cutting-edge graduates; hence returns to higher education are low. Tan and Gil (2000) explore this assertion using a brief regression analysis of the performance of different types of training institutions in Malaysia, by the probability of trainees working, the time taken to find work, starting pay and the relevance of training to work. They also note that data on unit training costs, if available, can help policymakers weigh different institutions against each other. In a similar vein, Universiti Kebangsaan Malaysia (UKM) consultants (2002) propose establishing career centres at every public university both to help graduates develop soft skills and secure jobs, as well as to maintain a database of graduates' job market experiences. With such data, universities could constantly hone their course offerings to enhance the employability of graduates.

Wage structures within the public sector

Despite continual efforts to make the civil service compensation structure dependent on performance (Embi 2005), pay grades are still locked into a pyramidal hierarchy comprising top management, management and professionals, and support staff. Some believe that this entrenched stratification generates inefficiency. The federal government's renewed emphasis on Key Performance Indices (Bernama 2009b) creates space for determining whether civil service wages are in tandem with worker productivity, and for advocating extensive restructuring if not.

Female Labour Force Participation

Besides boosting productivity, state administrators can strengthen Penang's potential GDP and thus her economic future by enlarging her workforce. One of the most direct ways to do this is drawing more

women into the labour force, as economically inactive women comprise approximately half of all working-aged women in Malaysia. Raising female labour force participation also has vast social benefit: in most cases, wages from female employment accrue to a family's disposable income, thus constituting welfare gains for several individuals.

Historically, Penang has had an unusually high female labour force participation rate, as women factory workers were integral to the burgeoning industrial sector of the 1960s and 70s (Ong 2001). In 2000, female labour force participation rate for Penang stood at 58.9 percent, against a national female participation rate of 46.6 percent. However, while female labour force participation for Malaysia subsequently increased to 48.0 percent in 2005, it declined steadily for Penang to 50.1 percent in the third quarter of that year (see Table 2). Since Penang's labour market differs from that of the country in aggregate (as with its comparative advantage in high-tech products, noted above), all the more reason for the state government to initiate employment policies that are tailored to Penang.

With respect to women and the workforce in Penang, the LFS can be highly informative because it captures those who do not appear on payroll lists or tax records, i.e. the economically inactive women who have employment potential. Moreover, it observes both social characteristics (e.g. marital status) and employment decisions (e.g. reasons for not working or for working part-time). This data can create a fairly nuanced understanding of female labour force participation, whether an analyst seeks to tease out the reasons behind the dramatic decline in participation rates or design policies that motivate more women to pursue employment. Such policies may encompass anything from training subsidies (if the data shows that women workers are underequipped) to improved public transport (if the numbers reveal that numerous unemployed women reside far from economic centres).

Besides this, inequality often lurks not only in employment rates but also compensation across sexes and occupations. Gustafsson and Jacobsson (1985) find that higher wages were the most important factor in raising female participation in the Swedish workforce. Analysing wage and salary distributions for Penang by sex, industry and occupation, perhaps from the LFS Wages and Salaries Survey, would offer a snapshot of the incentive structures for women in the workforce. Furthermore, such analysis could show how much of the male-female income gap is due to a concentration of women within low-wage sectors, and how much is due to discrimination within the same industry and occupational category (Gupta and Rothstein 2001). A related aspect for study is how taxation distorts the incentive to work. For example, in many countries the dependent spouse tax allowance results in married women being taxed more than single women (Jaumotte 2005).

Singapore's Ministry of Manpower calculates two metrics, the index of dissimilarity and the marginal matching index, to track gender inequality within each occupational group, with particular attention to traditionally male-dominated occupations (Ministry of Manpower Singapore 2000). Apart from this, it has gathered information from focus groups of economically inactive women, both to discern their reasons for not working and brainstorm ways to bring more women into the workforce (e.g. recruitment information in mass media, career reorientation). The government also uses such focus groups as training opportunities (Ministry of Labour Singapore 1995).

The following are specific measures that deserve further study as they could potentially amplify female labour force participation in Penang. Besides the immediate welfare gains for women employees, such provisions can help women make stronger commitments to their jobs and bolster the collective consciousness of gender issues.

Work schedule flexibility

Many women opt out of the formal labour force because they are providing what is termed "care labour" at home: supervising children, nursing the elderly, preparing meals and maintaining houses. However, some of these women would be available to work at certain hours of the day, e.g. while their children are at school, if flexible part-time jobs were available. If LFS data for Penang confirms that (a) a high percentage of women who are neither employed nor seeking employment are housewives, and (b) a high percentage of women who work part-time do so because they are housewives, the state government may wish to foster part-time job creation in order to help the economically inactive women in (a) become economic contributors in (b).

A frequently cited study of OECD countries concludes that states with a higher incidence of part-time employment among female work-

ers generally have higher female labour force participation rates (Jaumotte 2005). However, the study remarks that a massive influx of part-time employees could segregate the labour market, with women in part-time jobs excluded from skills development, employment protections and job advancement opportunities. To mitigate this, Jaumotte proposes legally guaranteeing parents flexible work schedules, as well as increasing financial aid to families that transition to dual full-time employment.

Another option would be empowering more women to work from their homes, which becomes increasingly viable as information technology takes root. Nonetheless, this may not be compatible with Penang's manufacturing- and services- oriented economy.

Parental leave

Although the Employment Act 1955 guarantees all women 60 consecutive days of paid maternity leave, this is often insufficient for both mother and baby. Furthermore, men in the civil service can only claim 7 days of paternity leave (Shahrizat 2005). In Sweden, renowned for both its gender equality and female labour force participation, parents are entitled to full leave until their child is 18 months old. Mothers also receive full maternity leave for at least seven weeks prior to and seven weeks after delivery (Sweden 2006).

Nevertheless, Jaumotte (2005) observes that excessive paternal leave could harm human capital development as well as promotions and raises. Another drawback to factor in is an increased reluctance to hire women of child-bearing age.

Childcare benefits

Adequate childcare is a key component to tilting the scales in favour of formal employment rather than unpaid care labour. Both Denmark and the United States saw strong growth in female labour force participation when childcare options and education for women became widely available in the 1960s (Gupta and Rothstein 2001). In line with this, Jaumotte (2005) advocates childcare subsidies to reduce distortions that arise from such obligations falling on mothers rather than fathers.

While it is far easier to award subsidies to women enrolled in tax records than to marketise care labour (i.e. pay women for their hours of family and household work), another potent action would be opening childcare centres at workplaces. In addition to enabling mothers to be in close proximity to their children throughout the workday, such centres can provide early education for future movers and shakers. It would be enlightening to see how many establishments in Penang have taken advantage of the federal government's launching grants for public sector employers and tax deductions for private sector employers who start childcare centres (Shahrizat 2005).

Almost ironically, the conflict over wages for foreign maids (Shyamala 2009; Kaur and Jamaluddin 2009) is building awareness about both the value of care labour and the need for adequate childcare services. Thousands of dual-income families throughout the country depend on domestic workers. While this has the unquestionable advantage of letting children spend the day in their homes, it also suggests that the market's solution may not be the best for overall welfare as it shifts scarce care labour remuneration away from the local labour force.

Education

At the 2005 National Statistics Conference, Thambiah pointed out that although Malaysian women register low employability, they posses better educational qualifications than their male counterparts. She noted that entrenched gender stereotypes often result in males underachieving and gradually moving from mainstream education into technical courses and the labour market. Conversely, many females outperform their male peers throughout their educational careers, but never bring their human capital into the labour market. This heightens the need to reassess the quality of local higher learning institutions and to track the employment patterns of graduates.

Apart from this, some women who have taken long periods of time away from the labour market may profit from retraining programmes. These may take the shape of skills upgrading, lessons in computer usage or labour market reorientation.

Policy Paths for the Penang State Government

The following are a few of many labour policy actions that the state government could undertake to make full use of existing resources.

Establish a centralised body for coordinating and disseminating labour market statistics, perhaps under the purview of the State Economic Planning Unit (UPEN).

As discussed in the first section, there is an urgent need for accurate labour market statistics in Penang. Much can be gained from developing a body of statistical indicators that is consistently channelled to stakeholders and made available for free to the public. As the DOS and MOHR publish their employment statistics separately at the federal level, the Penang state government could try to bridge this gap and produce a regular compilation of data from numerous government agencies for the state. Such information-sharing agreements are not unusual: the DOS, for example, provides 50 news agencies with economic statistics every month and has signed a Memorandum of Understanding with Bernama, a national news agency (DOS 2003).

Besides efficiency gains, centralizing labour market data would streamline the process of benchmarking and gauging the accuracy of different statistics, as other data would be on hand for reference.

Capitalise on electronic job portals, whether the ELX or the state government's Career Assistance and Training (CAT) Centre.

Notwithstanding the CAT's collaboration with the internationally recognised portal JobStreet, neither the CAT nor the ELX have as consequential a presence in the local labour market as they could. Of the two portals, the ELX's JobsMalaysia is far more established and can tap federal government resources. However, the state government has significantly more leverage over the CAT, despite current hiccoughs that include a paucity of job listings and a registration form that must be downloaded and printed rather than filled in electronically.

Whether the state government chooses to channel its limited resources to either the ELX or the CAT, or to maximise coverage by simultaneously administering the CAT and supporting the ELX, it must bear in mind both efficacy of recruitment and capacity for statistical output. Regardless of this decision, it is imperative that the state government invest in electronic job-matching systems, in part because it is only a matter of time before classified advertisements migrate to Malaysia's equivalent of Craig's List and in part because these job portals are a prime outreach to homemakers and other job-seekers who cannot invest much time or transportation costs in job seeking.

Offer incentives to establishments that have favourable employment practices.

For example, the state government could provide subsidies to employers who keep all workers' salaries above a certain minimum. Alternatively, additional criteria could be integrated in open tenders for state government contracts in order to reward companies that have a low percentage of foreign labour or a high percentage of women workers (Lee 2009). These measures would have the twin aims of offsetting the perceived costs of such employment policies and cultivating affirmation of these state-wide priorities.

Extend the PSDC model by engaging USM and private higher education institutions in stakeholder conversations about Penang's manufacturing future.

A manufacturing economy is undergirded by long-term investments, both in physical and human capital. As Penang climbs the value-added chain, its workers will need to have increasingly high skills qualifications. USM is well-positioned, if currently unprepared, to be a key supplier of such professionals. The university will itself benefit from industry involvement via continually updated know-how as well as an enhanced reputation, which will draw students and funding.

Maintain database of maternity, childcare and other family support benefits that various firms offer to female employees.

The purpose of such a database would be threefold. First, it would allow analysts to observe the impact of such benefits on women's availability for work (e.g. by comparing the extent of such benefits and the ratio of female representation on the firm). The government could then promote the most influential benefits. Second, jobseekers who have or

intend to have families would be able to make more informed decisions about where they opt to work. Third, this database would be an accountability mechanism of sorts for firms, thus raising consciousness about gender in the workplace.

Encourage employers to capitalise on the federal government's financial assistance for childcare centres.

In addition to making it easier for women to move into the labour force, these centres will in turn create more paid care labour jobs.

Conclusion

The U.S. sub-prime mortgage crisis has demonstrated how badly markets can fail with imperfect information and lax monitoring. The labour market in Penang is not at risk of so abject a collapse, but it stands to gain tremendously from establishing a workforce accounting system and implementing policies that are in line with the traits and aims of the state.

To get a clear sense of which directions to head in, the state government would do well to capitalise on national employment datasets, such as the LFS and the ELX. As the situation stands, only a fraction of useful ELX statistics see the light of day and ELX data are not calibrated to represent the labour market accurately. However, the state government could mitigate both of these deficiencies by coordinating data compilation, dissemination and analysis.

Such consolidated data would pave the way for enlightened policy approaches that could boost Penang's economic competiveness with respect to productivity and workforce size. Specifically, labour statistics can start to answer questions about the link between wages and productivity, whether from the areas of skills training, a possible minimum wage or foreign labour. Furthermore, such data can be formative in decisions about how best to attract women with families into the workforce, whether these incentives are parental leave, childcare benefits or flexible work schedules.

Whether the level of analysis is social justice or Penang's long-term economic edge, it is difficult to overstate the role of statistical indicators in labour policy, both in its formulation and in ongoing evaluation of its impact.

References

Bernama (Bangi). 2009a. "Minimum wage for four sectors to be announced soon". In The Malaysian Insider, 6 July 2009.

Bernama (Kuala Lumpur). 2009b. "National KPI to be introduced: Najib". <http://www.pmo.gov.my>, 12 July 2009.

Chan, Huan Chiang. "Population growth and distribution: Impact on regional development". Presented at the MIER National Economic Outlook Conference 2008-2009. 2007

Department of Statistics, Malaysia. "Malaysia: Country statement". Prepared for the SIAP/ESCAP Management Seminar for the Heads of National Statistical Offices for Asia and the Pacific. <http://www.unsiap.or.jp/completed_prog/workshop/ms/ms1/cp/cp_malaysia.pdf>, 2003.

Department of Statistics, Malaysia. 2009a. "Labour Force/Wages and Salaries/Migration Survey 2009". <http://www.statistics.gov.my/eng/images/stories/files/questionnaire/borangptb_m_gu.pdf>, 2009.

Department of Statistics, Malaysia. 2009b. "Metadata of the Labour Force Survey Report". <http://www.statistics.gov.my/eng/images/stories/files/metadata/item3.pdf>.

Embi, Muhamad Ali. Sistem saraan di Malaysia: Sistem saraan berasaskan merit (The compensation system in Malaysia: A merit-based system). Kuala Lumpur: Utusan, 2005.

Fold, Niels and Arne Wangel. "Labour shortages and industrial growth in Penang, Malaysia". Danish Journal of Geography 97: 111-8. <http://tidsskrift.dk/visning.jsp?markup=&print=no&id=72538>.

Gupta, Nabanita Datta and Donna S. Rothstein. "The Impact of Worker and Establishment-level Characteristics on Male-Female Wage Differentials: Evidence from Danish Matched Employee-Employer Data". Working Paper no. 347. United States Bureau of Labor Statistics, 2001.

Gustafsson, Siv and Roger Jacobsson. "Trends in Female Labor Force Participation in Sweden". Journal of Labor Economics 3, no. 1 (1985): 256-274.

Jaumotte, Florence. "Female labour force participation: Past trends and main determinants in OECD countries". Presented at the OECD Labour Force Participation and Economic Growth Workshop, 2005.

Kaur, Minderjeet and Nurul Huda Jamaluddin. "Minimum wage may lead to more illegal workers". The New Straits Times, 8 September 2009.

Lee, Hwok Aun. "Public procurement: Abuses and challenges". Aliran Monthly 2009:5.

Liew, Chin Tong and Francis E. Hutchinson. "Policy Innovation at the Sub-national Level: Implementing Pro-Employment Policies in Penang". Forthcoming. 2009.

Loh, F.F. "Expert: Minimum wage can help reduce crime". The Star, 20 April 2009.

Millea, Meghan. 2002. "Disentangling the wage-productivity relationship: Evidence from select OECD member countries". International Advances in Economic Research 8(4): 314-323.

Ministry of Human Resources, Malaysia. " 2009a. Labour Market Report". <http://www.MOHR.gov.my>, (various months) 2009.

Ministry of Human Resources, Malaysia. 2009b. "Labour and Human Resources Statistics 2008". <http://www.MOHR. gov.my/Statistik_Perburuhan_2008.pdf>, 2009.

Ministry of Labour, Singapore. "Women returning to work". <http://mom.gov.sg/publish/etc/medialib/mom_library/ mrsd/ms.Par.40674.File.tmp/873_op_02.pdf>, 1995.

Ministry of Manpower, Singapore. "Occupational segregation: A gender perspective". <http://www.mom.gov.sg/publish/etc/ medialib/mom_library/mrsd/ms.Par.35775.File.tmp/867_ op_11.pdf>, 2000.

Ong, Anna. "Fighting Poverty Through Globalisation and ICT". Economic Briefing to the Penang State Government 3(9):

5-8. Penang: Socio-economic and Environmental Research Institute, 2001.

Shahrizat Abdul Jalil. "Improved Maternity Benefits for Malaysian Women, Supporting Their Multiple Roles in Society". Keynote address. Kuala Lumpur, 2005.

Shyamala, R.K. "Minimum pay damper for Filipina maids". The Star, 30 June 2009.

Sweden, Government of. "Parental Leave Act (1995:584) with amendments: up to and including SFS 2006:442". 2006.

Tan, Hong W. and Indermit S. Gill. "Vocational education and training reform: Matching skills to markets and budgets (Malaysia)". World Bank, 2000.

Thambiah, Shanti. "Gender matters in human capital development". Presented at the National Statistics Conference 2005. See summary at <http://www.digitalibrary.my/dm-documents/malaysiakini/265_paper08.pdf>, 2005

Universiti Kebangsaan Malaysia, Consultants. "Study on the unemployment situation in Malaysia". Commissioned by the Economic Planning Unit, 2002.

Yusuf, Shahid and Kaoru Nabeshima. "Can Malaysia escape the middle-income trap? A strategy for Penang. Policy Research Working Paper 4971". World Bank Development Research Group, 2009.

Chart 1: Data Collected in the Labour Force Survey.

Source: Labour Force Survey Metadata, Department of Statistics

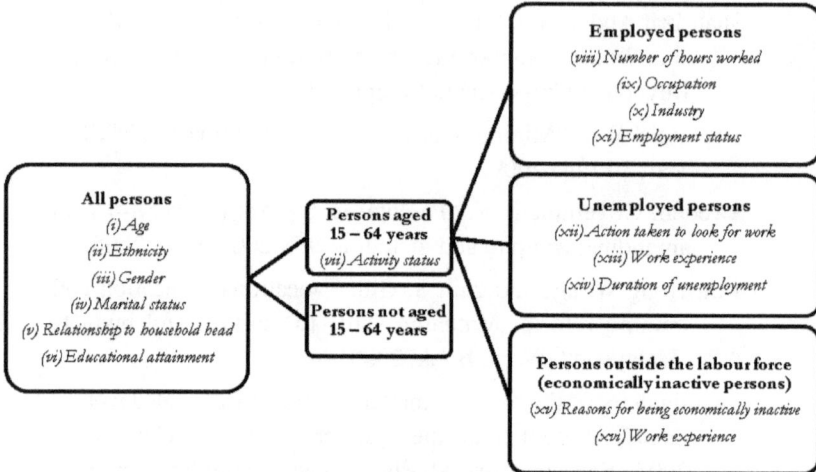

Employed persons
(viii) Number of hours worked
(ix) Occupation
(x) Industry
(xi) Employment status

All persons
(i) Age
(ii) Ethnicity
(iii) Gender
(iv) Marital status
(v) Relationship to household head
(vi) Educational attainment

Persons aged 15 – 64 years
(vii) Activity status

Persons not aged 15 – 64 years

Unemployed persons
(xii) Action taken to look for work
(xiii) Work experience
(xiv) Duration of unemployment

Persons outside the labour force (economically inactive persons)
(xv) Reasons for being economically inactive
(xvi) Work experience

Table 2: Female Labour Force Participation Rates for Penang and Malaysia, 2000-2005.

	2000	2001	2002	2003	2004	2005
Penang*	58.9	57.7	53.4	52.2	50.4	50.1 (for Q3)
Malaysia^	46.6	46.7	46.7	46.6	47.5	48.0

*Source: Department of Statistics, Malaysia. Retrieved from <http://www.penang.gov.m>y.

^Source: United Nations Statistics Division. Retrieved from <http://data.un.org>

7 Two classical studies in this mode were conducted by J. Medoff and K. Abraham: "Experience, performance and earnings" (1980) in the Quarterly Journal of Economics 95: 703-736, and "Are those paid more really more productive? The case of experience" (1981) in the Journal of Human Resources 16: 186–216.

Table 1: Comparison of Publications from the Labour Force Survey and the Current Population Survey.

	Labour Force Survey, Malaysia	Current Population Survey, United States
Frequency	LFS data are mainly published in a quarterly summary report and an annual volume titled the Labour Force Survey Report. The summary report for the first quarter of 2009 was published in June of the same year. The Labour Force Survey Report 2008 became available in July 2009.	The Employment Situation, a monthly news release of both CPS and establishment survey data is distributed two weeks after data collection is complete. This is soon followed by Employment & Earnings, a monthly periodical of detailed historical and cross-sectional CPS data.
Avail-ability	The quarterly report of the LFS is available online for free at <www.statistics.gov.my>. However, copies of the Labour Force Survey Report 2008 cost RM60 for print versions and RM120 in CD form. Unpublished data can also be requested for a fee.	Both The Employment Situation and Employment & Earnings are available at www.bls.gov as free PDF files. (For sustainability, the two- to three-hundred-page Employment & Earnings is now only available in electronic form.)
Depth	Eight of the ten charts and tables in the LFS report for the first quarter of 2009 present single-variable data (e.g. labour force participation by educational attainment), while only two contain cross-tabulated data (e.g. labour force participation by sex and age group). These charts and tables contain observations for between one and three points in time. The annual Labour Force Survey Report is considerably more detailed but publishes only annual averages and basic meta-data. It also lacks wage information.	In the June 2009 Employment Situation, every table incorporates at least two independent variables and shows observations for six different months. Employment and Earnings extends this level of detail in providing multiple classes of data (monthly/annual, seasonally adjusted/non-seasonally adjusted) as well as minute technical documentation.

[12]

The Embodiment of Social Justice in Employment Legislation and HR Practices

Ajit Singh Jessy

Justice Gajendragadkar in the Supreme Court case of J.K. Cotton Spinning and Weaving Mills Co. Ltd. v. Labour Appellate Tribunal [1963] II LLJ SC. said:

> *"... the argument that considerations of social justice are irrelevant and untenable in dealing with industrial disputes, has to be rejected without any hesitation.*
>
> *Social justice is something more than mere legal justice. It is a social philosophy imposed on the legal system. Industrial Courts and tribunals are not only not bound by the contracts of the parties, they can make new contracts and revise old contracts. They are not strictly bound by the law of master and servant. Otherwise there would be no point in creating such industrial tribunals. It is to free workers from contracts and obligations that were unfair and inequitable."*

His Lordship Justice Raja Azlan Shah (CJ) in the case of Non-Metallic Mineral Products Mfg. Employee's Union & Ors. v. South East Asia Firebricks Sdn. Bhd. [1976] 2 MLJ said:

> *"The Act (Industrial Relations Act 1967).. it seeks to achieve social justice, the Industrial Court is to a large extent free from the technical considerations imposed on ordinary courts."*

"No labour or social legislation can be considered by a Court without applying the principles of social justice."

"Quite apart from being a proprietary right, the right to liveli-hood is one of those fundamental liberties guaranteed under Part II of the Federal Constitution...Suffice to say that the ex-pression "life" appearing in Art. 5(1) of the Federal Constitu-tion is wide enough to encompass the right to livelihood.

The desire of Parliament to protect the nation's work-force from the harshness of an unbending and inveterate com-mon law and doctrines of equity, as expressed by the passing of the Act, may thus be seen to be entirely in harmony with the terms of the supreme law of the Federation. The high stan-dards of social justice so carefully established by the legisla-ture and by the framers of the Federal Constitution ought not, in my judgment, to be consciously lowered by any decision of this Court."

Over the last few years the Higher Courts, the Industrial Court and the Government have been chipping away at the hard-won rights of employees, and in many judgments of the Courts the concept of social justice has been eroded. The reasons for this are pressure from foreign investors, in particular some large multi-nationals, and the desire to at-tract more investments.

Until the decision of the Federal Court in the Dr. James Alfred case, there was no reduction from the sum awarded for unfair dismiss-al. Since that decision, the Industrial Court is now required to scale down monetary compensation and the reduction is to be made for the following reasons:-

a)   where the dismissed employee has been gainfully employed elsewhere between the date of dismissal and the hearing;

b)   when the dismissed employee had caused or contributed to his own dismissal

Whilst the Court of Appeal has stated that this should not be math-ematical calculation, nevertheless, reduction is arbitrary depending, on the good conscience and equity of the Chairman concerned. Thus deductions can vary from 10% to 50%, or even more.

The only remedy provided in the Industrial Relations Act 1967 for an unfairly dismissed employee is reinstatement. Prior to the decision in the Dr. James Alfred case and decision of the High Court in the Thilagavathy a/l Alagan Muthiah v Meng Sing Glass Sdn. Bhd. case, the only option that a dismissed workman had was to seek re-employment.

The well known labour laws scholar, C.P. Mill in his book, Industrial Disputes Law in Malaysia, says:

"the principle of mitigation of damages can have no logical place in a jurisdiction which is concerned primarily with re-instatement issues".

In February 2009, Parliament amended the I.R. Act to limit compensation to a maximum of 24 months, as well as made is mandatory that there must be a general scaling down of payments. Apart from scaling down post-dismissal compensation, the Courts have also limited compensation in cases of reinstatement to a mere 24 months. Prior to the amendments, the dismissed employee was entitled to payment from the date of dismissal to the date of hearing. Thus, if his case took five (5) years, he would be awarded 60 months..

de novomala fidemala fide "The way in which the Act is constructed, makes it clear that it is only the Industrial Court which is conferred with an adjudicatory function. The two preceding powers, namely, the Director-General and the Minister cannot therefore assume a function expressly reserved to the third. It follows that prima facie, considerations that are irrelevant to the Industrial Court's decision-making process cannot be, and are not relevant, vis-a-vis the referring authority."

The reason given by the Minister, that the drastic reduction is to clear the backlog, is thus against the very spirit and purpose of the Act.

The approach towards ensuring Social Justice is best portrayed by the example of Kayu Nasi Kandar, which operates a restaurant in Melbourne, Australia, when it was fined RM480.000. for underpaying a Malaysian chef over 18 months. The Courts and Human Resource

personnel must ensure that rules are interpreted so as to ensure social justice, as the workman has to largely rely on his employer's good conscience for fairness and justice.

[Epilogue]

Social Dimensions of Economic Development

Closing speech by P. Ramasamy
Second Deputy Chief Minister of Penang
(Penang Outlook Forum 2009)

The Rise of Social Inequality

I think it is safe to say that in the last fifty years, there has been a distinctive imbalance in how our country has developed. The focus of development has always been on material growth. We measure our success in terms of physical structures – the tall buildings we have built, the number of shopping centres we have, how many cars we have on the roads.

When it comes to social development, there's nothing we can brag about to the world, not even to ourselves. The gap between the rich and the poor in Penang is as wide as ever. Our goals as a nation have always centred on big, showy demonstrations of wealth. As if the size of our buildings can make up for our social deficits, for the lackadaisical way we continue to treat the poor, the handicapped, those who are different from the rest of us. We may have advanced tremendously in economic terms for the last fifty years, but as a society we have a long, long way to go.

The Need for Social and Economic Equity

And as long as we as a society do not resolve the issues of social and economic inequality, the growing income gaps between classes and races and gender, there will always be cracks in society's foundations.

We can't change things overnight. You can't alter a 50-year mentality or political and economic structure in a year or even four years. But we have to start right this minute. We are the state government. We are supposed to lead by example. If there is a problem with gender or racial disparity in the workforce, if we want the workforce in the private sector to reflect the demographic makeup of the country, or the state as a whole, then those of us in the public sector have to be the first to go this route.

There is no doubt at all that there is a significant employment disparity in the public sector. People found it a touchy issue when we raised it in the state assembly, as if we were trying to conspire against an entire race.

Look, we are not asking for a quota on race or gender, but the fact is there must be an emphasis on merit. There must be a balance in race and gender. We must show to everyone that in the state government at least our government is representative of all ethnic groups.

Restructuring Government and Society

Penang should be a cosmopolitan city, a plural city, where any Malaysian can come and not feel out of place. Now, we don't exactly have much power when it comes to labour matters, since the Federal Government controls that area, but we can still facilitate matters on a smaller, but no less important scale.

There are things we can do and will do to improve the labour situation here in Penang. Such as bringing biotechnology-based companies to Penang, and creating a "green economy", with "green jobs".

That is our priority right now: to make sure Penangites have jobs and are paid well enough to sustain themselves and their families.

We are kept up to date every week about the labour situation here on the island and on the mainland, on things like VSS, retrenchment and so on. The situation of the workers of Penang is one of our most pressing concerns within the larger social agenda.

Politics as the Art of the Possible

I was an academic for many, many years before going into politics. I've been asked many times before about the transition from the life of academia to politics. We university lecturers have often been called, for better or worse, "radicals" or "idealistic". As the DCM, I'm still called those things today.

And politics has been called the "art of the possible". This means that we often have to "compromise" in order get things done. We have to deal with competing interests and conflicting priorities.

We often deal with other people who have their own set of ideals – or none at all, but we won't get into that right now – and then try to come to an agreement, maybe even at the expense of our own personal ideals. This is why people like to say that every politician eventually sacrifices what they believe in.

Now, in my previous life as an academic, you could say that I immersed myself in all sorts of social theories and political ideologies. I've written papers and books. I became a teacher. I got into all sorts of debates and arguments. I've spent years overseas among other cultures and traditions.

And *because* of my work, not in spite of it, I've always kept one foot in the real world, and I've immersed myself in the plight of the downtrodden.

The Mandate of the People

I've fought for labour causes, for peace causes, for people Causes. I've fought for plantation workers and *orang asli*. I've always been – and this is true for the whole of DAP as well – a supporter of the working-class Malaysian. Not once did I find myself having to compromise my principles or my fight.

The question is: now that we have been elected into office, have things changed? Did we find ourselves having to compromise on this fight for social justice, in the name of "getting things done"?

All I can say is that, in politics, yes, unlikely partnerships will have to be formed in order to get anything done. That is inevitable in politics, when you have to work with other people with their own sets of views in order to get things done. But we were elected because of who we are and what we stand for. The working-class Malaysians, especially the hawkers, wage-earners and blue collar workers have generally been hardcore DAP supporters. They know that we've always represented

their views and fought for their rights. They know that we have always stood up for the marginalized, those who feel alienated, for the underdogs who have no one else to turn to.

And people who know us know that when it comes to issues of social justice we will fight for it. Regardless of the colour of your skin, regardless of which god you believe in, regardless of your gender and socio-economic status.

We are committed to fight for all Malaysians and that doesn't change now that we are now in the government. If anything, it emphasizes it more and more. Because now, instead of just highlighting this issue or that issue, we can actually do something about it. We were elected to implement social justice in this state, because the people of Penang felt that they weren't receiving it.

Social Justice and the Agenda for Change

Today, we will see that the concept of 'Social Justice' is linked to many papers and topics lined up to be presented this morning by our esteemed speakers. We can see that Social Justice is a favourite 'link concept' for academics to explore issues and theories connected to matters of the economy, society and government.

Many may think of the concept and subject of Social Justice as very abstract – something best left in classrooms, having little or no relevance to the real world.

My entire life has been firmly grounded in the pursuit of knowledge. I am always tempted to intellectually think through the barriers that separate the realms of theory and practice. As we academics teach and guide each generation along the endless quest for higher and more advanced academic qualifications, we are often prompted to do a great measure of soul-searching. This soul-searching often points to a question, a question that looms in our collective conscience.

Have we been doing the right thing? Is there anything we've done that we can say, wholeheartedly, that we are truly, truly proud of? Beyond merely making lots of money?

Have we done our part and fulfilled our obligation as government leaders and captains of society to actually put into practice the concept of 'Social Justice'? Or did we just push it all aside to concentrate on building our little financial empires?

Here is one thing I know: 'Social Justice' can be realized and practiced. Do it right – if you take it seriously, it can and will impact lives in positive and meaningful ways. But for this to happen, there has to be a systematic strategy and a strong political will to see that it is DONE. Not just talked about or analyzed or scrutinized endlessly. DONE.

Just preaching it won't be enough. That would merely be stating the obvious, and without action to back it up it just sounds like yet another campaign slogan.

What we should be more concerned about is not to be stuck on just analyzing the links in concepts and theories. If we do that, we will be trapped making theory after theory, with nothing to show for it but a piece of paper and it's never going to end.

So - How do we move on? How do we stop second-guessing ourselves with theory after theory? How do we begin to channel our resources towards understanding and applying 'Social Justice'?

Good Governance

The answer, ladies and gentlemen, can be found in the consistent practice of GOOD GOVERNANCE, and this brings us to the heart of the matter in my speech today. Good governance is the be all and end all, because at the end of the day, it is the success or failure of this practice by which we will be judged.

Don't we remember the past governments of Penang, which, repeatedly throughout our history, intervened to steer our State through economic turbulence, social-political issues and State versus Federal policy setbacks?

Good governance ensures that the leaders of the day actually practice what they preach. PRACTICE must follow THEORY. ACTION must follow VISION. And what you end up with is accountability to the society it governs, and the results of its practices and how society will evaluate its elected government.

And a government that doesn't just promise good things but actually delivers on its promises can bring unity and growth to society.

Closing the Social and Economic Gap

Promises like closing gaps: Social gaps, economic gaps, a category of divisions and dangerous cracks that exist in all societies around the world. If we do not address them immediately, they could tear down the foundations of society and the economy. Through the principles and practice of good governance, the government can step in with 'close gap' measures, intervention policies that acknowledge the power of divisive forces and work to overcome them step by step, policy by policy.

But what are the potentially divisive forces that may rise up to threaten unity and progress in Penang today?

I am certain the answers to this question, whether they be from political scientists, external observers or the man on the street, would be varied and wide-ranging, and all of them would a glimmer of truth.

But there is one factor that remains a core area of concern – one that we've observed in many developing countries. And that is the economic distribution of wealth and resources. And yes, the economic gap is the predominant threat to progress and unity. Bridging this gap is the most urgent task we as a state and nation face today. This is because in a society that is experiencing tremendous change and development, gaps that are clearly visible or less so, will appear as dividing fault-lines. These fault-lines have the effect of dividing society into camps – the haves and have-nots, the privileged and the downtrodden. We cannot afford to have these divisions if we are serious about building up a united society.

A fair society is a society where economic benefits are shared, and elected leaders are held accountable, and are equipped with a conscience and empathy for the people.

Lessons from the Past

Back in the 1970s, we experienced a flagging economy and rising unemployment. We credit the government of the day with taking firm, decisive action.

Smart and business-savvy leaders at the time implemented structural changes in the economic model, through intelligent policies that met the needs of the day and capitalized on the opportunities of that era. But today we need a government with more than just a good nose for business.

Smart strategies for economic growth are always welcome as a timeless formula for success. As the economy grows, society prospers. Yet we must be aware that, for the sake of long-term stability and unity, society must embrace equitable prosperity. Our growing wealth must be shared, for no one ethnic group or clan or class should ever think it's their right to have the entire cake while leaving everyone else out.

One concrete way to spread out the goods is to look out for employment equity. We are particularly concerned about redressing a lop-sided ethnic profile of employed staff at many GLCs agencies, local authorities, local councils, and so on.

Meritocracy and Productivity

Penang needs to see a new era of openness and fairness, where employment structures can be based on merit rather than skin colour. There needs to be more employment opportunities that are offered based on meritocracy, rather than a "network" of elitist and narrow race-based groups. Let us have the employment structures of the public sector actually reflect the racial and gender composition of our country, and not simply reflect the domination of a culture of any one group.

When employment opportunities are spread out more fairly, we will have moved in the right direction towards the end goal of social justice for the ordinary citizen. Employment is only one area. We are compelled to look at the other needs of the masses if we are serious about our Social Justice agenda. Increasing equitable employment options is vital, but not the sole expression of good governance. The government is looking for opportunities in different areas to enhance a balanced development in Penang, based on a transparent and accountable government.

The Caring Society and Social Safety Nets

For example, we have to improve assistance to those in society who can no longer work for a living; senior citizens, for example, whom we have neglected and forgotten far too often.

We have started a programme to assist senior citizens in Penang, with a 10-month registration process. We have printed forms, although we are not yet sure of the form of assistance to be given to senior citizens – the 'warga emas'. We have also looked at hardcore poverty, or 'kemiskinan tegar' – with over 700 families identified, but the list continues to be updated to ensure that we can wipe out hardcore poverty that was left unaddressed for 51 years. But we seem to have made a good impact, within 1 year, in our efforts to wipe out hardcore poverty, although it's a relative and not absolute term of reference. This area will receive special attention, as will employment aspects. This is to make the Penang government reflective of the interests of all citizens, regardless of religious or racial background. These then are some of the programmes underway. Besides bringing in foreign investments, the social agenda has to be addressed, which is very close to the Pakatan Rakyat, and the DAP's social democratic agenda.

Ladies and gentlemen, looking again at senior citizens, they've worked and served for the vast majority of their lives, but in their old age, they can hardly count on a society that marches on by without them, a society that works only towards economic development and the accumulation of wealth.

Social Justice means looking beyond jobs and the economy, to consider the services and institutions that make society liveable, civilized, and generous. This is why the government has been pressing hard for greater financial allocations to spruce up the education sector, because this area concerns nurturing a vital resource – young minds and talent that will help to build our society, block by block towards a better world.

It is also why the Penang government is striving hard to improve core services to ordinary citizens, like public transport which, in Penang, has until recently suffered embarrassing neglect and notoriety.

We acknowledge the importance of keeping Penang's environment clean and green. If we can't breathe clean air and live in a pollution-free environment, we can forget about loftier goals and other planned achievements. We believe first and foremost, in tackling the core areas and issues that impact Penang and the lives of Penangites who have entrusted us with the responsibility of governance and leadership.

Penang's Social and Cultural Heritage

We are also fully committed to keeping our island's historic treasures, such as heritage buildings and other priceless heritage resources intact, for the treasures of history are the tangible and intangible assets of today and tomorrow.

In our heritage lies our identity and pride as Penangites, and when we look after our treasured heritage, we nourish our roots and develop other qualities, from a strong Penang identity to increased revenues from tourism. The Penang government emphasizes all these aspects because, beyond a thriving economy, these things also help ensure an overall improved society for Penang.

Social Justice and Good Governance

In other words, this is the quest of returning Social Justice to Penangites and completing a balanced development. The government tries not only to preach, but practice the principles of good governance to expedite these measures, which would return long overdue Social Justice to the people of Penang that goes beyond economics.

Ladies and gentlemen, it is the practice, and not the theory of good governance that brings about real Social Justice. Real Social Justice is not a term or concept bandied around as a political tool. It is the results seen in the fulfilment of the social responsibility agenda of a government in power.

It is seen in the improvements to the quality of life, the state of the material environment, the maturity of the electorate to choose their leaders wisely, and the quality and integrity shown by elected leaders who profess to bring Social Justice to society.

Ideology and Social Justice

Ladies and Gentlemen, Social justice is not a "radical" concept. Social justice is not "radical politics". It is not something that only NGOs care about. And it is certainly not a privilege enjoyed only by the elite in this country. (And yes, I'm aware I'm addressing the Penang elite right now, the irony is not lost on me.)

At least it shouldn't be. Every Malaysian deserves justice; it is their right, regardless of how rich or poor they are, or if they have influ-

ential friends or not. So, going back to the question earlier of sacrificing ideology, the answer is no. Because our ideology is based around social justice for every Malaysian, regardless of race, religion or gender, and it is not something we can ever compromise.

Not if we want to maintain credibility among the people. Not if we want people to take us seriously at our word. Not if we want to live with ourselves and the consequences of our actions – or inactions.

And one thing people need to understand about social justice: it's not just an ideology you subscribe to. It is a commitment you make to the betterment of society as a whole, whether you are an academic or a politician.

Yes, we are very ideological. Our ideology factors into whatever decisions we make – but only because it *must* be strong. Our ideology is not a drawback to us; politically it is integral to our thinking process. It is not a weakness and it does not mean we are naïve and have our heads in the clouds with regards to how the real world works.

Our ideology is our strength. It defines who we are, what we do and how we do it. Without it, we would be a rudderless ship, lost and adrift in the seas, waiting for the *rakyat* to finally sink us in the next round of elections, or the next round of stock-taking, where the questions will be: What has the government done? What good governance principles have our elected leaders shown? What social justice has been returned to the people of Penang? If we fail to answer these questions properly, then we would have truly failed, because we would be no better than what had come before.

Let us adhere to social justice as a living principle, applied through good governance practices in day-to-day leadership, administration and interaction.

If we can do this, I'm confident we can finally move beyond theory and rhetoric, and lip-service ideologies, and begin to build a better tomorrow for Penang and her people. Surely they deserve no less.

www.ingramcontent.com/pod-product-compliance
Lightning Source LLC
Chambersburg PA
CBHW030641270326
41929CB00007B/155